Unity iOS Game Development

Beginner's Guide

Develop iOS games from concept to cash flow using Unity

Gregory Pierce

[PACKT] PUBLISHING

BIRMINGHAM - MUMBAI

Unity iOS Game Development
Beginner's Guide

First published: February 2012

Production Reference: 2170212

Published by Packt Publishing Ltd.
Livery Place
35 Livery Street
Birmingham B3 2PB, UK.

ISBN 978-1-84969-040-9

www.packtpub.com

Cover Image by Gregory Pierce (gregorypierce@sojournermobile.com)

Credits

Author
Gregory Pierce

Reviewers
Julien Lange
Clifford Peters

Acquisition Editor
Robin de Jongh

Lead Technical Editor
Meeta Rajani

Technical Editor
Pramila Balan

Project Coordinator
Kushal Bhardwaj

Proofreader
Linda Morris

Indexer
Rekha Nair

Production Coordinator
Alwin Roy

Cover Work
Alwin Roy

About the Author

Gregory Pierce has worked in software development and executive management, across a variety of high-technology industries, for over 18 years. Gregory started his professional computer software career as a software test engineer for the Microsoft Corporation in 2002. Since then he has gained experience across a variety of industries; while working in the defense and space industry for Sytex, Director of Research and Development for Bethesda Softworks and Zenimax Media, Software Architect for the Strategic Applications group within CNN, and later Time Warner, Technology Evangelist at JBoss/Red Hat, Vice President of Technology for Blockbuster, and finally Director of Global Software Development for the Intercontinental Hotels Group. A published technical author, Gregory has used his experience to give back to communities by lecturing on a variety of technology subjects, contributing to open source projects, and participating in organizations such as Junior Achievement. Gregory holds an MBA in Global Business from the Georgia Institute of Technology and a BS in Computer Science from Xavier University of Louisiana.

In this book, many of the chapters and artwork contained herein are commissioned by Sojourner Mobile, provider of the monetization platform that has made it all possible.

He co-authored Direct3D Professional Reference during the early days of DirectX.

I'd like to thank my wife Deirdre, son Gabriel, and daughter Sydney who sacrificed many nights and weekends to give me the time necessary to work on the book. I'd also like to thank my co-workers at IHG and all of my friends from Georgia Institute of Technology (Go Jackets) who provided feedback and encouragement when times were rough. Finally, I want to thank the fine people at Unity Technologies and all the mobile hardware manufacturers out there for kick starting the mobile revolution.

About the Reviewers

Julien Lange is a 30-year-old IT expert in Software Engineering. He started to develop on Amstrad CPC464 with the BASIC language when he was 7. He learned later Visual Basic 3/4, then VB.NET, and C#. For several years, until the end of his study, he developed and maintained several PHP and ASP.NET e-business websites. After his graduation he continued to learn more and more about software like Architecture and Project management, always acquiring new skills.

Julien was at work talking with a colleague in August 2009 and after discovering the high potential of iPhone games and softwares he decided to find an improved game engine allowing him to concentrate only on the main purpose of the game—developing a game and not a game engine. After trying two other game engines, his choice was Unity3D thanks to its compatibility with C# and its high frame rate performance on iPhone. In addition to his main work, he opened `iXGaminG.com` as a self-employed business in December 2010. This small studio specialized in advergaming and casual gaming using Unity3D.

I would like to thank my wife for allowing me to take some time in reviewing books on my computer. I would also like to thank Frederic for all the work we completed together with Unity. So, I do not forget to thank all current Unity Asset Store customers who are using my published assets and scripts.

Then I would like to thank my family, my friends, and colleagues, including Romain, Nicolas, Patrick I, Chang D, Alexandre, Philippe S, Philippe G, Marie-Helene D, Corinne F, Mathieu N, Christophe B, Christophe P, and Fabrice G, who knows me as an Apple(c) addict.

Clifford Peters is currently a college student pursuing a degree in Computer Science. He enjoys programing and has been doing so for the past 4 years. He enjoys using Unity and hopes to use it more in the future.

Clifford has also helped to review these books; Unity Game Development Essentials, Unity 3D Game Development by Example Beginner's Guide, and Unity 3D Game Development Hotshot.

www.PacktPub.com

This book is published by Packt Publishing. You might want to visit Packt's website at `www.PacktPub.com` and take advantage of the following features and offers:

Discounts

Have you bought the print copy or Kindle version of this book? If so, you can get a massive 85% off the price of the eBook version, available in PDF, ePub, and MOBI.

Simply go to `http://www.packtpub.com/unity-ios-game-development-beginners-guide/book`, add it to your cart, and enter the following discount code:

uigdbgebk

Free eBooks

If you sign up to an account on `www.PacktPub.com`, you will have access to nine free eBooks.

Newsletters

Sign up for Packt's newsletters, which will keep you up to date with offers, discounts, books, and downloads.

You can set up your subscription at `www.PacktPub.com/newsletters`

Code Downloads, Errata and Support

Packt supports all of its books with errata. While we work hard to eradicate errors from our books, some do creep in. Many Packt books also have accompanying snippets of code to download.

You can find errata and code downloads at `www.PacktPub.com/support`

PACKTLIB

PacktLib.PacktPub.com

PacktLib offers instant solutions to your IT questions. It is Packt's fully searchable online digital book library, accessible from any device with a web browser.

- Contains every Packt book ever published. That's over 100,000 pages of content.
- Fully searchable. Find an immediate solution to your problem.
- Copy, paste, print, and bookmark content.
- Available on demand via your web browser.

If you have a Packt account, you might want to have a look at the nine free books which you can access now on PacktLib. Head to `PacktLib.PacktPub.com` and log in or register.

Table of Contents

Preface

Apple's iOS has taken the world by storm and provided a game development platform, which for the first time gives average developers an opportunity to compete in the global multi-billion dollar entertainment software space. While there are several viable solutions for developing games for this platform, Unity has emerged as a leading platform for iOS and other platforms as well. With Unity's toolset, and this book, you will take the first steps on your journey to producing commercial quality games for the iOS platform.

This book takes a learning approach, focusing specifically on those things that are necessary to building an iOS title. From designing (from the mobile perspective) to scripting and creating game mechanics that are iOS centric, you will learn everything you need to get started. Throughout the course of the book you will build on lessons to design and publish a game with integrations to all of the components necessary to make a revenue generating title.

What this book covers

Chapter 1, What is Unity and why do I care? discusses the iOS development space, Unity, and why you want to use Unity as your game development platform for iOS and other platforms.

Chapter 2, Getting Up and Running details installing Unity and getting familiar with the user interface and its semantics.

Chapter 3, Hello World explores the creation of a sample application, provisioning the application using Apple's tools and the deployment of that application to a device.

Chapter 4, Unity Concepts discusses the Unity platform, how it works, and how you use the platform to assemble a game.

Chapter 5, Scripting: Whose line is it anyway? delves into scripting from the Unity perspective including a look at why scripting is core to game development with Unity, the C# interfaces, and building gameplay scripts.

Chapter 6, Our Game: Battle Cry! investigates some of the design topics of a Unity iOS game and outlines the mechanics of a sample iOS game that is built through the consequent chapters.

Chapter 7, Input:Let's Get Moving illustrates the many facets of input on the iOS platform and instructs the user on how to build a basic input system for touch based games.

Chapter 8, Multimedia focuses the user on the integration of movies, music, and audio into a game and how to produce and integrate content specifically for the Unity iOS platform.

Chapter 9, User Interface discusses building user interfaces for iOS games from the perspective of the standard Unity GUI API and Prime31's UIToolkit.

Chapter 10, Gameplay Scripting focuses on translating our gameplay requirements into iOS specific features in Unity and generating play mechanics such as particle systems, animation driven behaviors, collisions, and rag doll systems.

Chapter 11, Debugging and Optimization provides an overview of debugging and profiling while investigating object pooling and Beast lighting as specific means to optimize performance.

Chapter 12, Commercialization: Make 'fat loot' from your creation examines some of the approaches to commercializing an iOS application using Unity including iAds, In App purchases, and the Unity Asset Store. This chapter also illustrates how to track success with iTunes Connect.

What you need for this book

As iOS development is only officially supported on the OSX platform, you will need a machine that runs OSX, the XCode development tools, and a subscription to Apple's Development Program. You can find details for XCode and the Apple iOS Developer Program here: `http://developer.apple.com`.

Information for joining the iOS Developer Program, the Terms of Use, and other policies not specifically covered in this book, can be found there.

You also need access to the Unity development platform and the iOS plugin, which can be obtained at: `http://www.unity3d.com`.

Who this book is for

If you are a developer who is interested in developing games for the iOS platform and want to leverage the Unity platform, this book will provide the core knowledge that you need to get started. If you are a Unity developer looking to port an existing application to the mobile platform, this book will give you an overview of the processes involved in publishing specifically with the Unity iOS plugin.

Having an understanding of C# or Javascript will help, but if you are an experienced developer with either of these languages, you will still learn how to apply your skills to learn mobile development using this book, because much of the book is geared to an exploration of the concepts and implementation with Unity and the iOS platform.

The example code in this book is written primarily in C#. However, there are scenarios where Javascript is used as an instructional aid. While there is sufficient information to learn the necessary components of C# within the book, it is not a goal of the book to teach C# or its fundamentals.

Conventions

In this book, you will find a number of styles of text that distinguish between different kinds of information. Here are some examples of these styles, and an explanation of their meaning.

Code words in text are shown as follows: "Once downloaded (you should have a `.mobileprovision` file), double-click on the file on your machine."

A block of code is set as follows:

```
import UnityEngine
import System.Collections

class example(MonoBehaviour):

    def Start():
        curTransform as Transform
        curTransform = gameObject.GetComponent[of Transform]()
        curTransform = gameObject.transform
```

When we wish to draw your attention to a particular part of a code block, the relevant lines or items are set in bold:

```
IEnumerator Start () {

     iPhoneUtils.PlayMovie("Snowpocalypse2011.m4v", Color.black,
iPhoneMovieControlMode.CancelOnTouch, iPhoneMovieScalingMode.
AspectFill );

     yield return null;

     Application.LoadLevel("MainMenu");

  }
```

New terms and **important words** are shown in bold. Words that you see on the screen, in menus or dialog boxes for example, appear in the text like this: "Select the **Open Other...** button, navigate to where you installed the assets for the book".

> Warnings or important notes appear in a box like this.

> Tips and tricks appear like this.

Reader feedback

Feedback from our readers is always welcome. Let us know what you think about this book—what you liked or may have disliked. Reader feedback is important for us to develop titles that you really get the most out of.

To send us general feedback, simply send an e-mail to `feedback@packtpub.com`, and mention the book title through the subject of your message.

If there is a topic that you have expertise in and you are interested in either writing or contributing to a book, see our author guide on `www.packtpub.com/authors`.

Customer support

Now that you are the proud owner of a Packt book, we have a number of things to help you to get the most from your purchase.

Downloading the example code

You can download the example code files for all Packt books you have purchased from your account at `http://www.packtpub.com`. If you purchased this book elsewhere, you can visit `http://www.packtpub.com/support` and register to have the files e-mailed directly to you.

Downloading the color images of this book

We also provide you a PDF f le that has color images of the screenshots used in this book. The color images will help you bet er understand the changes in the output. You can download this f le from `http://downloads.packtpub.com/sites/default/files/downloads/0409_unityimages.pdf`

Errata

Although we have taken every care to ensure the accuracy of our content, mistakes do happen. If you find a mistake in one of our books—maybe a mistake in the text or the code—we would be grateful if you would report this to us. By doing so, you can save other readers from frustration and help us improve subsequent versions of this book. If you find any errata, please report them by visiting `http://www.packtpub.com/support`, selecting your book, clicking on the **errata submission form** link, and entering the details of your errata. Once your errata are verified, your submission will be accepted and the errata will be uploaded to our website, or added to any list of existing errata, under the Errata section of that title.

Piracy

Piracy of copyright material on the Internet is an ongoing problem across all media. At Packt, we take the protection of our copyright and licenses very seriously. If you come across any illegal copies of our works, in any form, on the Internet, please provide us with the location address or website name immediately so that we can pursue a remedy.

Please contact us at `copyright@packtpub.com` with a link to the suspected pirated material.

We appreciate your help in protecting our authors, and our ability to bring you valuable content.

Questions

You can contact us at `questions@packtpub.com` if you are having a problem with any aspect of the book, and we will do our best to address it.

1

What is Unity and why should I care?

Welcome to the world of Unity! In this book we will explore from beginning to end how to develop games utilizing what is one of the most exciting and accessible game development technologies available for mobile devices.

In this chapter you will learn the basics of getting up and running with Unity Technologies' game development product Unity. Together we will explore how to utilize this development platform to deliver games on iOS devices.

In this chapter we shall:

- Learn about the value of Unity as a development platform
- Install Unity
- Learn how to configure the Apple Developer Portal to support development and publishing
- Configure our development environment for publishing to an iOS device
- Publish a sample application to our iOS device

This may not sound like a lot, but with iOS development there are many things that you can do incorrectly, which will lead to difficulties when working with Unity. Rather than assume that you'll get it all right, we're going to talk through it step by step to make sure that you can spend your time building games and not trying to decipher mysterious error messages.

So let's get on with it...

Important preliminary points

This chapter assumes that you have already installed XCode and the Apple iOS SDK 4.x or later. If you don't have either of these tools installed, you can get them from `http://developer.apple.com`.

Further, it is assumed that you have downloaded and installed Unity from `http://www.unity3d.com`.

This chapter also assumes that you have set up an account at the iOS Dev Center located at `http://developer.apple.com`. Since iOS applications must be signed before they can be published to an application store, or distributed to devices, you must have an account set up and have the requisite certificates installed on your machine. There are a number of videos on the Dev Center website, which can help you get your certificates set up.

Also note that the screenshots in the book represent the Mac OSX version of Unity, as the OSX platform is the official development environment for iPhone applications.

What is Unity?

Imagine for a moment that you want to build a game for the iPhone and you want to take advantage of all the platforms' features, but you don't know Objective-C and you don't want to build a 3D engine. There are a large number of solutions in the marketplace for developing applications that will run on iOS – including the tried and tested method of creating an Objective-C project and writing a game engine using OpenGL ES that is specifically tailored to your content.

Given those facts, what is Unity and why should you care?

With hundreds of millions of mobile devices in the hands of consumers, and more arriving seemingly every day, it has become clear that the mobile device is one of the fastest growing areas for game developers. While the prospect of such an amazing audience is tantalizing, there are numerous operating systems, video technologies, touch interfaces, cellular network technologies, 3D accelerators, and so on that would make it difficult to truly deliver compelling content to this large an audience, profitably, without some mechanism to abstract above the platform differences and allow you to focus on what's important – delivering a great gaming experience.

Additionally there are a substantial number of approaches for delivering the various aspects of a game to the end-user. Consider for a moment the number of techniques available for providing sound, music, 3d artwork, physics, networking, or even force feedback for a game. Consider further the level of effort that would be necessary to have an environment where you can rapidly construct and test your ideas.

To truly be successful in this new multi-screen market you need an environment that allows you to focus your energies on creating great experiences and not the tedious details of the different hardware platforms on which the game will be played, or the mechanics behind how the game delivers that experience to the end-user. This is what Unity provides for you – and that is why you should care!

Getting a real application running on a device

To illustrate the type of content that is possible using Unity3d, we're going to get started by getting a real application running on a device. There are a number of steps that you have to perform to get this right, especially if you're a new developer to the iOS platform so I'm going to take some time to make sure you understand what's going on. iOS development can be very unforgiving if you don't do things the right way – but once you walk through it a few times it becomes second nature.

We are going to walk through each of the steps necessary to produce commercial content for Unity3 that can be deployed to an iOS device:

- Loading a project
- Selecting iOS as the target platform
- Publishing the application to our device
- Play our content on the device

Time for action – Loading a project

The first step is to start the Unity development environment by clicking on the **Unity IDE** icon.

If you're familiar with Unity version 2, it is important to note that there is no longer a separate application for Unity iPhone. One of the new features in Unity 3 is that there is no longer a distinct environment for every deployment target – you have one IDE for everything. This has a number of benefits, as we will see throughout the course of the book.

The first thing you will see when the environment starts is the Project Wizard. In this chapter we are simply going to load and deploy an existing project so that we can walk through the workflow of getting everything setup for publishing to the iOS device.

1. Select the **Open Other...** button, navigate to where you installed the assets for the book and select the `Chapter 1` folder.

2. Unity will then load this project and you will be greeted with the standard Unity interface:

3. If you noticed, in the middle of the previous screenshot, the title bar for the application you will see the standard VCR controls.

4. If you click on the **play** button, the game will start on your machine and you will be able to play around with the game in the Unity IDE. Play around with it for a second because you want to have some idea of how the application should look and behave when it is installed on a regular iOS device.

What just happened?

We have just loaded the sample game project in the Unity environment and run it on our development machine. In the normal development lifecycle you will find that you will perform the code-debug-test cycle on your machine and export it to your device to ensure that the performance is adequate or test the device-specific functionality.

Time for action – Select iPhone as a target platform

After we've had a chance to understand what our game will look, and play like, when it gets on our iOS device, it's time to deploy the application to our target iOS device. In the Unity IDE you accomplish this by changing the build settings for your project:

Next, let's examine the **Build Settings** dialog for the project:

In the **Build Settings** dialog there are a couple of activities we want to perform:

1. First, we want to make sure that we have something in our game world. Since you're loading an existing project you should already have scenes in your build. If for some reason you don't, you can press the **Add Current** button. This tells Unity that the scene that you've been playing around with is the one that you want to have included in your iOS game.

2. Next we want to make sure we're targeting the correct platform. In the platform list you can tell which platform is being targeted by looking for the one with the Unity logo next to it. In our case we make sure that it is next to "iOS"

I know your urge is strong to press the **Build And Run** button at this point. However, remember that iOS applications have to be signed before they can be deployed to devices, or sold on the Apple App store. Since we haven't told Unity anything about which developer profile and application identifier it should be publishing for, it will not be able to publish the application to the device. Thus, if you do follow through on this urge you will be greeted by this dialog box when you try to **Build And Run** for your device:

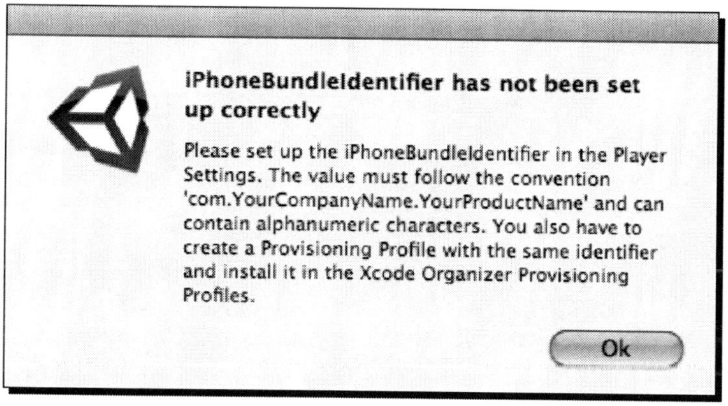

What just happened?

We have just chosen the publishing target for our game. Since Unity can publish to multiple platforms, you would perform this step for each platform that you want to target. Thus, if you are targeting Android, the web, or even a game console you simply select that platform in the dialog and Unity will produce a distribution that will run on that platform.

> At the time of this writing Unity provides publishing for other platforms such as Android, Xbox360, PS3, and the Nintendo Wii, with many other platforms in development. These additional platforms will require the purchase of the Pro version of Unity, in addition to any fees required to publish to the specific platform.

Time for action – Publishing to our device

To publish to our device we will have to provide a bundle identifier for Unity. To create one we will have to provide one within the iOS Provisioning Portal. This portal is located within the iOS Dev Center accessible at `http://developer.apple.com`.

On the main page for the iOS developer program you will find a link that will take you to the **iOS Provisioning Portal**. In addition, you will see links to the **iTunes Connect** portal that is used for publishing your product and getting information about sales and market performance:

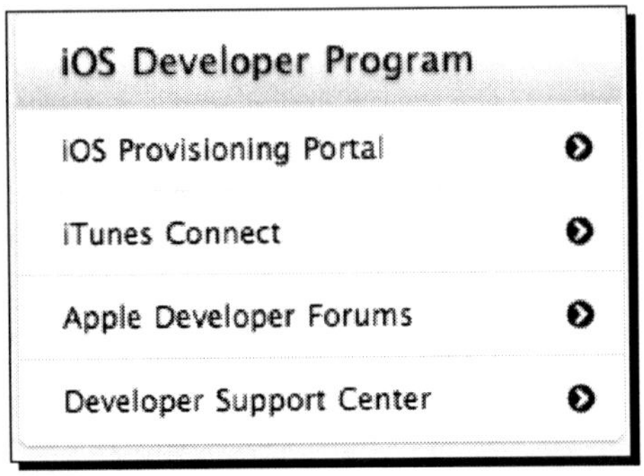

1. In the **iOS Provisioning Portal** you will select the **App IDs** setting so that you can create a new application ID (which is the same as the bundle identifier which Unity is looking for):

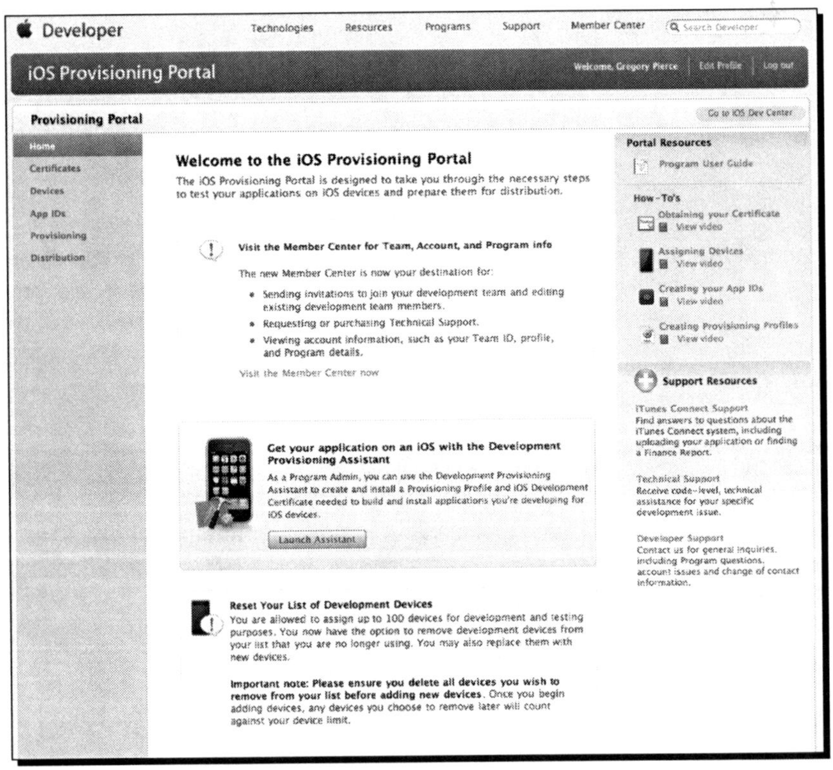

Let's take a look at how we create **App IDs** for our applications:

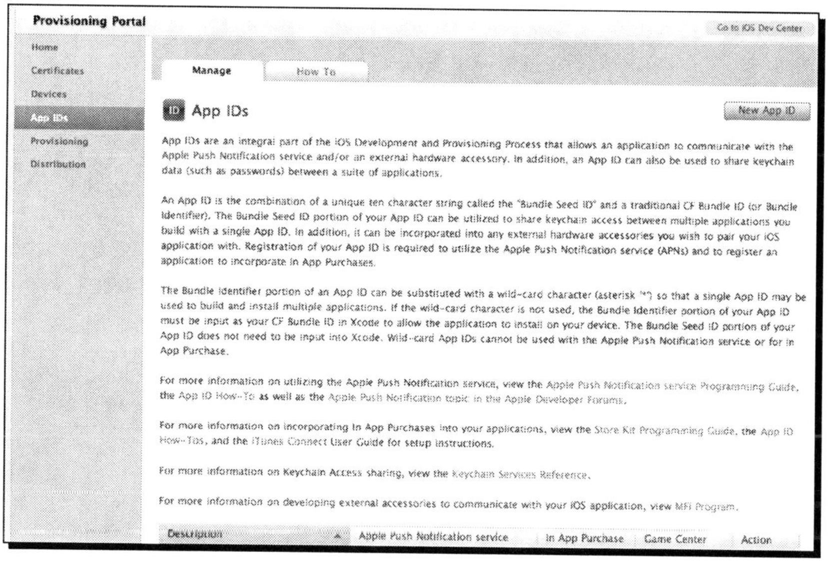

An **App ID** for an iOS application is very important, as it is the mechanism through which the application will be uniquely identified by Game Center, in App Purchases, Push Notifications, and inside of the Unity development environment:

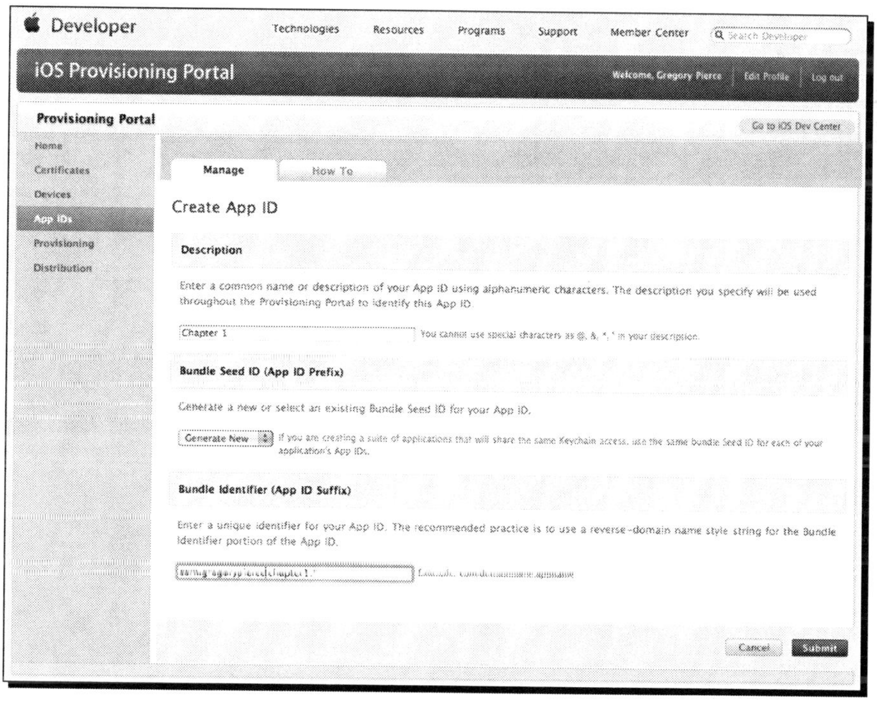

An application identifier has a description, a prefix and a suffix. The prefix is a collection of characters that are randomized for uniqueness, and the suffix represents the unique identifier for the application. When Unity refers to the **Bundle Identifier**, it is referring only to the suffix.

Create your **App ID** with a clear description of what this application is so that it will be easy to find it later. This is important, as over time you will end up with a large number of **App IDs** for all the games you will be creating. For the **Seed ID** itself, simply leave that set to **Generate New**.

For your **Bundle Identifier**, use the standard reverse-domain name notation to come up with the identifier for your app. Once this is created we just need a way to move this over to our development environment.

> For the bundle identifier make sure that you do not append a wildcard character to the end as this will limit you later as you seek to add more advanced functionality.

2. We now need to associate this application ID with a provisioning profile. If you already have a provisioning profile, you can modify the one you already have and change the **App ID** that it represents. If you don't have one, or don't want to modify an existing one, enter the **Provisioning** section of the **iOS Provisioning Portal**:

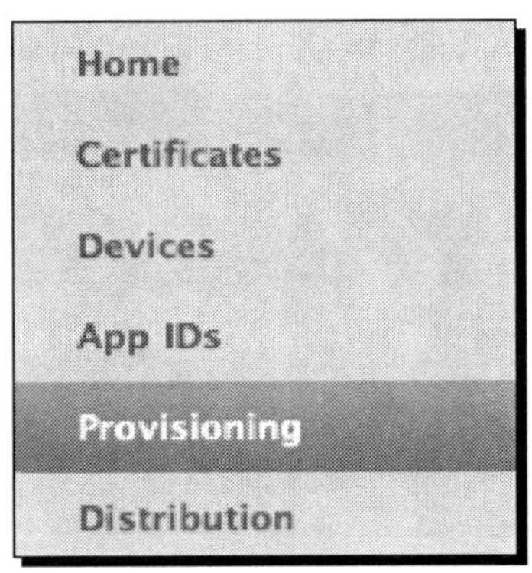

3. Once there, create a new profile for this **App ID** and fill in all of the fields, making sure to select the appropriate **App ID** in the drop-down list box:

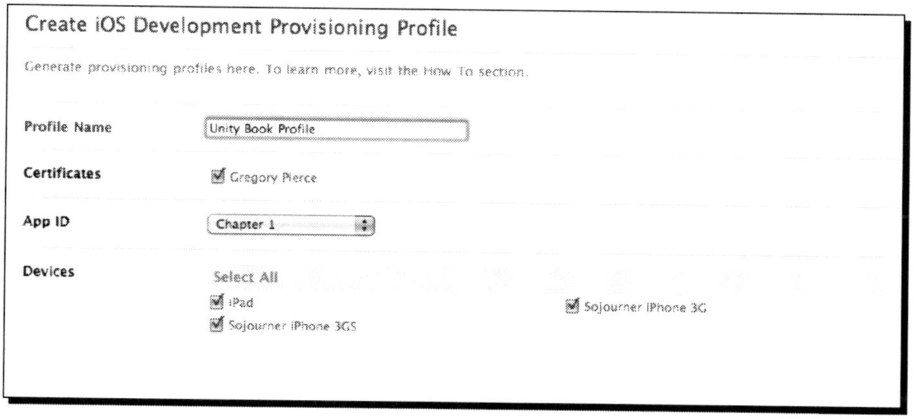

> You may not have noticed it, but this example illustrates what happens when you follow the bad practice of not coming up with very descriptive names for your **App IDs**. While in this case I know that I want **Chapter 1**, if I were developing several books – I would not be able to identify which Chapter 1 this App ID represented.

Notice that I have selected all of the devices that I want this application to be provisioned for. If you don't select a device here, you won't be able to deploy the application to that device.

4. Your provisioning profile is created, you now need to press **Download** so that it will be downloaded to your development environment:

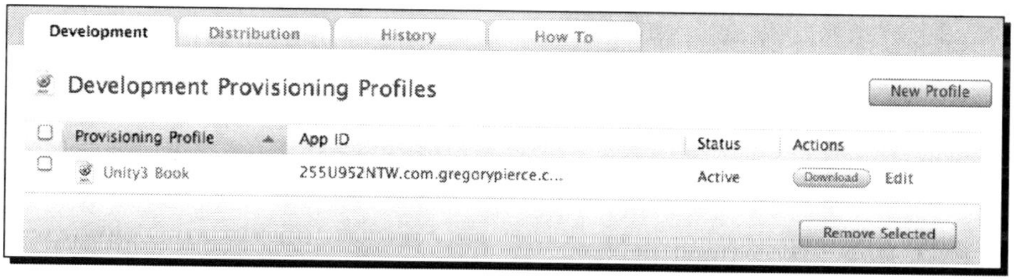

5. Once downloaded (you should have a `.mobileprovision` file), double-click on the file on your machine. As this is a registered file type for XCode it should install it into XCode for you.

   If for some reason it doesn't, you can open up the Organizer in XCode (**Window | Organizer**), select the **Provisioning Profiles** entry in the organizer. XCode will then install the profile and it will be synchronized to all devices that can accept the profile:

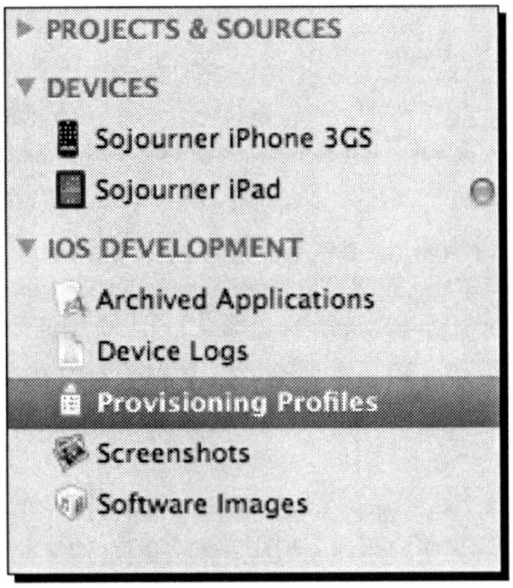

   XCode has the ability to automatically provision devices that are configured in the iOS developer portal within XCode. This makes it easy to ensure that your profiles are added to your target devices. To do this, ensure that the **Automatic Device Provisioning** checkbox is checked:

   Once performed, XCode will communicate with the iOS developer portal and download all of your configured devices and display them in the Organizer:

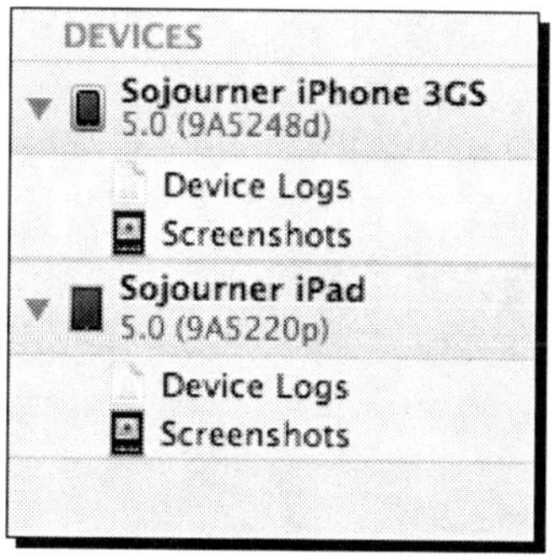

6. We are now able to configure Unity to publish content for this application ID on our target device. We accomplish this by entering the **Bundle Identifier** and setting the **App ID** suffix for our application. In the case of our example, it would be `com.gregorypierce.chapter1`:

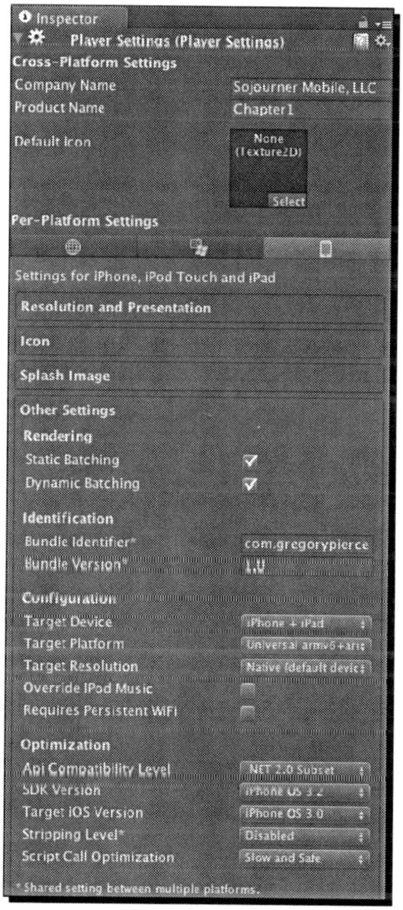

With that step completed, the hardest part of building games for Unity is over!

7. Run this application by selecting the **Build and Run** option from the File menu (**File | Build and Run**). This time when you select "Build and Run," Unity will build a player for your content and deploy the application to the iOS device connected to the machine.

   Don't be alarmed when you see XCode open and start building your application, as this means that the process is working and very shortly you should see the sample application start on your device.

What just happened?

What Unity is doing behind the scenes is taking all of the assets and scripts from the Unity IDE and putting together a player that will be able to playback the content and all of its scenarios based on input from the user. This is a very important concept to understand as the content within the Unity IDE is largely platform agnostic and can be readily redeployed after a simple recompile within the Unity environment. This player is what becomes the actual application that is deployed to the iOS device.

We spent a large number of steps creating some artifacts within the iOS Developer Portal. These artifacts were: the certificate, the App ID, and the provisioning profile. These artifacts form a circle of trust between the developer, Apple, and the iOS devices in the hands of developers and consumers.

The certificate is a credential that is created in the Apple environment that allows content to be signed specifically by the developer, so that it is clear who authored the content. Without a certificate it is possible that someone could claim to be the developer and sign applications on his/her behalf.

The App ID is a unique identifier that allows the iOS device and the Apple services to know, without ambiguity, which application is trying to do something. Finally, the provisioning profile defines.

The provisioning profile associates the certificates, devices, and an app ID. Without a provisioning profile on your machine you will not be able to sign or deploy applications to either a device or to the application store.

Once we provided Unity the App ID, it was able to communicate with XCode and tell XCode which profile and certificates should be used to sign our application and deploy it the iOS device. On the device itself, when XCode deployed the application it transferred the provisioning profile to the device, so that the iOS device could identify that this was a device that it should run, even though the Apple App Store did not provide it.

We have just performed all of the steps necessary to setup our development environment and publish content to Unity. Further, we have built our own mini testing lab using Unity Remote so we can utilize our device yet debug the game in our development environment. This is a crucial milestone as we can now focus entirely on customizing Unity and building games.

Pop quiz – The fundamentals

1. Which of these platforms can Unity not publish content for?
    a. Web
    b. Consoles
    c. iOS Devices
    d. Android Devices
    e. Linux
2. Where can you go to set up an application ID for your iOS device?
    a. Apple Developer Forums
    b. XCode Organizer
    c. iTunes Connect
    d. iOS Provisioning Portal
    e. XCode SDK
3. There remains uncertainty about whether or not Unity developed applications can be published to iOS devices within Apple's Terms of Service? (true/false)
4. If you have the following App ID 255U952NTW.com.gregorypierce.chapter1, what should you provide to Unity as your Bundle Identifier?
    a. Chapter1
    b. com.gregorypierce.chapter1
    c. 255U952NTW
    d. 255U952NTW.com.gregorypierce.chapter1
    e. 255U952NTW.com.gregorypierce.chapter1.*
5. You can publish an iOS application without creating a developer account? (true/false)

Summary

In this chapter we learned a lot about how to set up everything for publishing to iOS devices.

Specifically, we covered:

- How to load Unity and open a new project
- How to create an Application ID for signing and publishing an application
- How to deploy an application to an iOS device

Now that we've learned about setting up our development platform we're ready to really dive into Unity and explore its capabilities – which is the topic of the next chapter.

2
Getting Up and Running

In this chapter we will examine the Unity Interface in detail, explore all of its views and tools while personalizing them to suit our particular development style, and configure our environment for remote debugging using Unity Remote. In this chapter we will finish laying down the foundation for building applications and explore all of the Unity options that we need.

In this chapter we shall:

- Explore the Unity user interface
- Customize our interface with new custom layouts
- Configure and deploy Unity Remote for debugging
- Test our application using Unity Remote and our new custom layout

So let's get on with it...

Welcome home

If you've ever used a 3D modeling tool or written an application using any modern software development IDE you will find Unity 3 very familiar and fairly straightforward. The Interface for Unity is composed of a Toolbar area that consists of 5 basic control groups and a number of user customizable areas that can contain Views.

Transform tools

The transform tools are used with the Scene View and allow you to manipulate the objects in the scene. We will take a moment to walk through these tools since we will spend much of our time using them.

Working our way from left to right the first of the tools is a multi-use tool that is used to manipulate the camera in the scene. The camera you're moving is of your view of the scene and has no relationship to what is actually shown in the game.

In the default mode, the **Hand** tool will simply translate the camera around. Pressing the left mouse button and dragging will translate along the X-axis of the camera. If you have a mouse wheel, scrolling that wheel will move the camera along the Z-axis.

Holding the *Alt* key or the right mouse button will cause the Hand to change into an Eye. In this mode you can orbit the camera around its current pivot point in the scene. The Scene Gizmo in the upper left of the scene view reflects this. As you pivot the camera, the gizmo will update to reflect the current camera pivot.

Holding the *Control* key allows you to zoom the camera as you move the mouse around in the scene. This is particularly useful if you need to get in close to where some critical action should be taking place.

Transform Gizmo Toggles

There are two gizmos that determine how the updates to an object, using the Transform Gizmo, will impact on the object. The Transform Gizmo is just as it sounds, it appears in the Scene View and allows us to change the position or rotation of an object. These toggles determine where the Gizmo will appear.

The first toggle is the **Position** toggle. If set to **Center**, the Transformation Gizmo will appear in the center of the object's bounds that you want to transform. In most cases this is what you want if you are laying out an object in a scene. However, if you want to change an object's position based upon its pivot point, select **Pivot** for the setting of the toggle.

The second toggle is the **Rotation** toggle. Here you will determine whether or not rotations will be relative to the object's Local coordinate system or based upon the Global or world space coordinate system.

VCR Controls

The next set of controls is used to drive the gameplay in the Game View. The visual representation of these controls is so commonplace that they almost require no explanation.

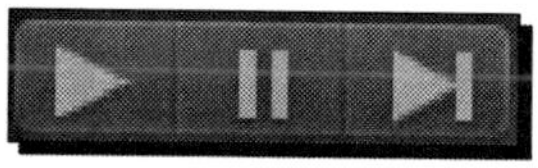

The **Play** control will cause the game to start playing. If you want to stop and look at things you press the **Pause** button. When the **Pause** button is pressed, Unity will switch to **Scene** view (unless already displayed) so you can examine the details of the scene. Pressing **Pause** again will cause the game to continue where it left off. If, while paused, you want to determine what will happen in the next cycle, you can press the **Step** button. Pressing the **Step** button while a game is playing will cause it to enter a paused state.

> If the **Scene View** is on a separate tab you will be able to see both views at the same time.

Layers drop-down

As you develop your applications you will create layers in the **Scene View** which represent groups of game objects that you want to display in the view. This helps to unclutter the display in a very complex scene.

In the **Layers** drop-down you can select what layers you want to see and which ones you want to hide. The hidden objects are still there and will display in Game View the next time the game is run.

Layout drop-down

During the development of creating a game you will find that some tools are useful for some scenarios and not useful in others. Custom layouts allow you to define a collection of views, and their position and configuration, while providing a unique name for the layout so that you can switch to it later.

The **Layout** drop-down will display all of the layouts that are available for you to switch to, allowing you to rapidly move between multiple IDE arrangements so that you have the tools that are important to you when you need them.

Project view

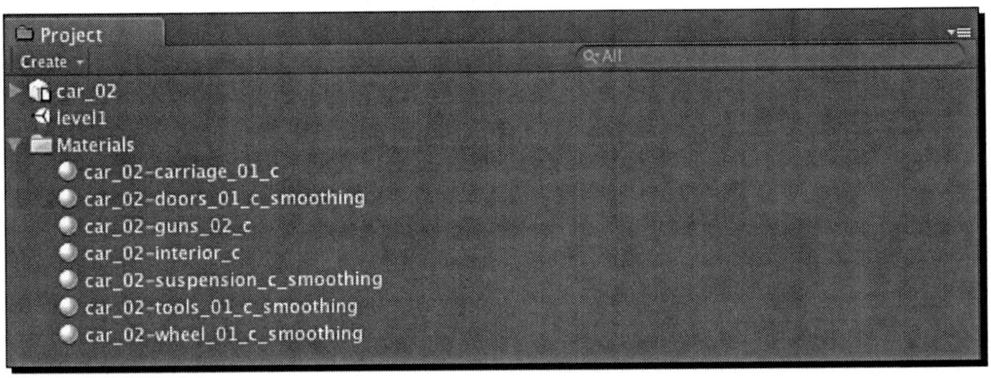

The **Project** view is where you will manage all of the assets that are in your project. However, if the files in those folders get updated (that is, you change the mesh of an object in some other tool), those updates will be changed in Unity as well.

> This view corresponds to the Asset folder of your project, but you should NEVER make changes to the project folder directly, you should make your changes in the Unity Project view.

You can add new assets to your project by simply dragging them from the desktop, or file system browser, right into the project view and Unity will import the content for use. Under the covers, Unity will also move the assets into the project's Assets folder.

Hierarchy view

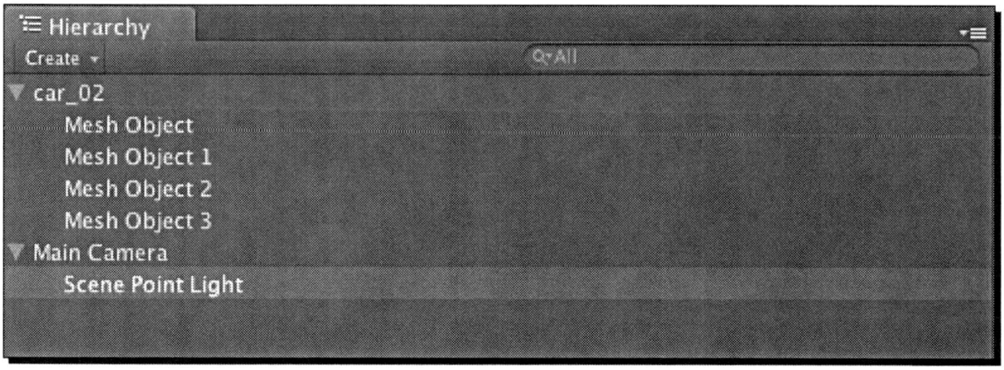

The **Hierarchy** view is a close peer to the **Project** view. Where the **Project** view is responsible for managing the assets that are available to your sandbox – the **Scene** view, the **Hierarchy** view is used to manage the objects that are in the scene and the parent child relationships of those objects. For example, you may have a vehicle object in the scene that has a light attached to it. In the **Hierarchy** view these objects would have a parent child relationship, such that the light would be the child of the vehicle object. The result would mean that as the parent object changed through transform, rotation, or other the child object would be impacted.

In large projects there will be a large number of objects in the **Hierarchy** view. To make it easier to find particular objects, or types of objects, Unity provides the search box in the **Hierarchy** view. When you enter the name of an object, Unity will filter the **Scene** view such that the objects you have entered are clearly visible in the view while the other objects are grayed-out. For example, suppose you are trying to find the steering wheel component of a scene that consists of a large number of game objects. If you enter **steering wheel** in the search box it will only provide texture, color, and so on to that object so that it is easy to find. Similarly, if you enter a type of object, such as **light**, in the search box the scene will only highlight the lights in the scene – even if the word 'light' isn't in the name of the Game Object.

Scene view

The **Scene** view is where you will you will spend most of your time. It is in the Scene view that you will build your game, position the camera, change environment settings, observe occlusion levels, and so on:

Game view

The **Game** view is where the action takes place. Whenever you press **Play** in the VCR controls, this view will use the active camera in the scene and render what that camera sees to the **Game** view:

The **Control Bar**, in the **Game** view, contains useful controls for adjusting the Game view to deliver information useful in rendering the **Game** view closer to the actual target display:

The first tool in the **Control Bar** is the **Free Aspect** drop-down that allows you to change the aspect ratio of the **Game** view to different values. This is particularly important for iOS development as you can select the aspect ratio of your target device and get a better idea of how your content will look with the appropriate perspective applied.

The next tool is the **Maximize on Play** toggle which, when enabled, will display the **Game** view in full screen. In the case where this **Game** view is not the same resolution as the screen, you will note that the **Game** view maximizes to cover the entire display, but only renders the scene at whatever resolution / aspect ratio you have set in the **Free Aspect** drop-down.

The next control is the **Gizmos** control. This will force Unity to render all of the Gizmos that are present in the **Scene** view in the **Game** view.

The final control is the **Stats** control. When enabled this will show the Rendering Statistics window overlaid on the **Game** view. This is an extremely useful control to have active, as you will gain insight into how your application is performing at a high-level, without having to delve into the **Profiler** view while playing the game.

Inspector

The **Inspector** view contains all of the properties for the selected Game Object in a view. The properties that the Inspector shows are entirely context sensitive based upon the Game Object selected:

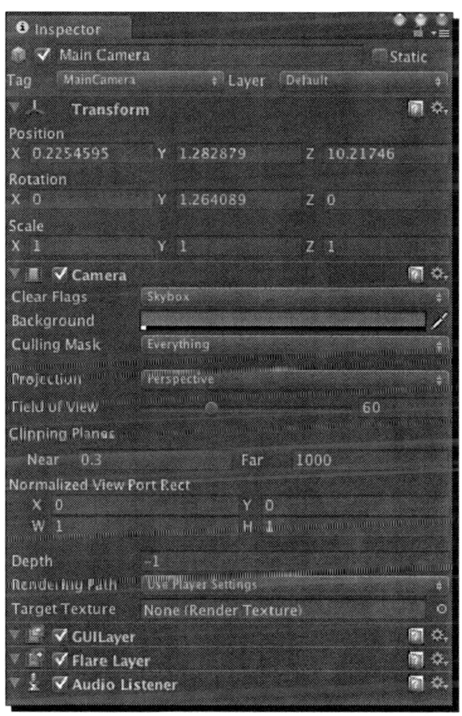

As Game Objects in Unity are composed of components such as meshes, scripts, transforms, and so on. each of the components that make up the Game Object will have its editor appear in the **Inspector**. So, for example, in our example **Inspector** we've selected a camera in the scene. As you can see the Transform, Camera, and so on each have editors that show up for this Game Object.

Console view

The **Console** view shows all of the messages that come from your game. These messages may come from the Unity engine, or may represent messages which you have sent to the **Console** view using the script commands, such as `Debug.Log()`. If you double-click on the messages that appear in the **Console** view, you will be taken directly to the script that caused the message:

Profiler view

The Unity Profiler is your best friend when building games with Unity, particularly when developing for an iOS device. While the tool is only available with the Pro version of Unity, it deserves special attention as it provides substantially more information than the Rendering Statistics window in **Game** view:

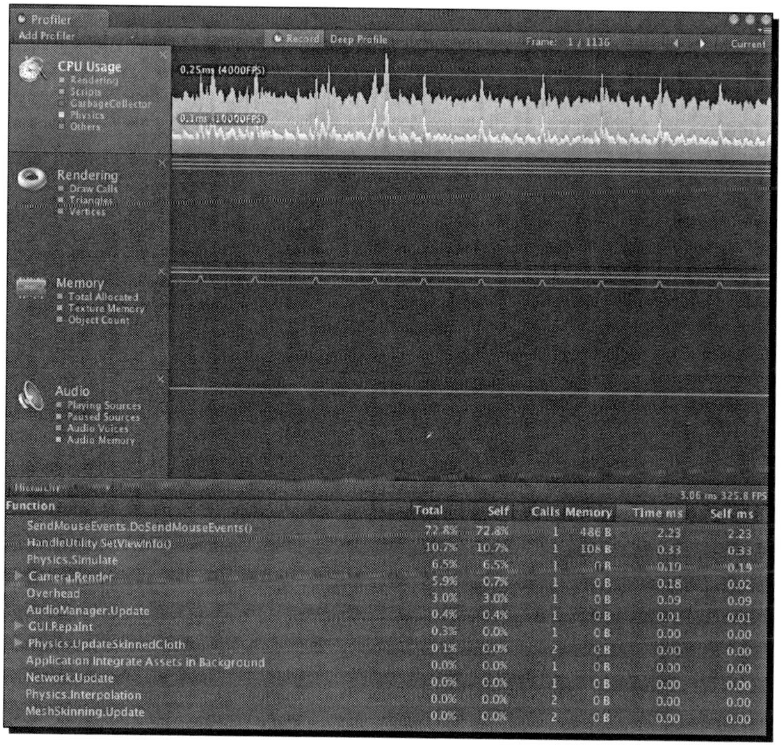

In the top are profile tools that provide information about CPU Usage, Rendering, Memory, and Audio statistics. Next to each Profiler is a histogram representing the values retrieved from the instrumentation process on each frame. You can click and drag the mouse across the histogram and see the results across multiple profile tools, which will help to correlate specific performance issues with other events that occur in the application:

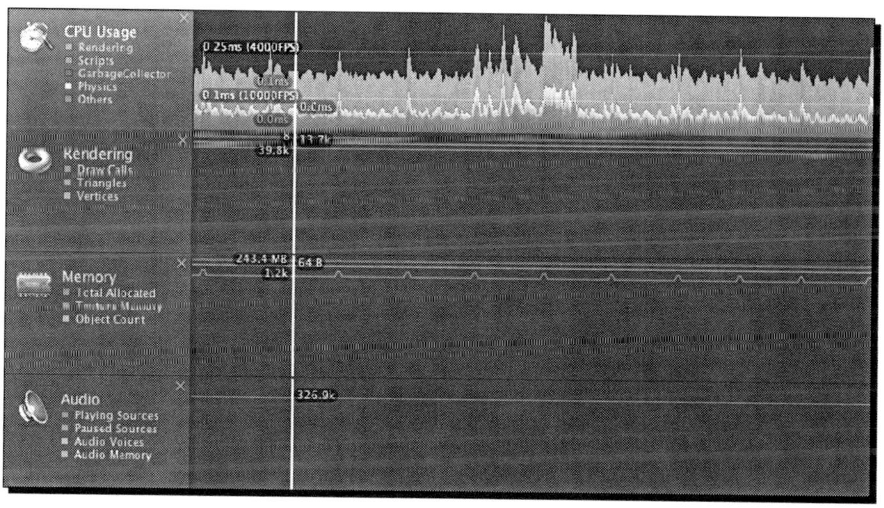

The bottom provides information about function calls that are being made by the application. This is done by instrumenting the code and determining how often the functions are being called. This can help determine where the hot spots are within an application so that you can focus your attention and get your game performing well on your target platform:

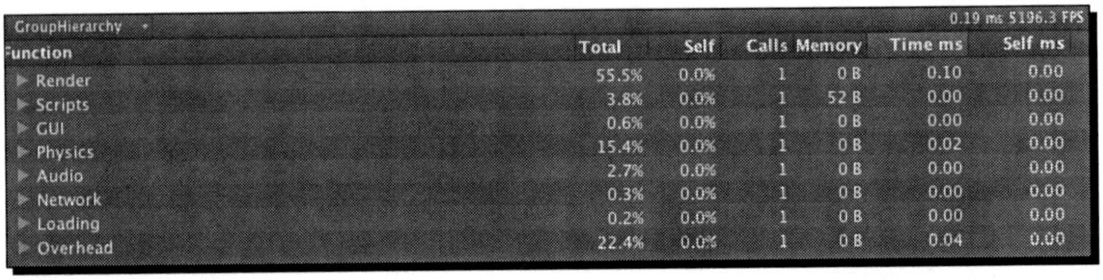

Time for action – Creating a new layout

While the Unity environment has a lot of features and options, it is possible to become entirely overwhelmed by the amount of data, or not realize that something has gone awry. We will look at building out a simple customization for our environment that contains the views we need, as well as some of the views that don't appear in the interface by default, in order to prepare ourselves for testing applications. If you're familiar with the Eclipse development environment you may be thinking that Unity opens views depending on what action you're performing, but Unity doesn't do that. However, we are going to emulate some of that functionality by creating a new layout that is well suited to profiling an application.

1. Our first step for creating a new layout is to start with a base layout and customize it. Unity has several default layouts to choose from, but for our purposes we will choose the Wide layout. In the **Window** Menu, select **Wide** layout:

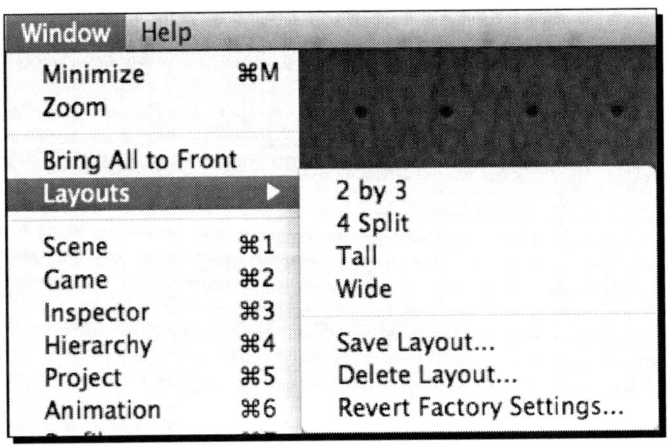

2. The next, step to creating our layout, is to decide which views are most important for getting things done. Since we're planning to profile an application it makes sense to bring in the **Profile** view into our environment. Selecting the **Window** menu and Profiler will show the new view. However, you will notice that it is a standalone window and not attached to the rest of the environment. Unity doesn't require that all of the views live within the same window as the others. In fact, this makes it easier for users with multiple screens as you can have different groupings of views on different screens. However, for our purposes we will assume that we have one screen to work with.

3. To position the Profiler inside our interface select the **Profiler** tab and drag it. This will result in a grayed out version of the tab appearing in the interface. As you move this grayed-out version into places where it can be docked, it will change shape to illustrate what it will look like if you dock it in that position. For now let's release it right above the **Hierarchy** view and the **Project** view:

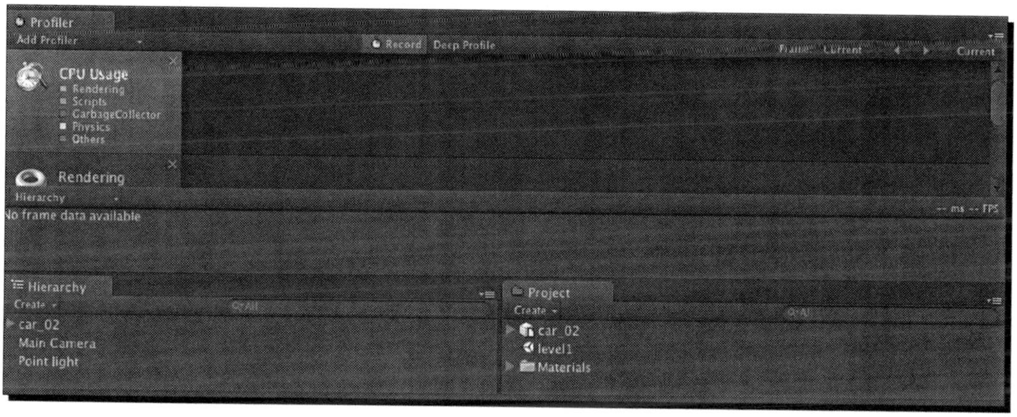

Since we're profiling our application we probably don't really need to know much about the Project's layout so we can remove the **Project** view from the layout. To accomplish this we need to select the **Menu** drop-down which appears in the upper right of the view and select the **Close** tab. Once done, the **Project** view will no longer be in the layout. Don't worry, if you ever need to bring it back you can always go into the **Window** menu and dock it in the same manner in which we introduced the **Profiler** view.

Now we probably also want console messages, as they represent feedback from our game session. We will introduce the console by selecting **Window | Console**. When the console menu appears we will drag it right next to the **Hierarchy** tab, such that it appears as a tab in the same row with the **Hierarchy**. This represents the other layout option that Unity provides, which is to have rows of tabs for views:

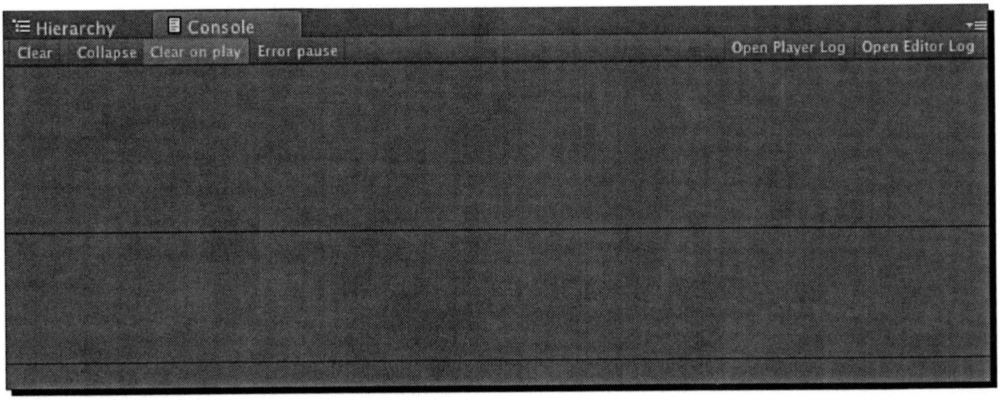

What just happened?

We have created a new layout specifically for profiling an application and saved it, so that whenever we are ready to dive deep into debugging and application profiling we can simply switch to it, without having to otherwise clutter our environment when we are simply designing our game. This has some very substantial implications for productivity as the interface can be set up for a particular purpose, such as level editing, scripting, or testing and you can focus the environment on specifically what you need. While it may not seem like a large detail right now, as your projects get bigger you will be glad this level of flexibility is there.

Time for action – Saving a new layout

1. Now that we have created our new layout, we need to save it so we can reuse it later. In the **Window** menu select **Layouts | Save Layout**:

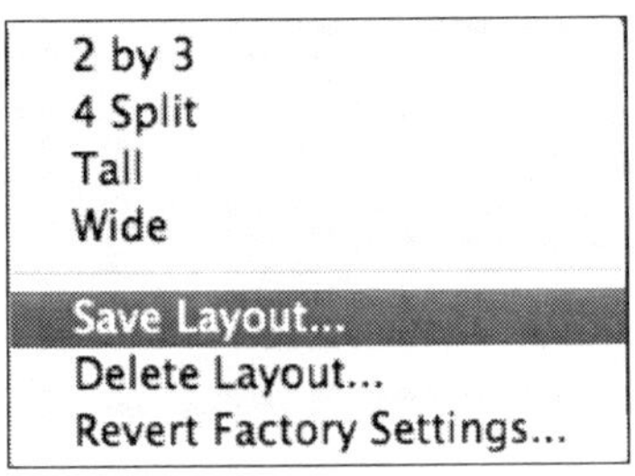

2. You will be presented with a simple dialog box that will ask for the name of the layout. Enter **Profiler** into the text box and press **Save**:

3. Now that your layout has been saved you can switch over to it at any time by selecting **Window | Layouts** and selecting your layout:

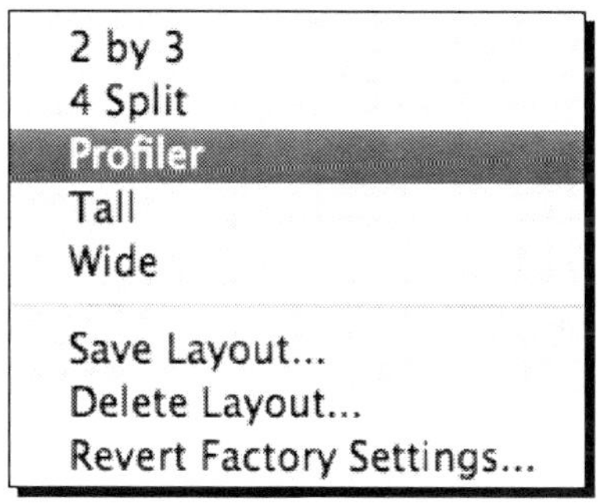

What just happened?

We have just saved our layout so that we can reference it later in our development process. In addition, we can share our layout with other developers by giving them the layout files that Unity stores.

Layouts are stored with the .wlt extension in the following folder :

1. on Mac OSx :

   `Users/username/Library/Preference/Unity/Editor/Layouts/`

2. On Windows 7

   Unity 3:

   `c:\users\username\AppData\Roaming\Unity\Editor-3.x\Preferences\Layouts`

   Unity 2.x:

   `C:\users\username\AppData\Roaming\Unity\Editor\Preferences\Layouts`

3. On Windows XP

   Unity 3

   `C:\Documents and Settings\username\Application Data\Unity\Editor-3.x\Preferences\Layouts`

   Unity 2.x

   `C:\Documents and Settings\username\Application Data\Unity\Editor\Preferences\Layouts`

The best way to see this in action is to deploy a real application and look at it from two different layouts to see how it will change the way you interact with your environment. This is also a great time to install Unity Remote, as we want to use it when we are doing rapid prototypes.

Time for action – Deploying Unity Remote

One of the hardest things to do when building an application for an iOS device is to be able to get some real time feedback from the device, while still having the richness of the development environment to work with. Unity solves this problem with the Unity Remote application that will allow you to play test your application within Unity, while using the iOS device as a controller. Unity Remote accomplishes this by streaming the game to the iOS device through WiFi and gathering the input actions from the device and injecting them into the Unity environment. With Unity Remote you can avoid having to build and deploy your application to your device every time you make a change.

There is only one problem with Unity Remote when it comes to testing our application – we need to build it specifically for our device.

> Remember, all iOS applications must be signed before they can be installed on the device.

We are going to walk through each of the steps necessary to produce commercial content for Unity 3 that can be deployed to an iOS device:

1. The first step is to open the Unity Remote project in the XCode environment. The Unity Remote source project is not in the distribution for Unity and needs to be downloaded from the Unity website. Unity Remote is an official Unity extension on the website and can be downloaded at `http://unity3d.com/support/resources/unity-extensions/unity-remote`:

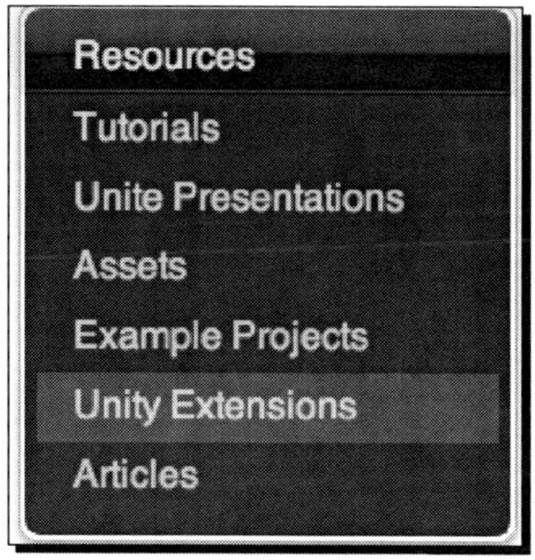

2. Once this project has been downloaded, select the **UnityRemote.xcodeproj** to open this project in XCode. As we did in the last chapter, we need to create an **App ID** for Unity Remote in the **iOS Provisioning Portal**:

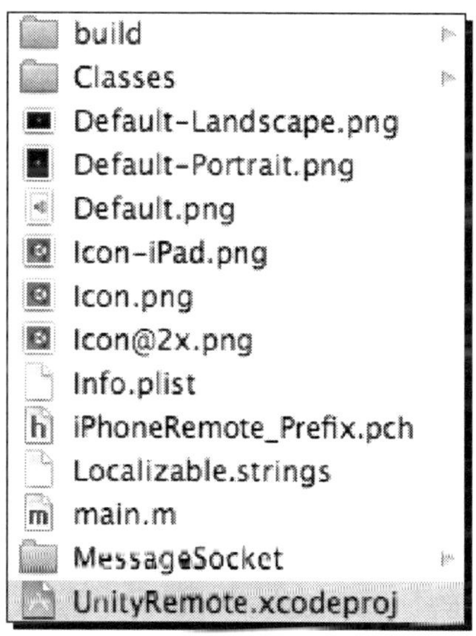

3. With our **App ID** created, we need to enter that **App ID** into the XCode project so that the application will build with that **App ID** and be deployed to our iPhone. While Unity takes care of these steps for us, we will need to do them ourselves for Unity Remote as this is a regular XCode application.

> Don't worry, once we get Unity Remote installed we won't need to do this again.

4. Open the project settings using the **Edit Project Settings** in the **Project** menu in XCode. This will display all of the settings that XCode will use to build and deploy your application:

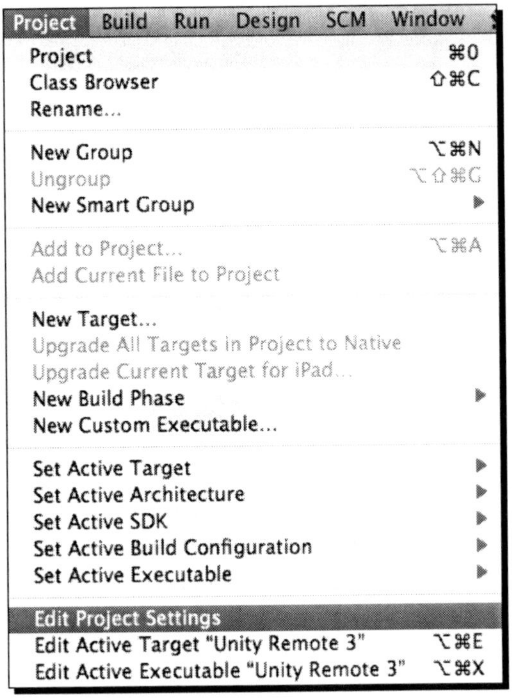

There are two groups of settings that we are interested in for this project: Architectures and Code Signing.

5. In the Architectures section we want to make sure that we have set the project's Base SDK to the appropriate version for our device. For example, if our device is running iOS 4.0 we want to make sure that we don't have the Base SDK set to build for iOS 4.2. Simply select the drop-down list on the Base SDK line and XCode will tell you what the valid options are for your configuration. If XCode doesn't show an SDK here, it is because it is not installed properly and XCode will not be able to build with it.

6. In the Code Signing section you will want to select the Any IOS entry under the Code Signing Identity item. When you select the drop-down for this item it will display all of the possible code signing options for this project. Simply select the one that corresponds to the App ID you just created in the iOS Provisioning Portal.

7. With those settings updated for your App ID, and device, you can now build the project in XCode from the Build menu by selecting Build and Run. This will build the Unity Remote application with XCode and deploy it to your device.

8. Make sure that you have the target device plugged in when you run this command or XCode will complain profusely:

> If you aren't running the standard iOS 4.0 SDK that the Unity Remote project expects you will encounter a particular error.

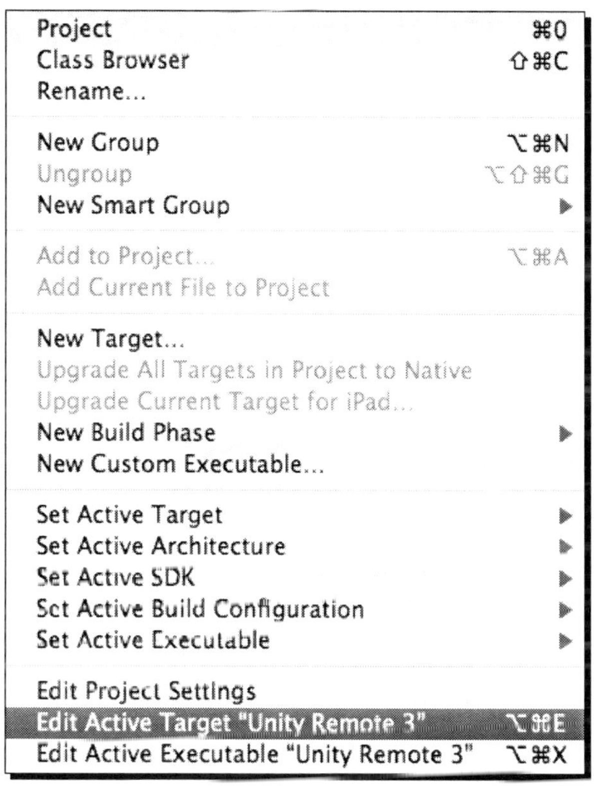

What this error is saying is that the Unity Remote was expecting iphoneos4.0 to be installed as the SDK. This is represented in the toolbar, as well in the build configuration drop-down as **Base SDK Missing**. Depending on when you've begun your trek into iOS development, iphoneos4.0 may be a distant memory. To remedy this you will have to adjust the settings for the project to match the SDK that you have installed by editing the Active Target for Unity Remote:

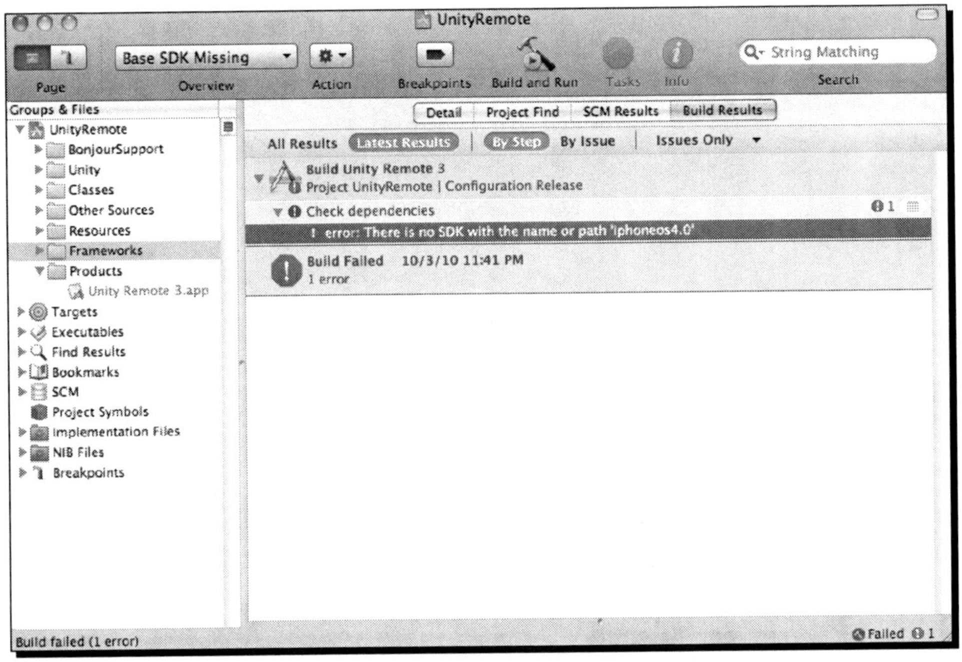

> In the **Architecture** section you can change the Base SDK to whichever SDK you desire. Generally, the best option is to set this to the **Lastest iOS** unless you have a particular reason to do otherwise. With this setting changed you will see that the **Base SDK Missing** error is gone from the toolbar and when you build the project it will successfully install on your device.

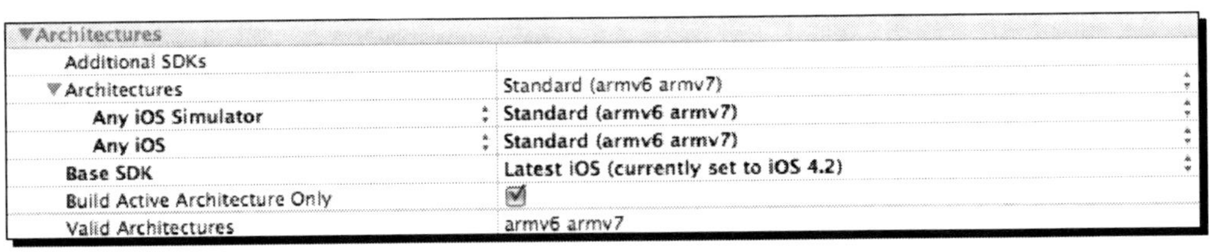

What just happened?

We have just built and deployed Unity Remote to our device. This allows us to use our iOS device as an input to our game and test the behavior of the game from the iOS device, without having to deploy the application on the device. This is useful as it will speed the development process and reduce the number of code-compile-deploy cycles we have to perform.

Time for action – Testing our application using Unity Remote

Now that we have Unity Remote deployed we can get to the business of using our iOS device as a controller in our game development environment:

1. Run Unity Remote on your device and a list of the machines ready to provide data for Unity Remote will appear in the list. If, for some reason, yours doesn't because of specific DNS or Bonjour security, you can enter the IP address of the machine you want to control by selecting the button in the lower left. If you don't really care to simulate the visual interface of the game on the iOS device you can change the radio button for **Show image** to **Off** and the game's frames will not be displayed on your device, yet you will still be able to control the game inside of Unity with your iOS device acting as a controller:

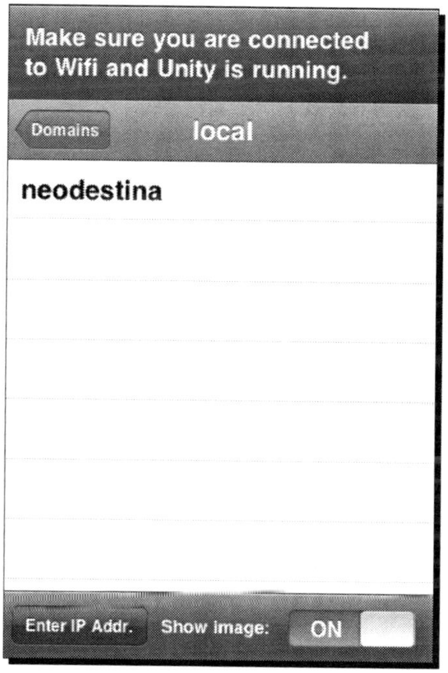

2. Press **Play** in the Unity toolbar. This will be the signal for Unity and Unity Remote to begin exchanging data. The content that is in the **Game** view will begin to appear on the iOS device, though you may think something is wrong the first time you see it as it will appear to be a much lower resolution version of your game:

Game View representation of the game in Unity

If you recall, I mentioned that Unity streams the game to the iOS device. What the IDE is doing is actually streaming the video of what's happening in the game to your device so you will see a variety of compression artifacts, depending on your Wi-Fi connection speed and other factors:

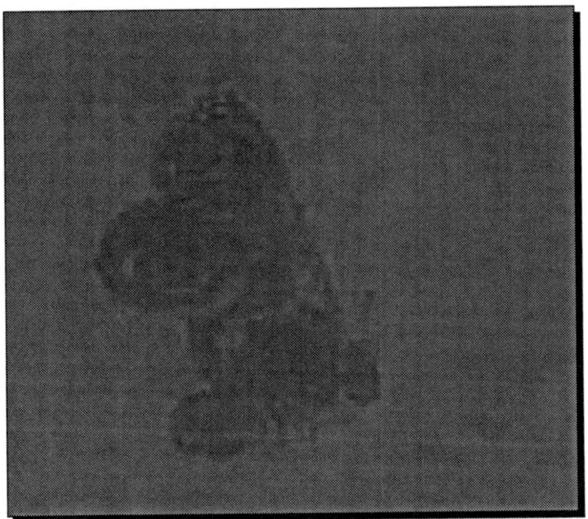

View of the game on Unity Remote

3. This is a normal behavior of Unity Remote (and one of the reasons for the Show Image radio button) and should not detract in any way from your ability to perform your testing. Remember, this is purely a testing tool to enable rapid development so visual fidelity is not necessary. If you really need to know exactly how its going to look, you can deploy the game to the device – but bookmark this chapter as you will find that after some time the benefit of knowing how great your content looks on the device will pale into comparison to being more productive using Unity Remote.

What just happened?

What Unity Remote is doing behind the scenes is getting the frame buffer of the application and compressing that into a video stream and streaming that over to the iOS device. Any device input that is gathered through the iOS device is then transmitted through Wi-Fi to the Unity IDE and used to direct the objects in the environment. Whenever you enter **Play** mode in the **Editor**, your device will become the remote control for testing the game.

While this approach is very useful for rapid application development, it is important to note that performance using this approach is approximated at best and you will still want to build and run your application on your device exclusively every so often, to confirm that performance and gameplay is as you expect. Similarly, it is important to note that this approach is very dependent on your Wi-Fi connection. If your device isn't showing a full Wi-Fi signal you can expect significant performance implications.

We have just performed all of the steps necessary to setup our development environment and publish content to Unity. Further we have built our own mini testing lab using Unity Remote so we can utilize our device, yet debug the game in our development environment. This is a crucial milestone as we can now focus entirely on customizing Unity and building games.

One last thing about Unity Remote that is worth noting, while I had you build the remote application yourself you can actually download this in the App Store. Given this you may be asking yourself then why did you have me build it? As an iOS developer, even one using Unity, there are a number of times that you will find yourself needing to debug what is happening under the covers with XCode. In addition, you may find yourself wanting to integrate with some native feature of iOS that isn't supported in Unity. In all of these scenarios you will find yourself digging through the underlying XCode project, so now seemed to be the best time to get familiar with how things are put together.

Links to the Unity Remote :

1. Unity Remote 3 for iPhone :
   - `http://itunes.apple.com/fr/app/unity-remote-3/id394632904?mt=8`
2. Unity Remote 3 for iPad:
   - `http://itunes.apple.com/fr/app/unity-remote-3/id394632904?mt=8`
3. Unity Remote < 3 for iPhone:
   - `http://itunes.apple.com/fr/app/unity-remote/id305967442?mt=8`

Pop quiz – doing the thing

1. Where can Unity views be displayed?
   a. Toolbar
   b. Undocked on different screens
   c. In Tabs
   d. Remotely on the iOS device
   e. On other Unity machines
2. Where can you go to set up an application ID for your iOS device?
   a. Apple Developer Forums
   b. XCode Organizer
   c. iTunes Connect
   d. iOS Provisioning Portal
   e. XCode SDK
3. The Unity interface can only be customized for one user and use case? (true/false)
4. Unity Remote works over 3G Connections? (true/false)
5. You have to build Unity Remote in order to perform remote debugging? (true/false)

Summary

In this chapter we explored the Unity environment and learned how to customize it for a particular purpose.

Specifically, we covered how to:

- Customize the Unity interface
- Customize the iOS deployments
- Deploy Unity Remote
- Test an application using custom layouts and Unity Remote

While we have spent some time reviewing the Unity interface, we have done so at a relatively high-level. To get more in depth coverage of the Unity interface and its options, it is recommended that you read through the Unity documentation.

With the first two chapters under our belts, we can now leave behind the pre-built projects and begin building games from scratch, which is the subject of the next chapter – Hello World.

3
Hello World

In this chapter we will build a new project from scratch and produce the first reader created application that we can run on our iOS device. While we have experimented with deploying applications to our device before, these were pre-built applications. It's time to take the training wheels off and take the environment for a test drive.

In this chapter we will:

- Compose our first scene
- Test our application in the editor
- Customize the iOS settings
- Deploy this application to a device

This is where the fun really starts...

Composing our first scene

In our first application we're going to follow software development tradition and create the typical first program Hello World. As we're using Unity to create our game it seemed to make sense to actually create a 3D world and deploy it to our device. When we're done we should be able to see the earth on our device:

The final output of our Hello World game

Start with the basics

For our first game we're going to start with the basics.

1. Create a scene

2. Create sample objects
3. Customize sample objects
4. Control the camera
5. Deploy to the iOS Device

Time for action – Creating a scene

1. Our first step is to create a new Unity Project by selecting **File | New Project**. In the Project Directory specify where you would like Unity to create this new Project and press the **Create Project** button:

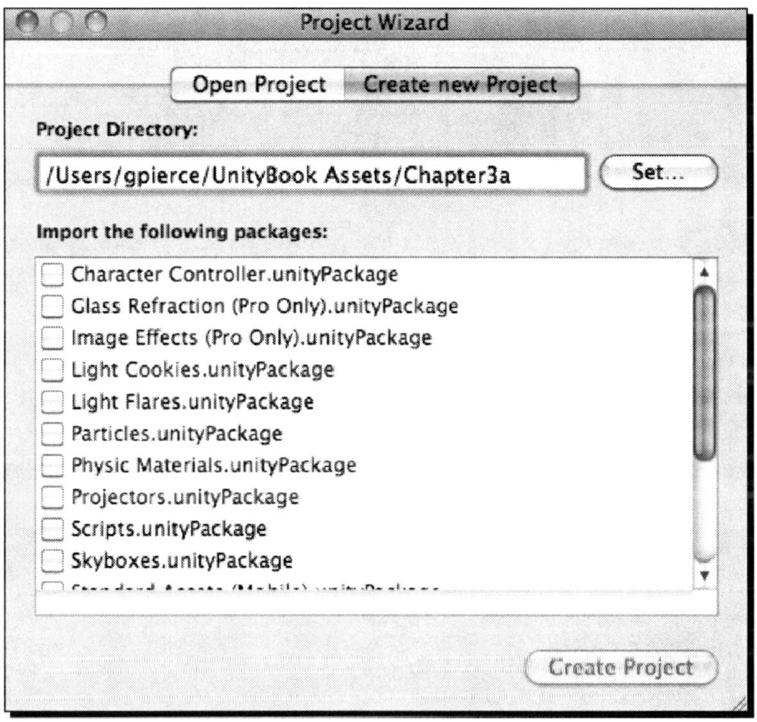

Unity bundles common sets of scripts, assets, and other reusable functionality into distributable files referred to as Unity Packages. These single file archives end with the `.unityPackage` extension and represent the primary mechanism for sharing in Unity. We will not be importing any packages into Unity for these first applications so don't worry about selecting any of the packages.

Most games are broken up into scenes or levels and Unity is designed around this concept. A scene in its most basic state is just a container pointing to all of all the art assets, scripts, behaviors, and so on. You can, of course, put all of your content into one big scene, but that is more suitable for very small games or those that stream all of their content from the Internet. With the constraints of most iOS devices and the speed of even 3G Internet connections it would be impractical to do that so we will focus on level-based design.

2. When Unity created our project, it created a default scene for us – it simply needs to be saved. Unity will put all of the scenes in the `Assets` folder of the project. Save the scene as **level1** and you will find that the new level is represented in the **Project** view:

Once you start creating multiple scenes, you will be able to simply double-click on the scene in the **Project** view and it will change the **Scene** view and **Game** view to represent the new state.

What just happened?

We have just created a simple scene for our game. At the moment it's very empty, but is ready to be filled with actors, scripts, and other functionality to become a real game.

Time for action – Creating objects in a scene

Next, we need to create some objects in our scene or we will have a very boring game. The first object we need to create is something to represent the ground. Yes I know there is no ground in space, but to illustrate some of the available features we need the ground.

1. In the **Main Menu**, create a new plane by selecting **GameObject | Create Other | Plane**.

2. We also want to give this Plane a unique name, so in the **Inspector** view change the name of the object from Plane to Ground by selecting the **Plane** text in the **Inspector** by simply replacing it with **Ground**. Unity will now refer to this object as **Ground** as well. This will come in useful later when we're trying to do things with the ground plane:

3. In the **Inspector**, increase the size of our ground plane by changing the **Scale** to (**100**, **1**, **100**). This should give us plenty of room to move around:

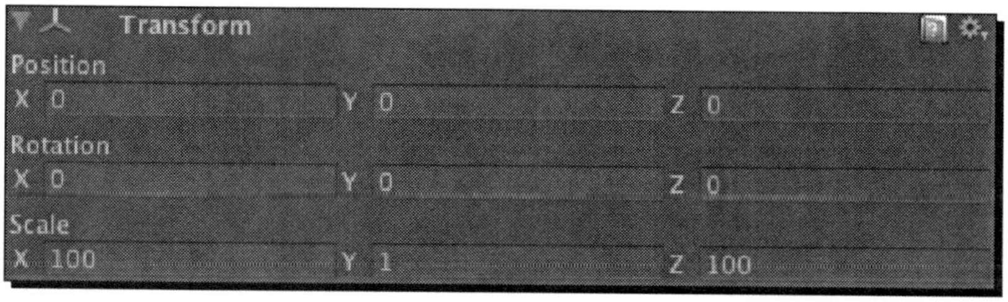

4. One new feature of Unity 3 is the ability to get a quick render of what the world looks like from the camera's perspective without having to play the game. In the **Hierarchy** view select the **Main Camera** object and you will see in the **Scene** view that there is a **Camera Preview** window that is showing you what the camera sees. This window is a real-time preview as well, so as objects change in the scene, the **Camera Preview** will update to reflect those changes:

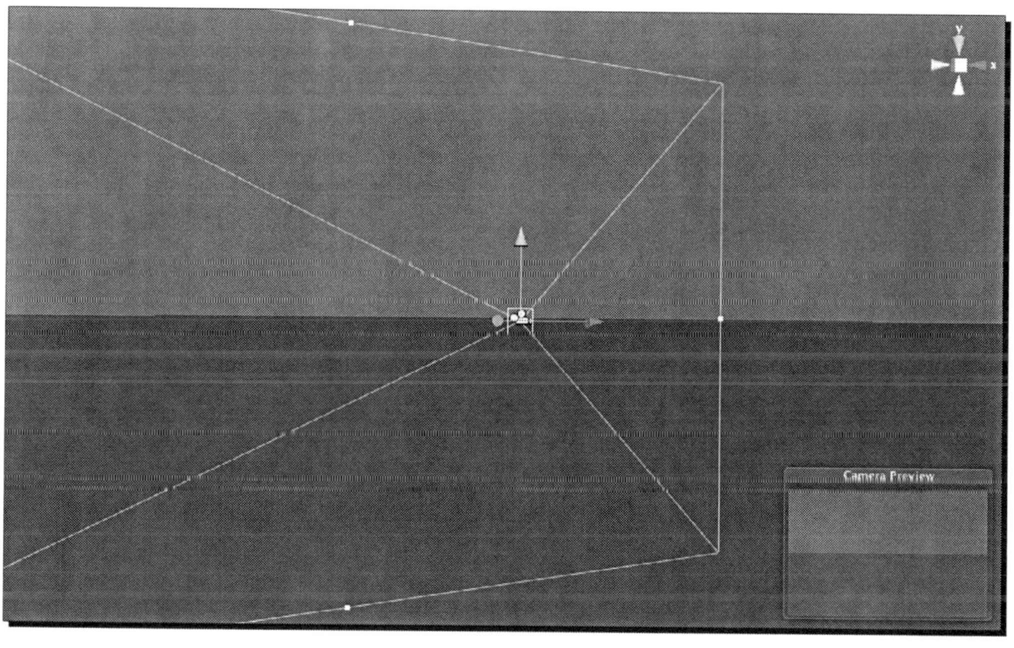

What just happened?

We have just created a simple ground object for our Hello World scene and explored how we can preview the world with the Camera Preview.

Time for action – Let there be light

One of your most important assets in Unity is lighting. With the right lighting effects your game can go from looking pedestrian to revolutionary. Unity has a very sophisticated lighting engine that can handle dynamic lights, baking lights with the Beast lighting system, and deferred lights.

1. For now we will create a basic light by selecting **Create | Point light** which will add a **Point Light Game** Object to our scene:

2. Now that you've created your point light, let's position it above the scene so that it can reflect on other objects. In the **Inspector**, change the **Position** to (**0,5,0**). This should put it above the scene:

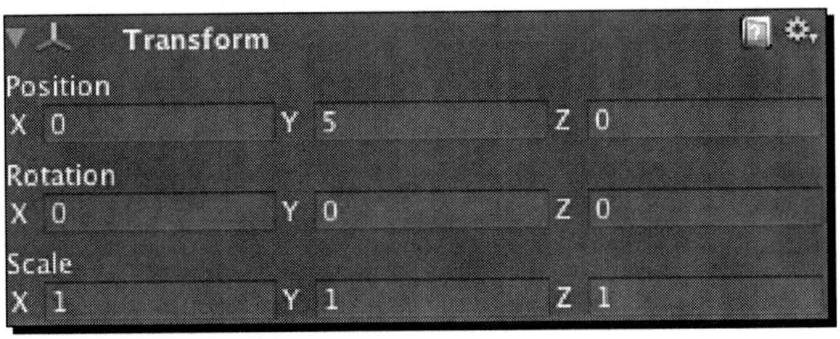

3. Let's center the editor on this light by pressing the shortcut-key F, which will focus the scene on this object:

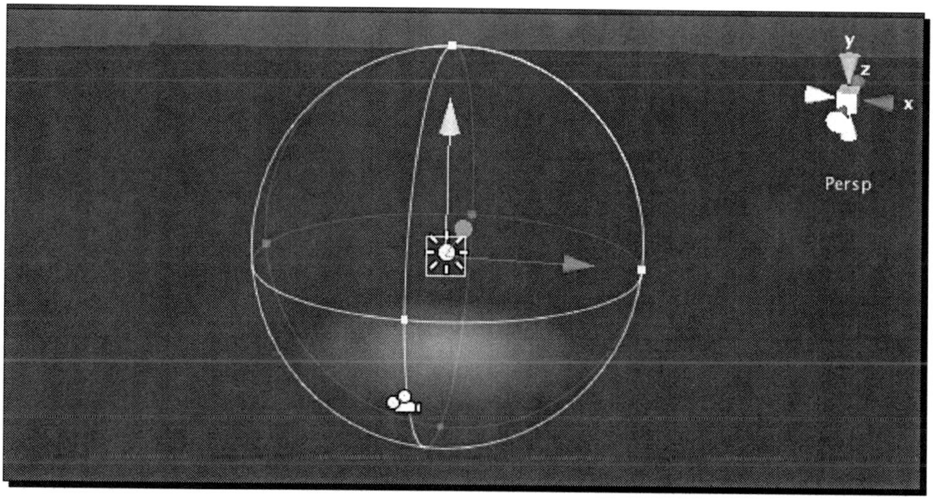

4. Just to make sure our light is bright enough let's set the **Intensity** to **4**. You can either use the slider or just enter **4** in the text box next to the slider:

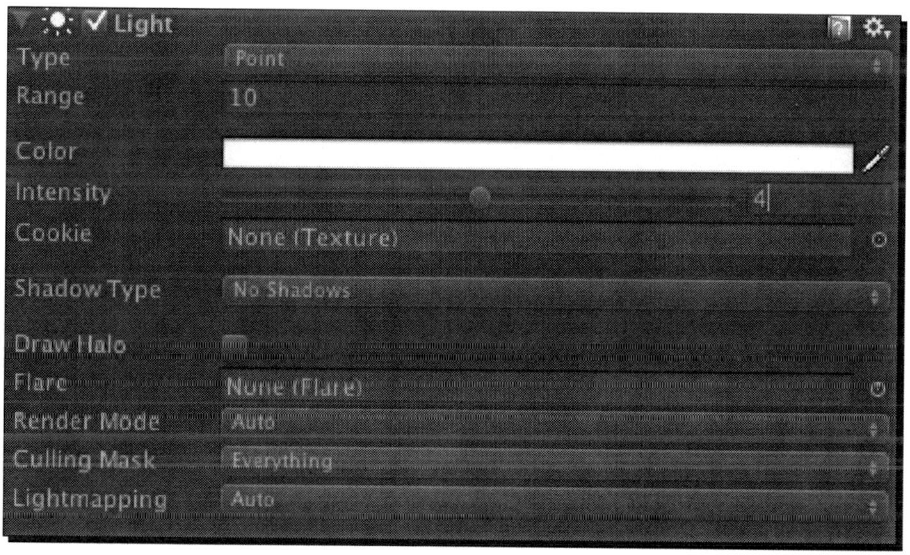

You can also see that the intensity of the light has increased as there is now more light in the scene:

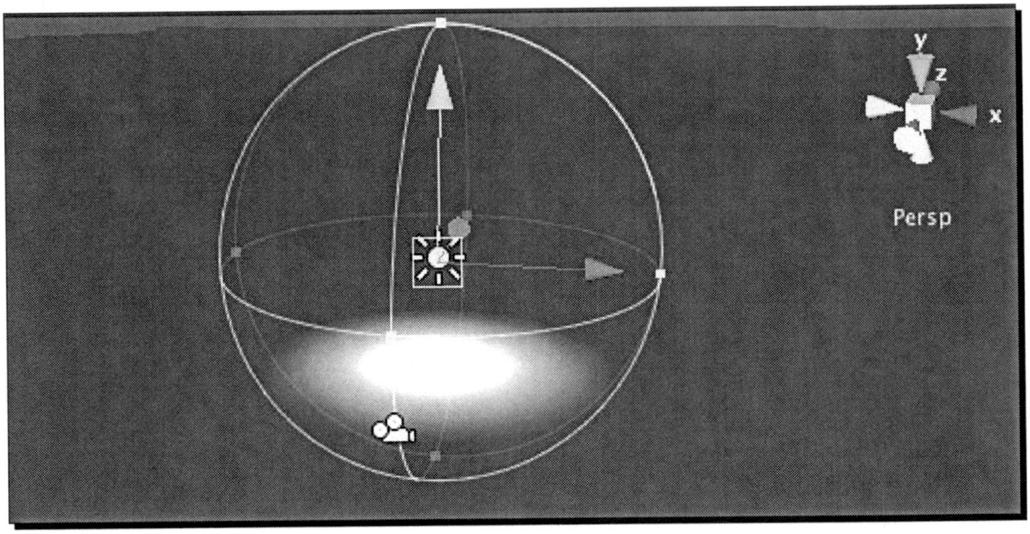

5. Select the **Main Camera**, you will see a **Camera Preview** that shows the light shining down upon the ground plane:

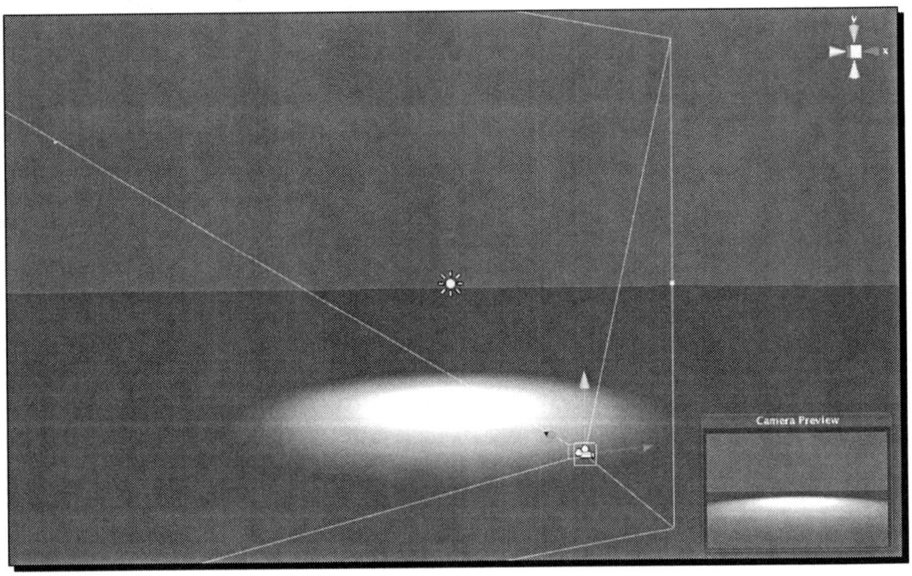

What just happened?

We have added some lighting to our scene so that we will be able to see what's going on in our scene. Remember, that in the absence of lights in the scene there won't be much for the gamer to see. While we have created a simple lighting model here, you will see that lighting is perhaps one of the most important features that you can add to your game as it will provide a significant amount of visual fidelity to your objects.

Time for action – Hello "World"

What good would a Hello World chapter be if we didn't actually put the world in it.

1. In the **Hierarchy** view, create a **Sphere** with **Create | Sphere**.
2. Rename this Game Object to **World** in the **Inspector**.
3. Let's move it a little off-center so that we can see the effect lighting has on this sphere to **Position** (**-2**, **2**, **0**). While this is interesting, this doesn't much look like the world:

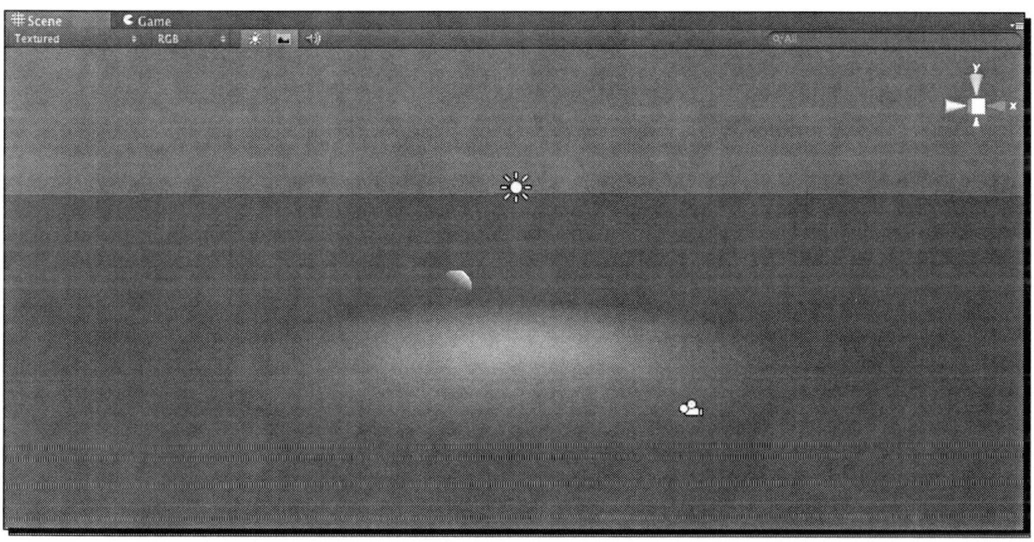

4. In the `Chapter 3` folder you will find a file called `earth.jpg`. Select the **Project** view and drag this texture right into the **Project** view. Your Unity environment may pause for a moment while Unity imports this file.

5. Select the earth texture in the **Project** view and you will see the details for this texture:

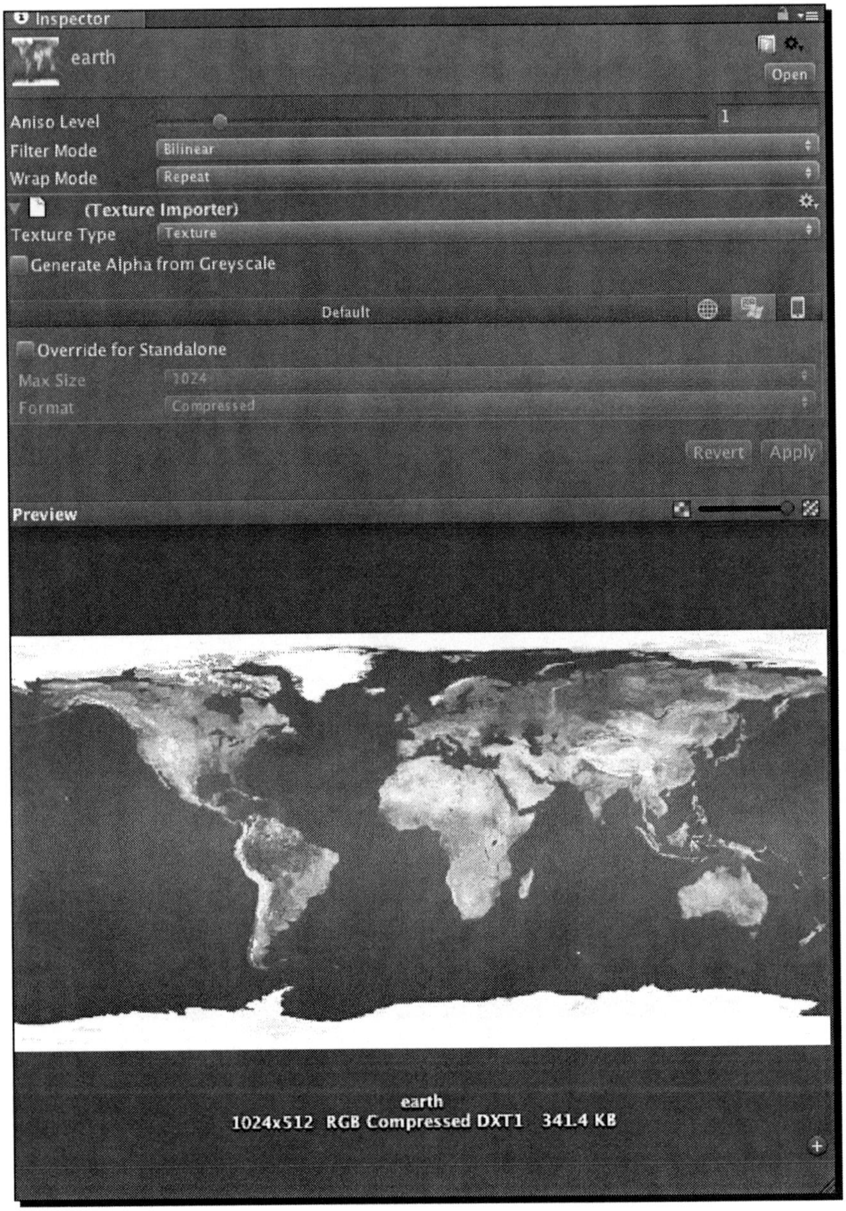

6. It would be nice if we could just plop this texture onto our sphere and have a rendering of our world. The Unity developers thought this would be nice as well. Consequently, you can drag the earth texture from the **Project** view onto our sphere in the **Scene** view and it will automatically texture it.

7. Select the **Scene** view and examine the rendering of our scene. We're getting closer to a true Hello World:

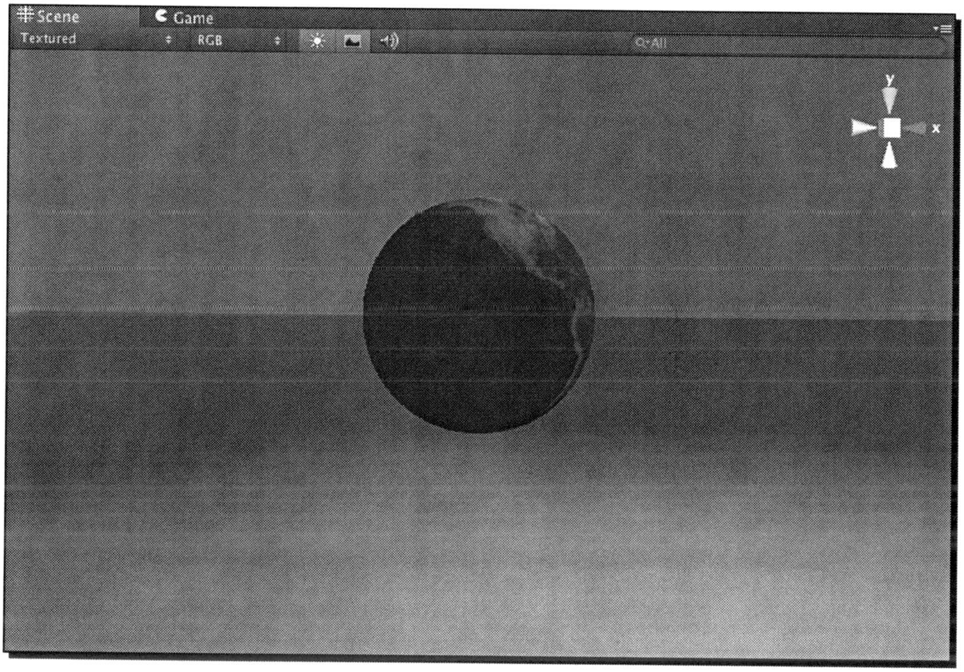

What just happened?

We have just added the first actor to our game. In this case our actor is a very simple sphere model with a texture on it, but we have just performed the basic steps that are necessary to get objects into a Unity scene.

Time for action – Controling the camera

This is all very interesting, except that we're fairly far away from our creation and we lack the ability to move around the scene. With traditional iOS devices we can accomplish this by accessing the accelerometer within the device:

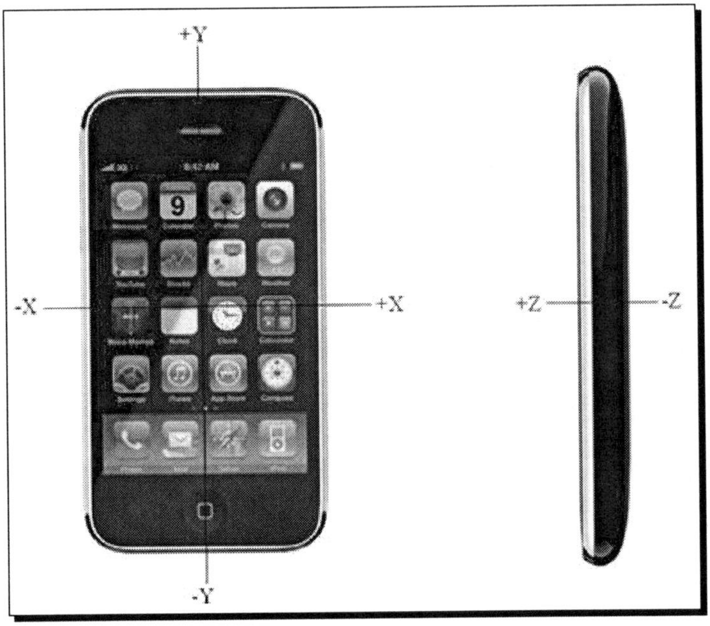

Unity encapsulates all of the functionality of the accelerometer into the `Input` class and we can use its attributes and methods to connect to the accelerometer and determine what is going on with our device.

> Those of you coming from Unity iPhone will notice that all of the Unity Input for iOS has been encapsulated in the `Input` class. There is no longer a need to use the `iPhoneInput` class.

1. In the **Project** view create a new JavaScript script by selecting **Create | JavaScript**. This will create a new script named `NewBehaviourScript`.
2. Double-clicking on this script will open the script in Unity's default editor **Unitron**. We will cover the other Unity-provided tools that can be used to develop scripts, MonoDevelop, when we deep dive into scripting.

3. In the script window we simply enter the code for the script in the `Update` function:

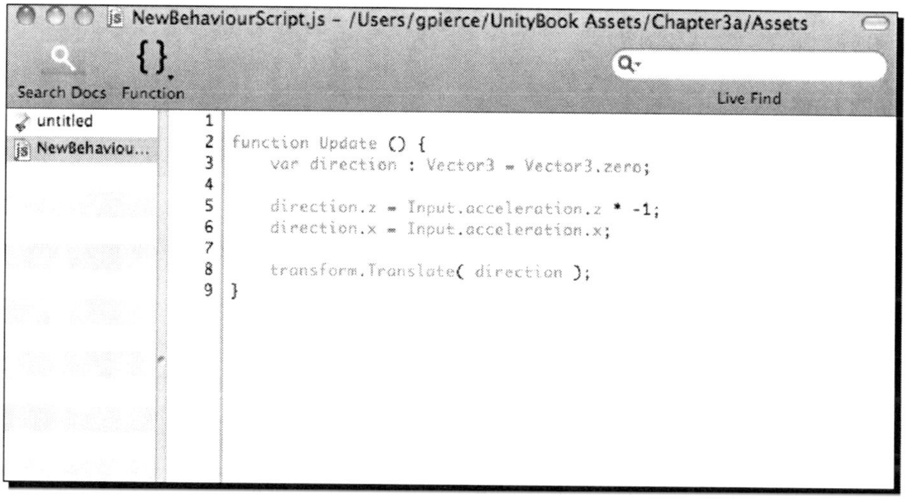

> **Downloading the example code**
>
> You can download the example code files for all Packt books you have purchased from your account at `http://www.packtpub.com`. If you purchased this book elsewhere, you can visit `http://www.packtpub.com/support` and register to have the files e-mailed directly to you.

Scripts must, generally, be attached to Game Objects to do anything useful. In our case we want to move the camera around so we need to attach this script to the camera. There are two ways to accomplish this in Unity. As with texturing, you could simply drag the script onto the camera.

4. In the **Hierarchy** view select the **Main Camera** object.

5. Then, in the **Project** view drag the script from the **Project** view onto either the Camera in the **Inspector** view or onto the object in the **Hierarchy** view.

   The other way to accomplish this task is to select the **Main Camera** in the **Hierarchy** view and, subsequently, in the Unity menu bar select **Component | Scripts | New Behaviour Script**.

   In either case you will find that Unity has added your script to the camera:

What Just happened?

We have just examined how scripting is handled in the Unity environment. Every part of your gameplay functionality will be implemented as a script and you've just seen how simple it is to add these behaviors.

Time for action – Deploying to the iOS device

Now that we've created an application that does something useful, it's time to deploy our new creation to our iOS device and explore our scene using the accelerometer. As we've run through this process before we can cover these details at a high-level, it's important to walk through this again just so that the process feels right.

1. The first thing we need to do is to make sure that we're deploying the right type of application. When Unity originally created our new project it created it for desktop deployment. We need to change this in the **Build Settings** (**File | Build Settings**):

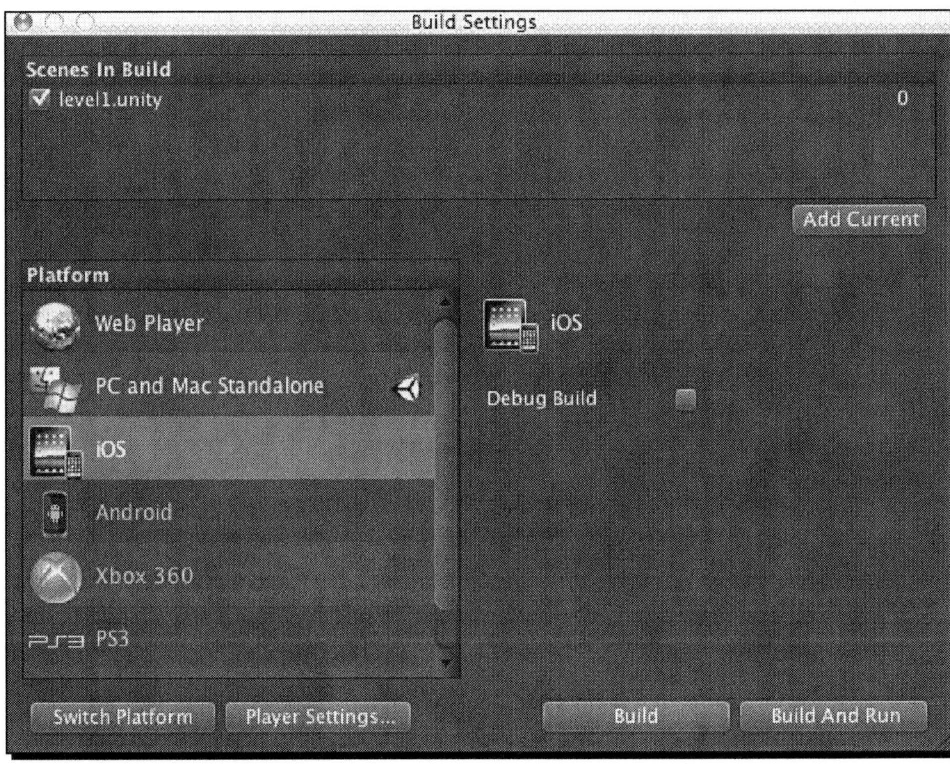

2. An important step here is to make sure that any scenes that we want included in the build on our device are included.

3. Click on the **Add Current** button and our level1 scene and all of the assets necessary for that scene will be included in the application when it is packaged for the device.

4. Select the iOS platform as the target platform and click on the **Switch Platform** button. Unity will pause for a moment and make the necessary changes to the project so that it can be deployed to the new target platform:

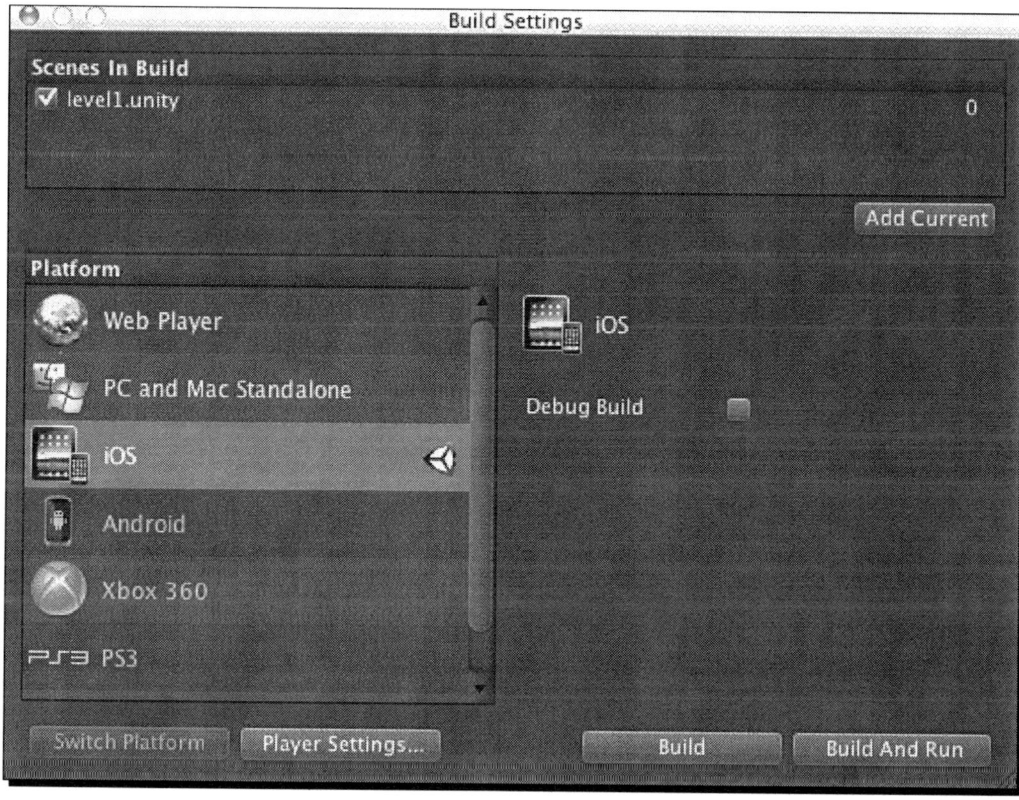

With this done the only thing remaining is to change the build settings for the project so that Unity can communicate with XCode and have it construct the application for deployment.

5. As before, we need to create an **App ID** and deploy a provisioning profile to our development machine so that Unity can accomplish this. Enter the **iOS Provisioning Portal** and create a new **App ID** for our new application. While we could use the same **App ID** we used before, recall that doing so would replace our old application with the one we just built:

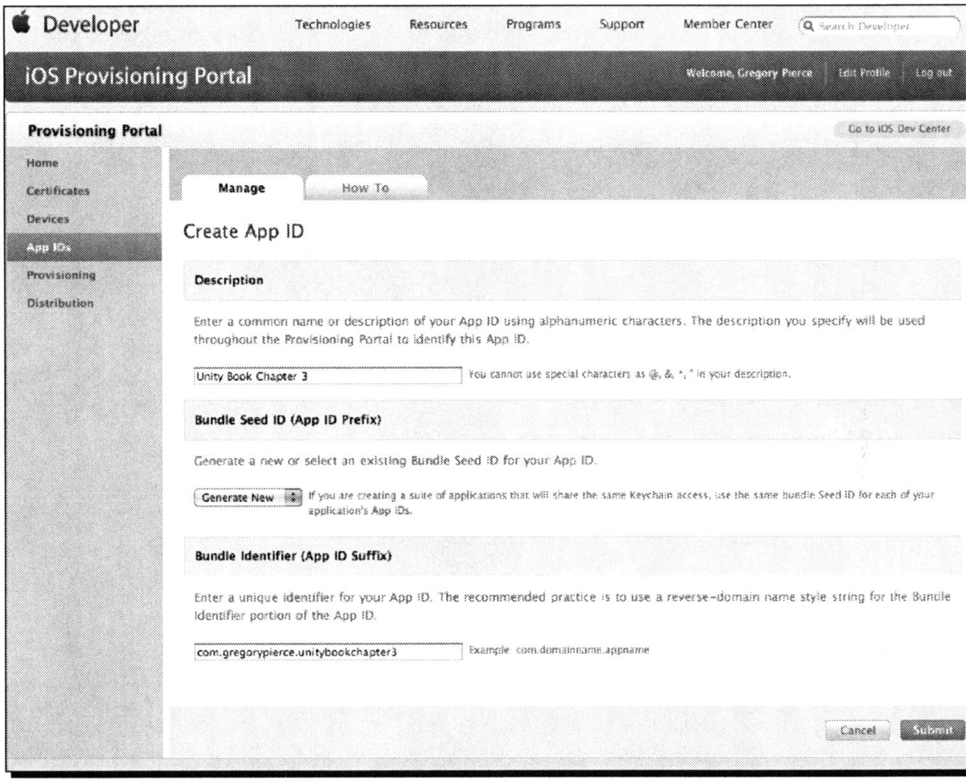

6. Next we need to create another provisioning profile so that we can deploy the application to the device:

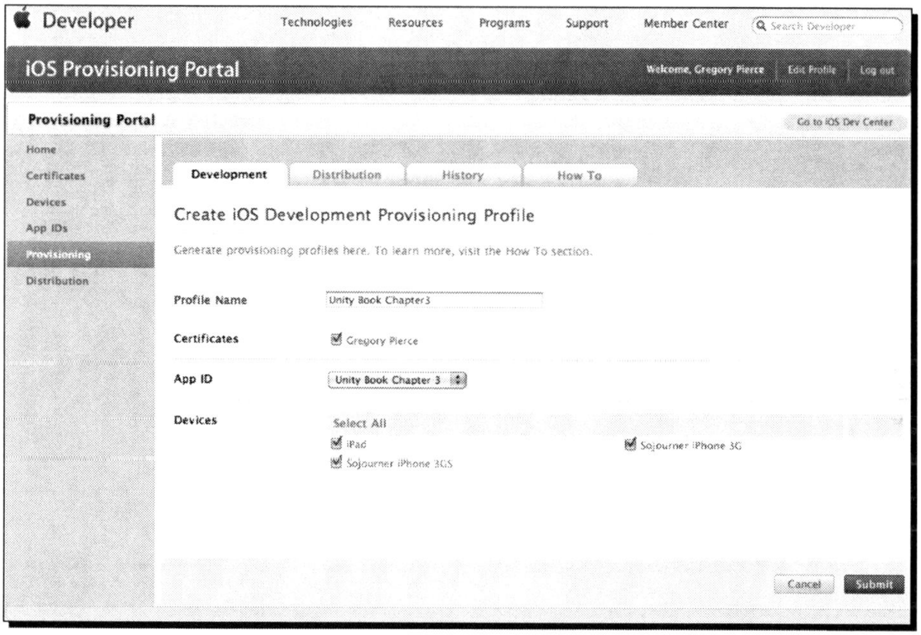

7. Once the provisioning profile is created you need to download the provisioning profile so that XCode can deploy the application to your iOS device:

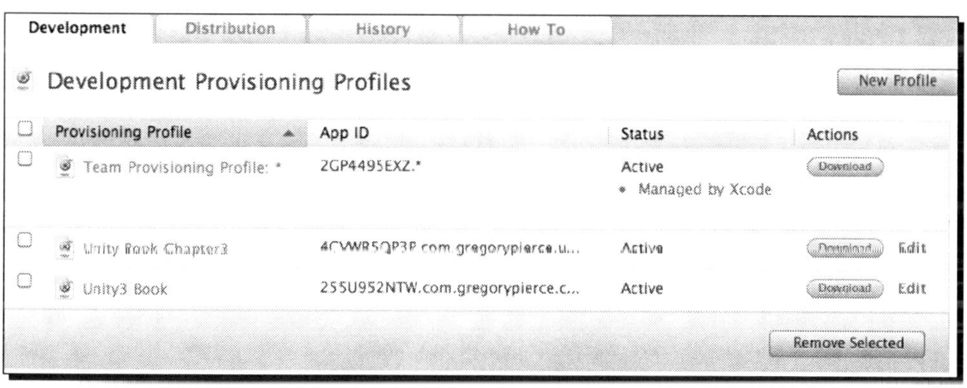

8. Double-clicking on the provisioning profile will open XCode's Organizer and deploy the provisioning profile to your device:

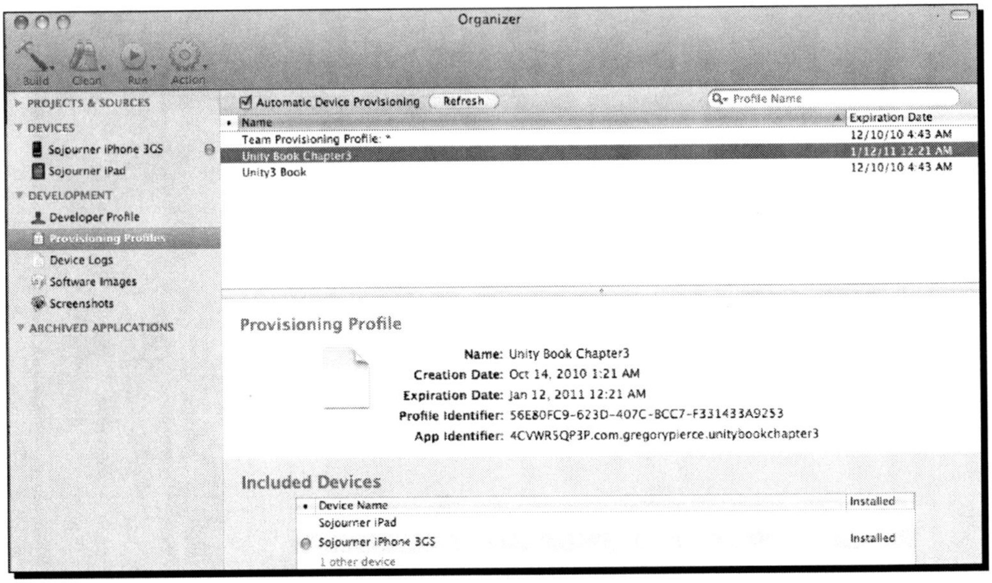

9. With this completed all we need to do is inform Unity of which **App ID** it should be using by entering that **App ID** in the **Bundle Identifier**:

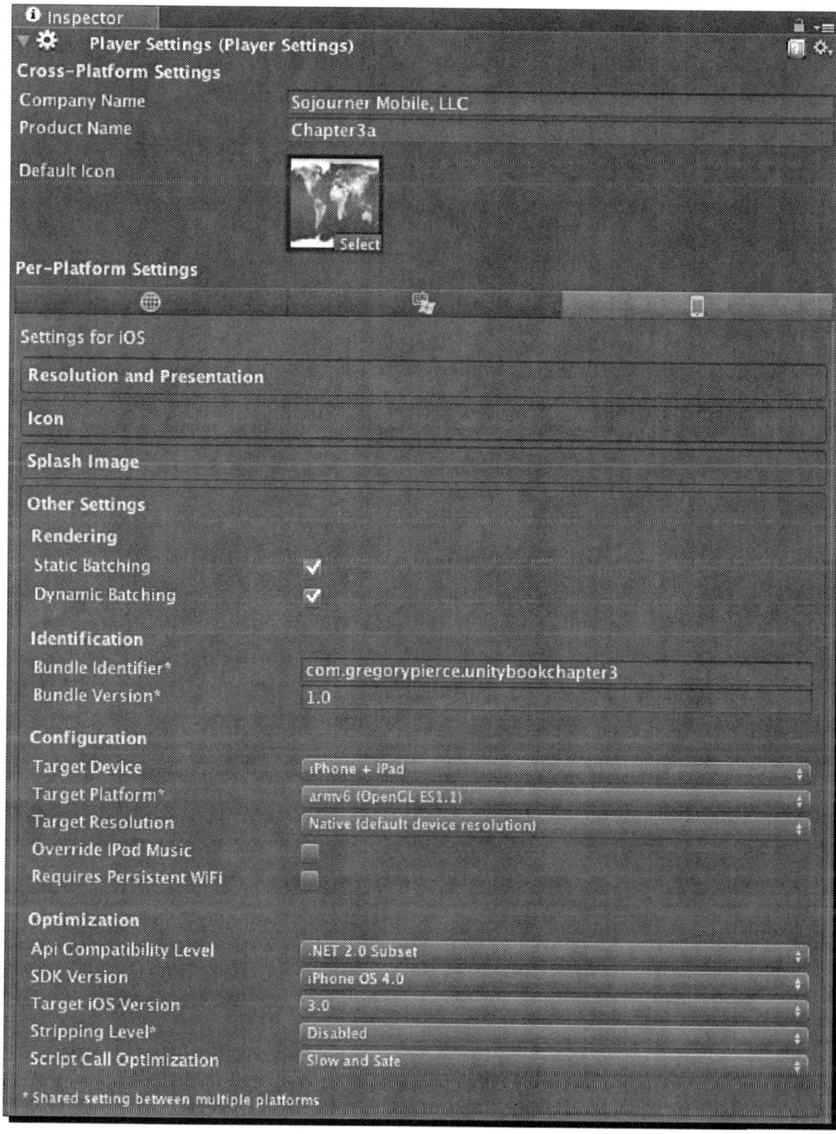

It would be nice to use our own icon rather than using the stock Unity icon. The icon that you use should be an asset in your unity project and can be any texture you want. Simply drag that texture onto the Default Icon box and Unity will do the rest.

10. With all of these steps completed, the last action we need to perform is invoking Unity's Build process so it can have XCode compile our game and install it on the phone. We can accomplish this through **File | Build & Run**.

11. Shortly after you've performed these steps, Unity will start on your iOS device.

Remember that we have the accelerometer active so as soon as our game starts we will start moving around the scene.

What just happened?

We just built our first game application from scratch. It doesn't do much right now, but we have just opened the doorway to building great games for the iOS platform. This should also give you a feel for how you would normally interact with the Unity environment. Unity is a sandbox where you can add all sorts of assets and then create scripts that will allow behaviors for those assets.

Summary

We built an application that actually does something worth showing to people in this chapter. While it's not likely to make millions of dollars in sales or garner celebrity status, this is a critical milestone for developing games in Unity as we have just touched a lot of the game development workflow.

Now that we've built our first scene, we need to take a tour of the Unity core concepts, as without a clear understanding of how Unity works, it will be difficult to really take advantage of the environment. The Unity Concepts will form the basis of the next chapter.

4
Unity Concepts

Now that we have built our first application and have a taste for what Unity is capable of, it's time to learn the core concepts of Unity so that we can build much more complex and compelling games. We have briefly discussed some of the core concepts already, but to build compelling content it is necessary to have a more in-depth understanding of how Unity uses these concepts.

In this chapter we shall:

- Learn the core concepts of Unity
- Create the core components within the tool

Basic concepts of Unity development

When studying a foreign language you will spend some time immersing yourself in its nouns and verbs so that you can understand the concepts and begin creating sentences.

Asset

An asset represents the atomic unity through which you can construct a scene in Unity. Anything that you bring into the environment is considered an asset including sound files, textures, models, scripts, and so on.

You can import assets into a Unity project by either dragging and dropping them from the desktop into the **Project** view, or by using the **Import New Asset** menu (**Assets | Import New Asset**). Once in the **Project** view the asset is something that can be used in your game. Think of the **Project** view as your palette from which you will paint your world.

Assets are managed on the file system by Unity. If you go into your project folder and look at the `Assets` directory you will find all of the assets that are in your project. When Unity imports your assets, it will store the imported asset and all of its metadata here.

> It is important to note that you should never try to manage assets in this folder directly.

While you can make changes to textures, audio, models, and so on, in this location with your various tools you should never move them as this will break the link between the asset and the Unity metadata for the asset. In effect, Unity will behave as if you just brought this asset into Unity for the first time and any relationships, settings, and so on will have to be newly created.

Time for action – Exporting asset packages

There will be times when you want to share a collection of assets with other users on your team or within the community. Unity makes this easier by providing a simple mechanism called Packages. A **package** is just a collection of assets bundled together in a single file.

In this exercise we're going to explore how one would share assets from an existing project with other developers:

1. Open the project for this chapter named **HelloWorld2**. In it you will find a version of our original Hello World demo with some additional assets.
2. Select the assets that you want to export as part of the package:

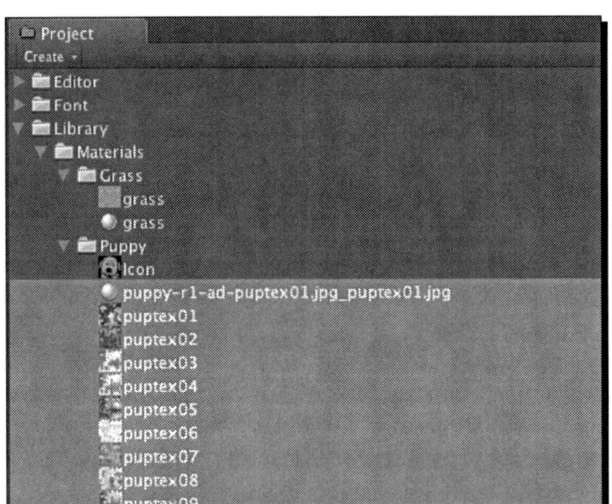

In the above illustration the **Materials** element within the **Project** has been selected. There are **Puppy** and **Grass** materials that are a child of the **Materials** element and they will be bundled in the package as well. If you only wanted to share the **Puppy** materials you would simply select the **Puppy** element and only those materials would be packaged.

3. Next let's create a package using the **Export Package** menu (**Assets | Export Package**). When selected, this will create a package starting with the selected item in the **Project** view and anything that is a child of this element.

4. Unity will then display a dialog with all of the assets that will be exported. If there are assets that you want to remove, uncheck its checkbox:

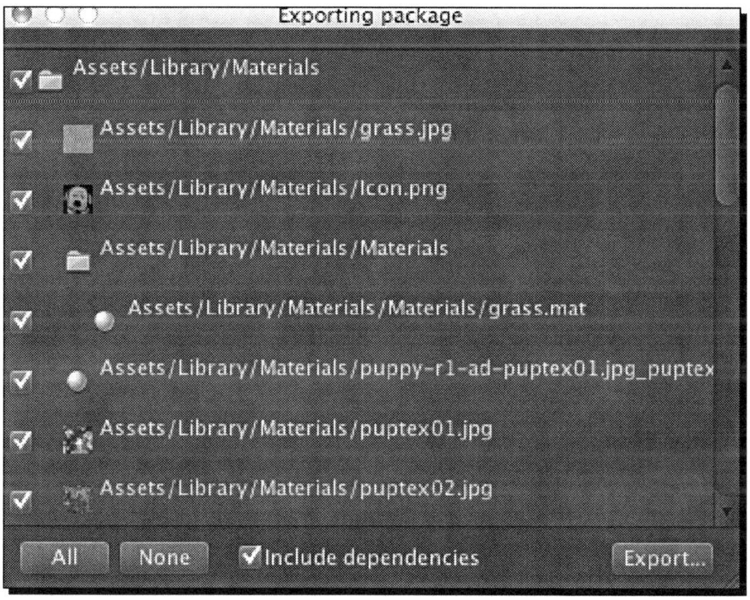

In addition, there is a checkbox labeled **Include dependencies**. If your assets have other assets, such as scripts, that they depend on, keeping this box checked tells Unity to include those assets in the package.

5. Select the **Export** button and, in the subsequent file dialog, provide a name for the Unity package file. Unity will create and compress the assets into a file with the extension `.unitypackage`:

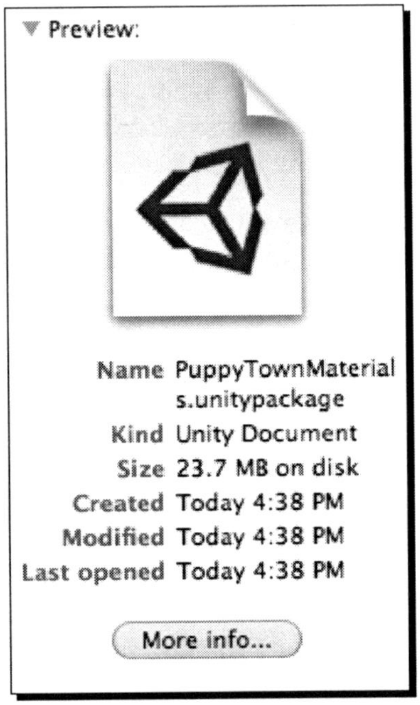

What just happened?

We have created a Unity package that contains all of the assets we selected. This is the ideal way to share assets with your team as any settings, hierarchies, and so on will be preserved when those assets are imported.

Time for action – Importing asset packages

There are a growing number of third party companies who are providing assets specifically packaged for Unity developers, including the Unity Asset Store which can be accessed from within the Unity product. All of these solutions provide content through the same `.unitypackage` format described in the section Time for Action – Exporting asset packages. With assets from the Unity Asset store, the process of including the assets in your project is automatic. However, there may be times when you have received assets from others and need to import them into your project yourself.

1. Create a new Project in Unity called **Project Import.**

2. Using the `.unitypackage` file you built from the Exporting Assets Time For Action, import into your project by dragging the `.unitypackage` file into the **Project** view at the location in your project hierarchy where you'd like them to be stored, or by using the **Import Assets** menu (**Assets | Import Asset**):

3. Once performed you will find that Unity has imported in the `.unitypackage` file in the **Project** view, but it has not expanded the assets into the familiar hierarchy that we had before. Unity doesn't know if you want all of the assets in the package and it is giving you the option to decide, rather than pollute your project with an unknown list of assets.

4. Double-click on the `.unitypackage` file to have Unity expand the package into its component parts.

   You will be presented with a dialog that lists everything that is in the package, as well as a note letting you know whether or not the assets are new. This is useful when sharing assets across projects, especially when the assets might have the same name.

5. Select the **All** button to have Unity include all of the assets in the package:

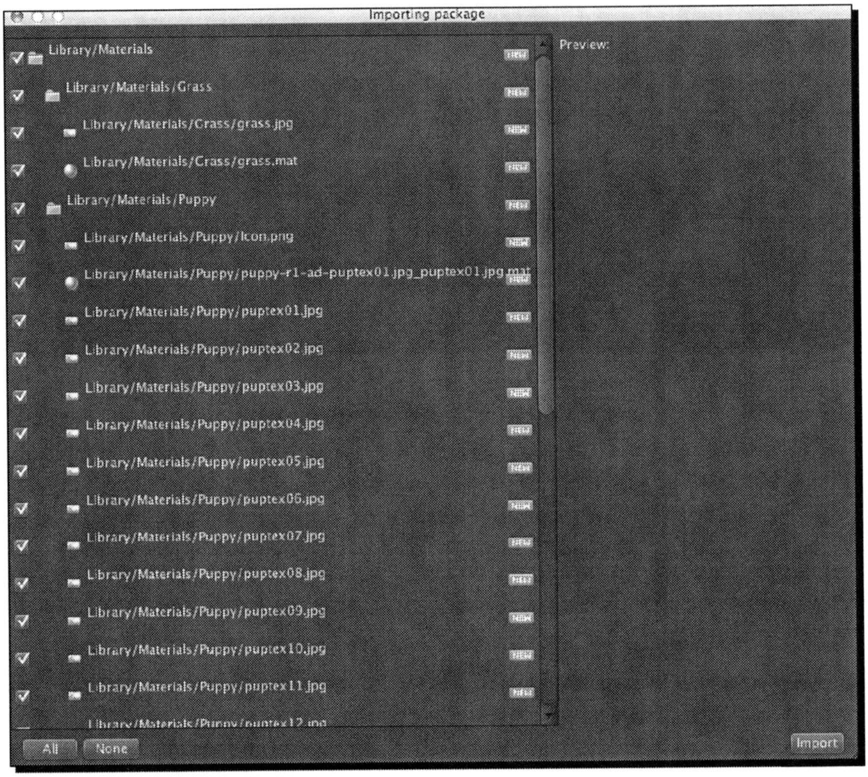

6. Observe the **Project** view and you will find that all of the assets that you selected have been included in the Project and that the hierarchy for the assets has been preserved:

> Although we didn't have a Library element in our package, or one in our Puppy Test project, Unity created this hierarchy and imported in the assets accordingly. It is this sort of information, and the settings associated with it, that would be lost if you managed the `Assets` folder manually.

7. Delete the `unityproject` file from the Project Hierarchy since we have extracted the assets we're interested in.

What just happened?

We have just imported assets into a new project preserving the original hierarchy of the assets from the original project.

While we have chosen to import all of the assets from the `unityproject` it is not necessary to do so. You can preview the assets that you want to import and uncheck those you'd rather not be included in your project.

Game Objects

Normally when you think of a Game Object you think of an animated soldier, a particle system, or a Sprite within a game. However, a Game Object is more of an abstract concept, a base object with no behaviors or functionality. Game Objects gain the ability to perform functions by having behaviors added to them. The approach through which this is done is the **Decorator** design pattern, which allows some arbitrary number of behaviors to be added to some base class. These behaviors, known as **Components** in the Unity vernacular, are what give a Game Object true meaning and definition. It is through Components that Game Objects have the ability to exist in a scene and have a position, rotation and scale.

Components

Components are decorators for Game Objects that provide additional behaviors and configuration to assets. Many of the core tenets of rendering, physics, audio, lighting, and so on are all accomplished by adding Components to objects. As such, many of the Unity concepts that we will cover have a computer graphics definition and a component which when attached to that Game Object provides the behavior. The best way to illustrate this concept is through some examples.

You might think that the easiest way to have a light is to have some concrete Light type that is defined in the system. However, suppose that you want a regular object such as a starship engine to have the ability to emit light? Certainly you can create a Light object and associate it with the engine model, but suppose that you also want it to emit smoke and be affected by physics, and play a sound? Immediately you would notice that your scene would be polluted with objects that aren't really relevant to the game – nevertheless they would show up in your hierarchy and you'd have to manage them. The more elegant way to accomplish this is to say that you have a starship engine and it has certain behaviors. These behaviors are the components that we'd associate with the object.

Even our standard Game Object gets its ability to have position, scale, and rotation from a Transform Component. In Unity's Inspector view what you are really looking at is the stack of components that are applied to this Game Object.

Let's take another example.

Time for action – Adding components to Game Objects

1. In Unity, create an empty Game Object:

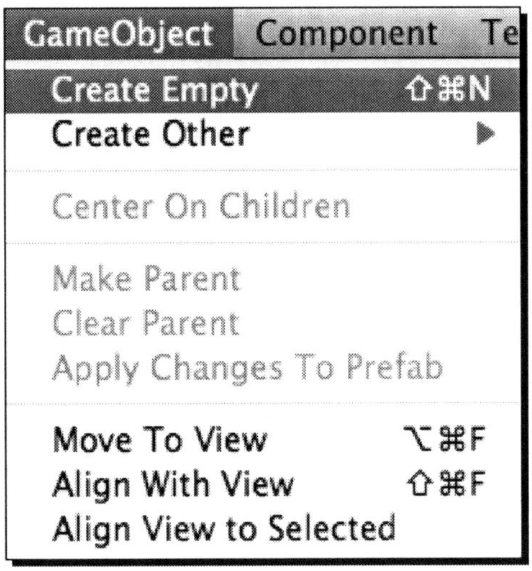

Now let's add some components to this Game Object.

2. In the **Component** menu you will find all of the components that you can add to this Game Object. In the **Rendering Submenu**, select the **Light** option:

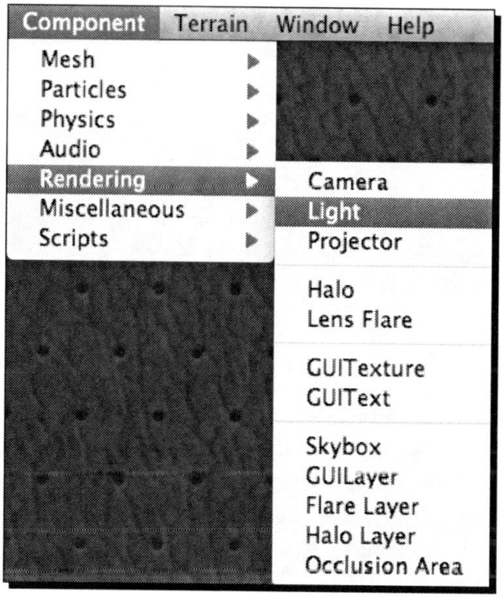

What just happened?

In Unity you will note that your Game Object now has a light behavior associated with it:

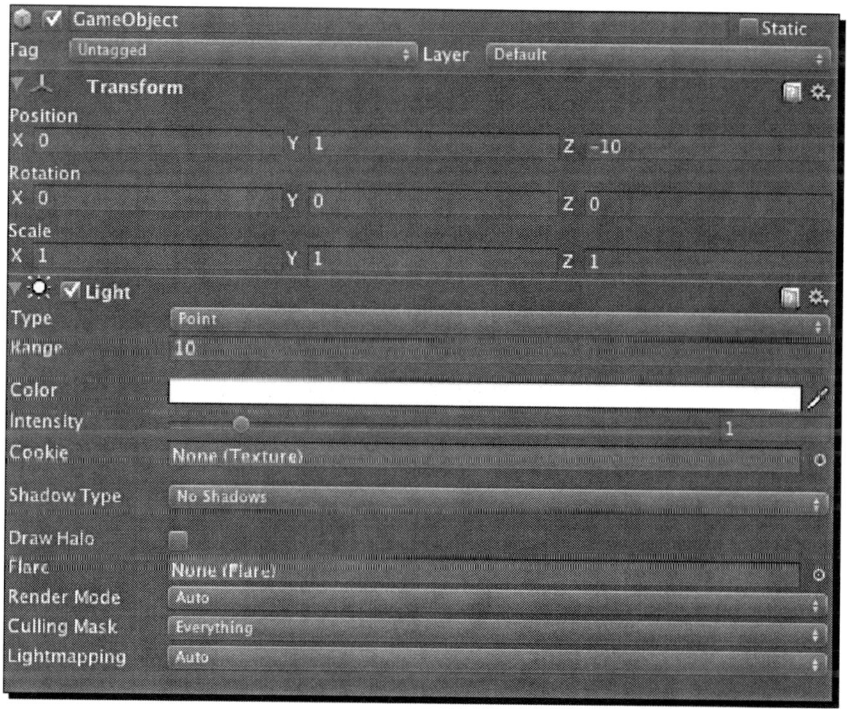

If you were to create a regular Light object from the **Hierarchy** menu you'd find that both objects are the same. This is because the **Light** Game Object is simply an empty Game Object with a **Light** component – simply configured appropriately for the type of light that you wanted to create. If you explore, you'd find that you could configure your light exactly the same as the stock light object.

All of this should show you the possibilities that you have. You are not constrained by an arbitrary construction of objects by the Unity developers. In fact, you can create your own custom components as well and add those components to any Game Object that you desire.

Transform

A transform is the base concept of something in 3-dimensional space. It represents the position, rotation, and scale of an object and can contain links to child objects in a hierarchy. Every object in a scene has one of these, even if nothing is rendered. The **Transform Component** is the base component that every Game Object has and it is also the one that you cannot remove as it is necessary for your object to exist in 3D space:

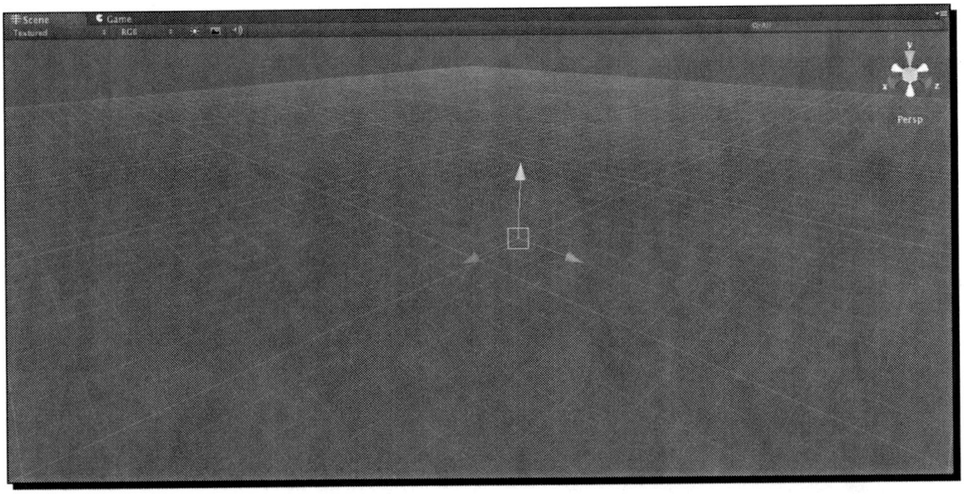

Time for action – Positioning, Rotating, and Scaling a Game Object

1. Create a Cube Game Object.
2. Change the position of the cube by changing the X value of the **Transform Component** to **10**.

   You will notice that the cube's position in the scene reflects this new location.

3. Change the rotation of the cube along the X-axis to **45**.

   You have now rotated the cube 45 degrees along the X axis.

4. Change the scale of the cube's **Transform Component** to **10** on the X-axis.

   You have not scaled the object along its X-axis.

What just happened?

You can refine the location of an object within the scene by changing its **Position** attributes. These attributes represent where this object is in world space coordinates – the coordinate system of the scene itself. In addition, you can change the orientation of an object by adjusting its **Rotation** attributes. Finally, you can define an arbitrary scale for an object by updating the **Scale** attributes:

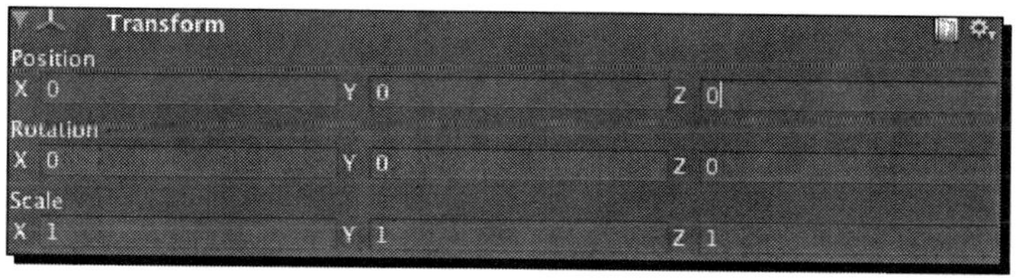

Camera

The **Camera** provides the viewport through which the user can view the content within your scene. The camera will capture everything that is within its frustum and project that content onto the frame buffer for rasterization onto the 2D display. The frustum defines a geometric shape, which is used to clip Game Objects in the scene. If a Game Object isn't within the frustum, the **Camera** assumes that it is not visible to the user and doesn't waste cycles trying to draw it. This concept is important and will become even more important, when we discuss occlusion culling later in the book. For now, just note that the Near Clip plane, the Far Clip plane, and the **Field of View** define the shape of this object and all of these settings can be configured easily in the **Camera** Component:

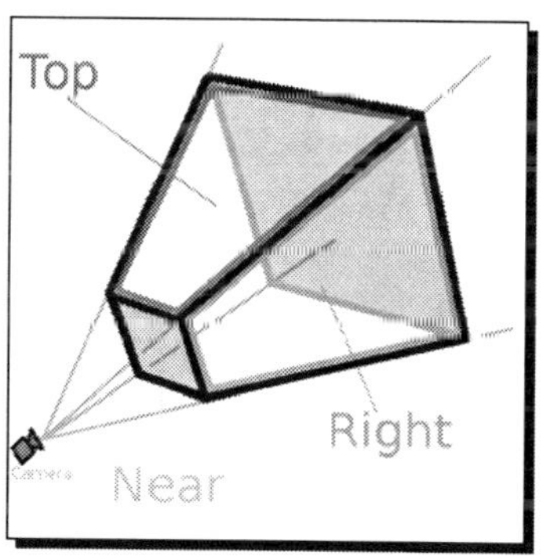

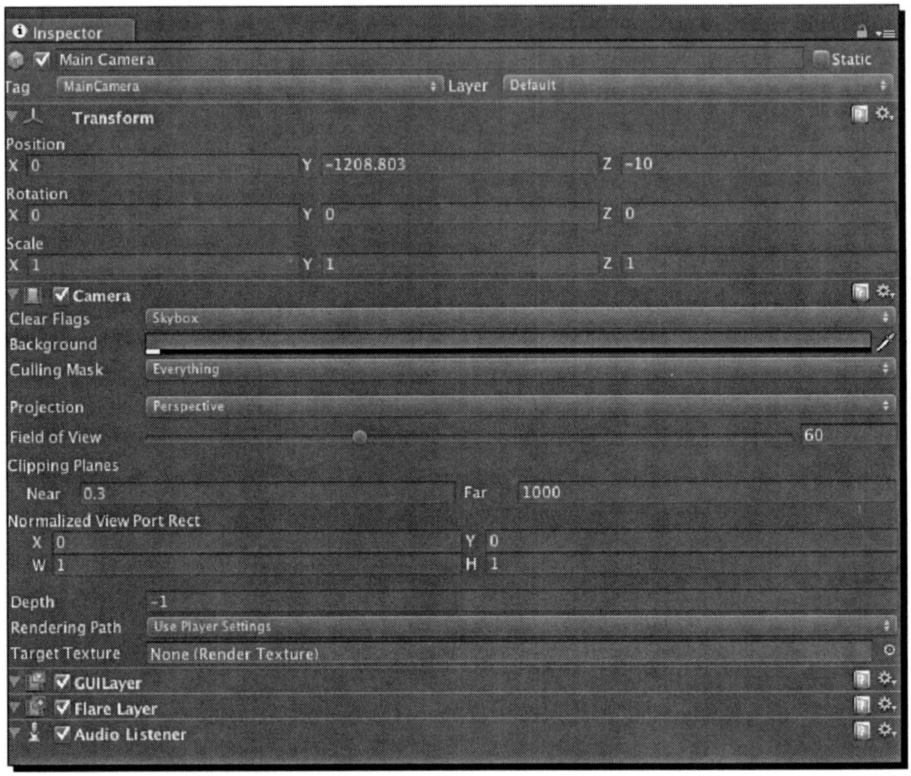

Camera properties

The Camera Component has several properties that define how much of the world the user will be able to see when the scene is rendered.

Near Clip

The near clip plane defines a plane such that objects closer to the camera are no longer displayed. This setting normally places the near clip fairly close to the camera so that objects can get close to the 'viewer' and not get clipped.

Far Clip

The far clip plane defines a plane such that objects beyond this distance are too far away and should not be drawn. The setting you choose for this will have a fairly substantial impact on your game's performance. While you may be able to increase this setting very far in the distance, realize that those objects far off in the distance are being rendered and consuming resources as if they were closer. So if you raise the far clip out to your virtual horizon and there is a city out there, but it's only a few pixels in size, you're still drawing that city in all its splendor and taking the performance hit to do so, even though it's scarcely visible.

Field of View (FOV)

The field of view defines how wide the viewport is along its Y-axis. This will impact how perspective of objects is computed and result in the object being taller/fatter based upon this setting:

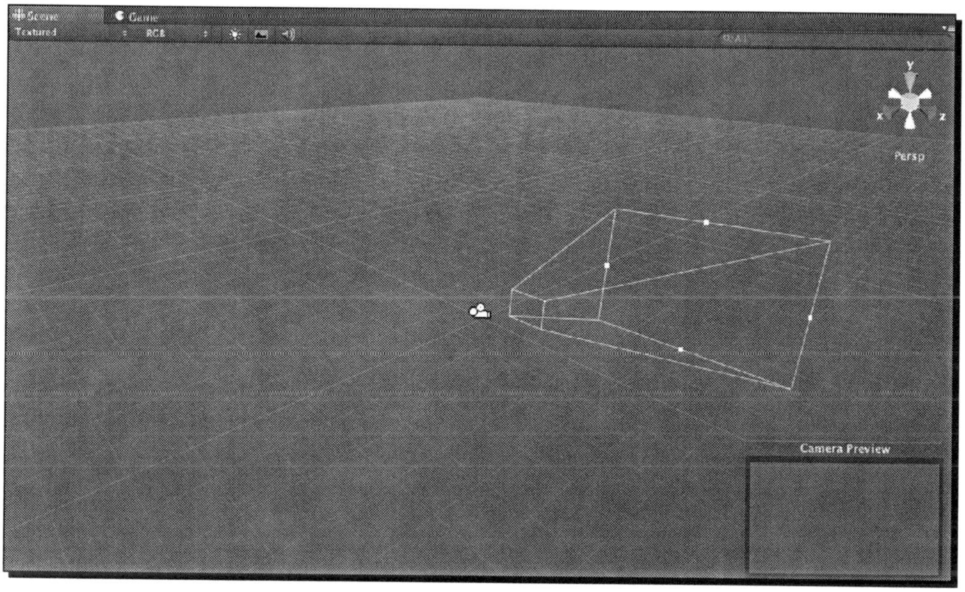

Camera projection types

You can set any Unity camera to one of two projection types: orthographic projection and perspective projection. These projections determine how the world seen by the camera is rendered.

Orthographic projection

A camera with orthographic projection removes the perspective correction from the camera's view and ensures that no matter how far an object is from the camera its distance will remain the same. The orthographic camera will be important when we build traditional 2-dimensional user interfaces and particularly important for 2D games.

Perspective projection

The perspective camera takes into account the distance of a Game Object from the viewer, and based upon this applies a perspective correction such that objects further away appear smaller than they really are. For most games this is the primary mechanism used to draw content.

It is important to note that there are no constraints in Unity that require you to use one camera projection type or other in a scene. In fact, it is quite common to use multiple cameras for different purposes. You could, for example, have an orthographic camera that is responsible for drawing your user interface elements and a perspective camera that is responsible for your regular scene elements.

Lights

Lights are straightforward in concept. They illuminate objects in the scene so that they can be seen. Without lights, objects will appear to be dark and lifeless. With lights you can add mood to a scene and, through the shadows that they cast, add depth to the world. There are three primary types of light in Unity: Directional lights, Point lights, and Spot lights.

Directional light

A Directional light is one that has an infinite distance from the scene. While you can position it in Unity, only the direction of the light is used in determining how the objects in the scene are lit. Directional lights are the cheapest lights that you can use in your scene. This is the fastest way to do global scene illumination as the position of the light doesn't impact how 'lit' something is within the scene, only the direction of the light.

Point light

In contrast to the directional light, the Point Light is a light source that has a position in the scene, but no direction – emitting light equally in all directions. This light is of average computational complexity and generally used for most effects in a game.

Spot light

The most expensive light type, spot lights simulate the same effect that you would get from flashlights – a cone of light. This cone also has a fallout, such that light in the center of the cone is brighter than that at the edges of the cone. While there may be some situations where you might want to use a spot light, the expense of doing so on iOS devices makes this highly prohibitive.

Lightmapping

While you can accomplish tremendous things with lights that approach realistic lighting, to do so requires an exceptional amount of computing power. When considering the computational and graphical capabilities of mobile devices, computing lights in real time is a sure way to ensure that our games and applications will have poor performance. This can be remedied by using light maps.

Light maps are best described as lighting a scene and baking the effect of those lights on the scene. Since it is computationally cheaper to blend light maps with material textures, we can accomplish through light maps what would normal have required more expensive lights. As luck would have it, Unity has built in support for light maps through the industry-leading Beast light mapping system.

With Beast you will be able to place lights in a scene, as you normally would, and Beast will compute the impact of those lights on the textures in the scene and create light maps for us. We can get exceptional results quickly and cheaply doing this.

Lights and Beast light mapping will be covered in more detail in the chapter on lighting.

Sound

Sound is an often-overlooked part of a good game and helps set the mood for the player. Watch your favorite movie (not a silent movie) with the sound turned off. You will notice that the experience is not as compelling as it was when the sound was on, and if this movie is something you know very well – you will find that your brain tries to fill in the blanks by recovering the dialogue and music from the movie in your memory. Sound is crucial for engagement and Unity has an arsenal of audio capabilities that cover the spectrum.

Audio listener

In the real-world, sound must be heard and if you are too far away from the emitter of the sound, you won't hear anything. Unity handles this concept of hearing through the audio listener. This Game Object is normally attached to the player's avatar, character, or other representation in the scene. The audio listener then acts as a microphone within your game world and anything that it hears – the player hears through the speakers.

By default, the audio listener is placed on the Main Camera in the scene. If you want the user to hear from the perspective of some other object, simply remove the audio listener from the Main Camera and attach it to the Game Object that you wish to represent the users center of hearing. In Unity, you cannot have multiple audio listeners active at the same time. While the audio listener is a component, it doesn't have any configurable properties.

Audio sources

Audio sources represent things that make noise in the game world. You can add an audio source to a Game Object by selecting the Game Object and choosing **Component | Audio | Audio Source**. This will add the **Audio Source** component to your Game Object:

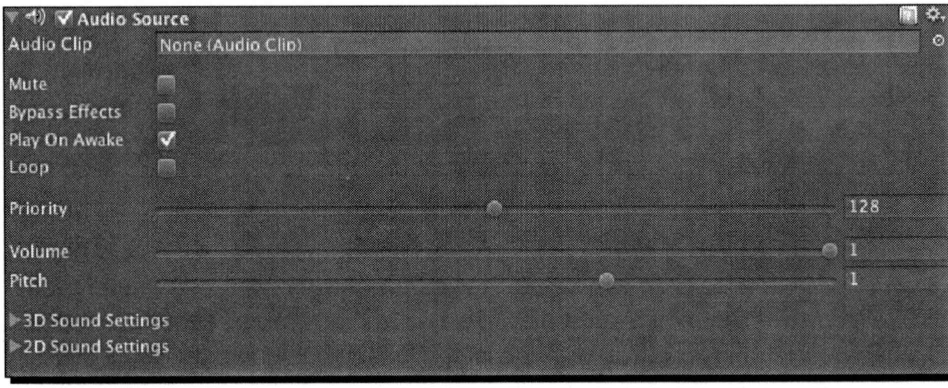

You will also see that in the **Scene** view your Game Object has a speaker icon on it. This denotes that this Game Object has an audio source component on it and generates sound:

Audio clips

While we have created an audio source, we have not associated an actual sound with it. This sound is what Unity refers to as an audio clip. Unity supports audio clips in pretty much every format you can encode sound to including `.aif`, `.wav`, `.mp3`, `.ogg` and even the tracker formats of `.xm`, `.mod`, `.it` and `.s3m`.

Time for action – Adding audio clips

1. From the project folder for `Chapter 4` select the `dog_1.mp3` file and drag it into the **Project** view.
2. The audio clip will be imported into Unity and will appear in the **Project** view designated by a speaker icon:

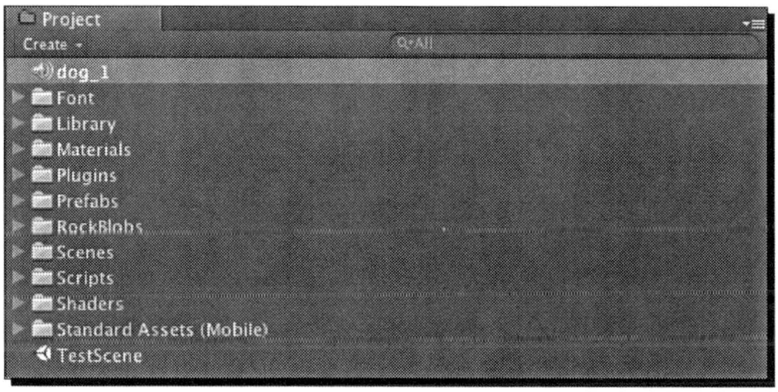

3. Select the **Audio Clip** in the **Project** view. The **Inspector** will fill with all of the settings for the **Audio Clip**:

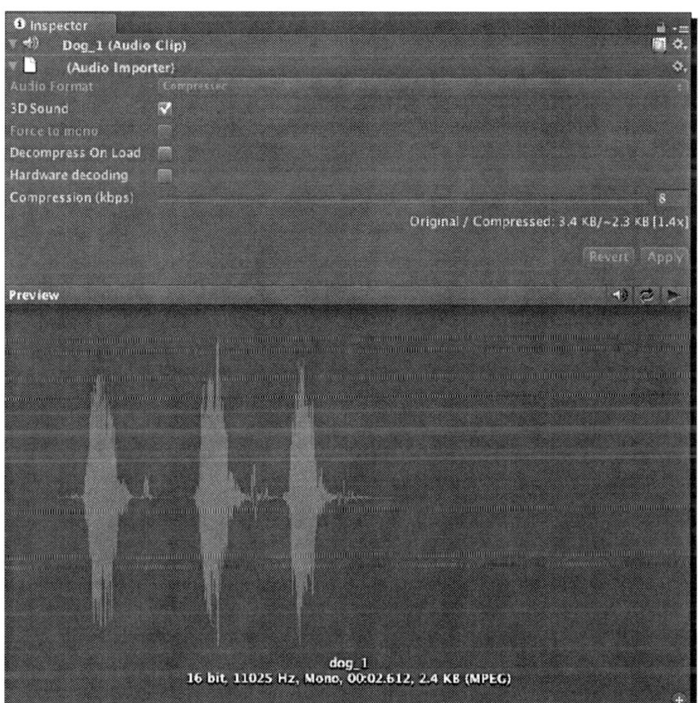

4. Create a Cube Game Object.
5. Add an **Audio Source** to the Cube Game Object.
6. In the Audio Source Game Object select the **Loop** checkbox to designate that we'd like this sound to play indefinitely.
7. To the right of the **Audio Source** property is a small round button. Press it to bring up the **Asset Browser**.
8. Select the **dog_1** asset from the browser:

What just happened?

You have just added sound to an object. Now when you play your scene, if you are close enough to that Game Object you will hear the sound. If you are having trouble, make sure that **Play on Awake** is checked in the **Audio Source**.

Scripts

When you create a script in Unity you are creating a new behavior that will be attached to a Game Object and that behavior will be invoked as Unity communicates with the Game Object during the rendering pipeline stages. Unity ships with a number of pre-defined scripts to do basic things such as FPS Control, iOS Joypad controls, and so on. However, you will find that for most things that you want to do you will be creating a script yourself.

Unity supports scripting using Javascript, C#, and Boo as the primary scripting languages, but given that Mono will work with any .Net language it is entirely possible to write your scripts using F# or even Java. However, you may find that since these paths are not officially supported, the cost to self-support your custom path may not be worth the effort.

Internally, Unity utilizes the Mono/.Net compilation path for all of the scripts that you have in your project. The underlying language implementation for C# and Javascript scripting within the Unity frameworks are all extending functionality from Boo. You will find that it is very easy to create new scripts, import functionality from .Net assemblies, or even extend the language by interfacing directly with the **abstract syntax tree** (**AST**) generated during the build phase. During the build phase, Unity will cause all scripts to be compiled statically, embedded with your application, and deployed to the device.

Editors

There are two editors available for scripting with Unity: Unitron and MonoDevelop.

Unitron is the original script editor that ships with Unity and will be active by default. It is lightweight and fast, but lacks all of the modern conveniences of a traditional IDE. As your projects get more complex, you will find that having a robust IDE is essential and may want to move to a more professional editor:

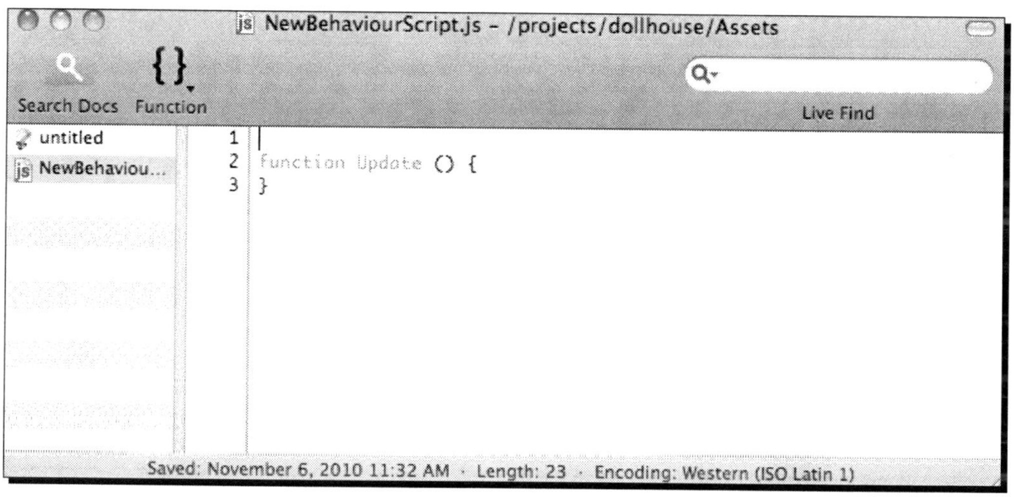

MonoDevelop was introduced in Unity3 as a higher productivity option for developers that needed something that had support for functions such as code completion, better key binding support, add-Ins, refactoring, metrics, and so on. **MonoDevelop** is a solution that has been around nearly as long as Mono, and since it is open source and supported on all the platforms that Unity utilizes it makes an ideal choice for development:

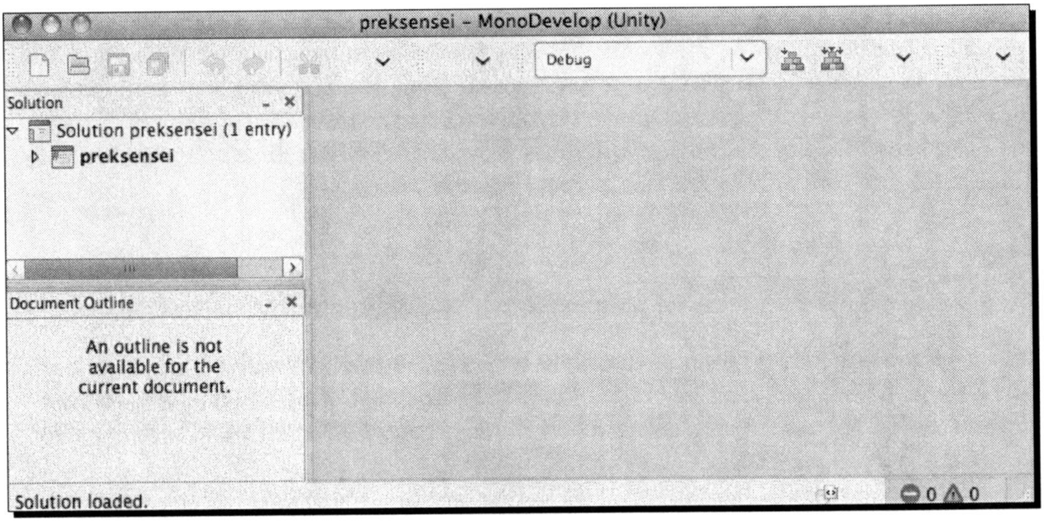

To change which editor you use, enter the **Unity Preferences** (**Unity | Preferences**) and in the **General** tab change the **External Script Editor** to your editor of choice. If you want to use **MonoDevelop**, you will find it in the `/Applications/Unity` folder. After selecting it, when you double-click on a script from any of Unity's languages the editor will launch and allow you to update the script. Changes you make to a script and save will be available immediately to Unity, and any errors in the script will immediately show up in the **Unity Console** view:

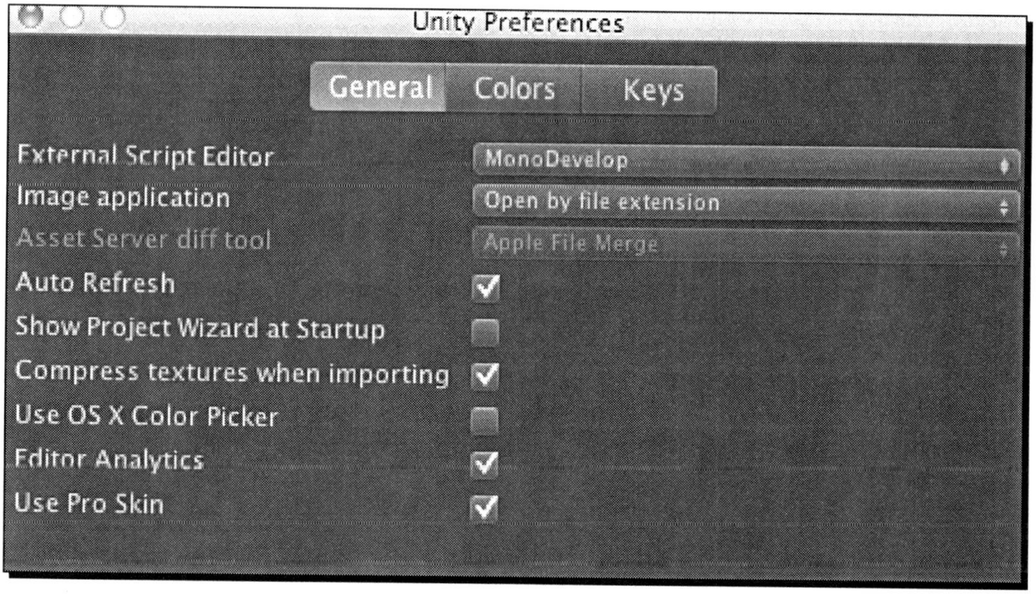

We will cover scripting in more detail in the next chapter.

Prefabs

A Prefab is a reusable collection of meshes, scripts, animations, and so on that you want to use in a scene. Prefabs are a core component of any Unity project, but when starting out it may not be immediately clear why you want to adopt them.

Let's pretend that this is our enemy in our hot seller "Red Cubes must Die" and we need to add more red cubes. We don't want to go through all the steps to try to create this cube again. Your first thought might be to copy/paste the cube, and that will work. But now you've decided that instead of a red color you want a red flame texture. Do you go back to all of the cubes in the scene and change the texture? This may work for a small number of objects, but imagine doing this in a complex scene.

Worse still suppose you've just imported a lot of mesh data and set up the textures for a zombie in your hack and slash game. You scaled him to fit your scene and made sure all the animations work properly. However, this is just one of the many zombies you plan on putting into this level. Certainly you don't want to have to do this for every zombie that is going to be in the game.

Time for action – Creating prefabs

1. Create a new scene in the project by selecting **File | New Scene**.
2. Save the scene.
3. Create a Cube Prefab.
4. Create a new **Material** from the **Assets** menu by selecting **Assets | Create | Material**.
5. Select the **Material** in the **Project** view.
6. In the **Inspector**, select the **Main Color** selector and set the color of the material to **red**.
7. Assign the Material to the Cube by dragging the Material onto the Cube in the **Hierarchy** view:

8. Create a new **Prefab** in the **Project View** by selecting **Create | Prefab**:

9. Let's rename it to **EvilBox** so that we know that when we use this **Prefab** we are creating the Red Cubes that have to die:

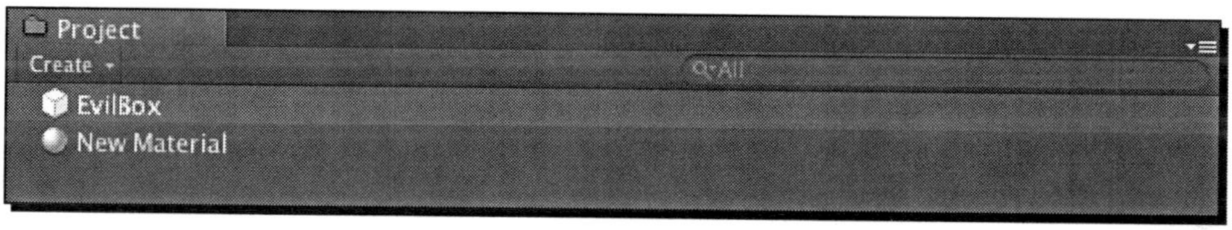

10. Next we will take the Red Cube that we created earlier and drag it onto the **EvilBox** prefab. When you do this you will notice that the Cube and the **EvilBox** prefab are both highlighted in blue. This notes that the prefab now has all of the settings of the original object:

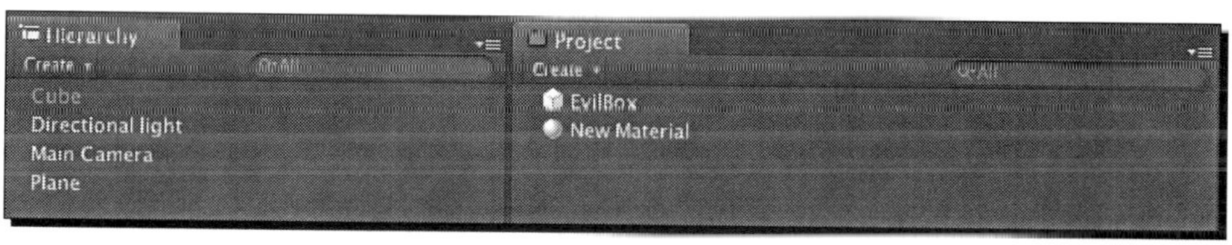

11. Delete the original Cube from the **Hierarchy** view.

12. Drag the **EvilBox** prefab into the scene several times and you will notice that new objects are created in the **Hierarchy** view. These new **GameObjects** are **Instances** of the original prefab template:

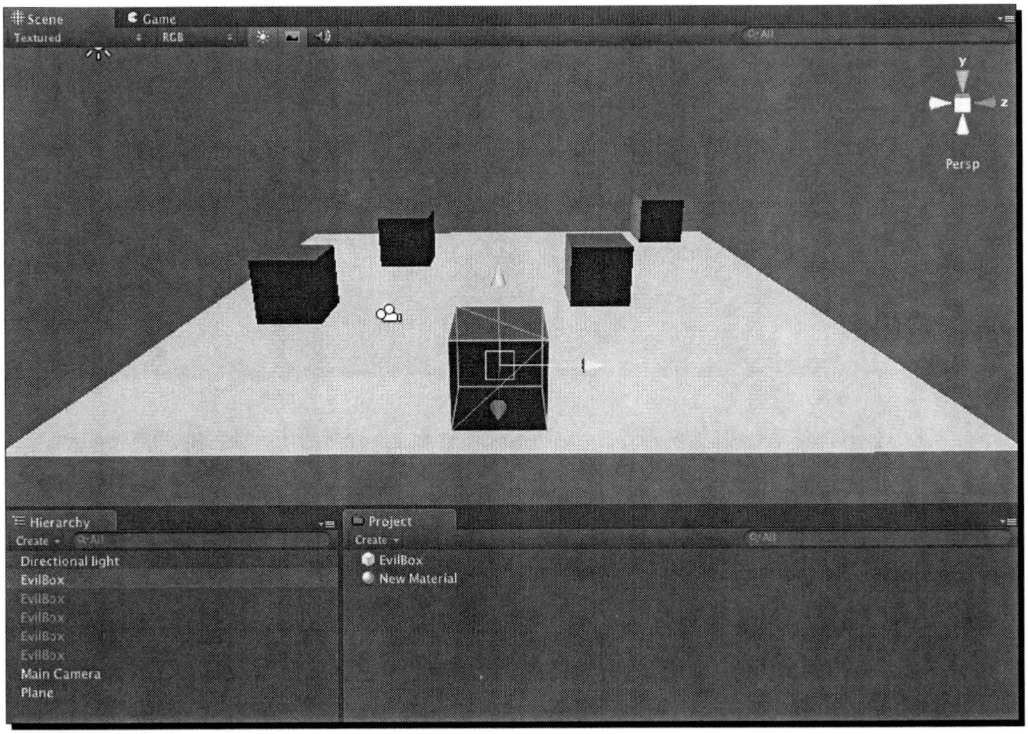

What just happened?

We have just created a reusable prefab object for our game. This Prefab object has a well defined appearance and behavior which can be duplicated over and over. More important still, if you need to change the **EvilBox** because someone told you that it's really blue boxes that are evil, you can select the **Prefab** and change its settings and all of the instances will change accordingly as every instance of a prefab is tied to its template's properties.

If, for some reason, you change one of the instances of a Prefab Instances in a material way, the Instance will change from being blue back to the default gray color. This denotes that the Prefab no longer represents the Instance. But suppose that you wanted to take the settings of the Instance and make it the new default? To accomplish this, drag the child instance that you changed from the Hierarchy over to the Prefab and you will see that the settings of the Prefab are updated with those of the instance and that the instance itself is now linked with the prefab again.

Scene

The Scene is the place where all of your action takes place. From a Unity perspective the words Scene and Level are synonymous and there are times when the tool uses the terms interchangeably. You can create new scenes from the **File** menu:

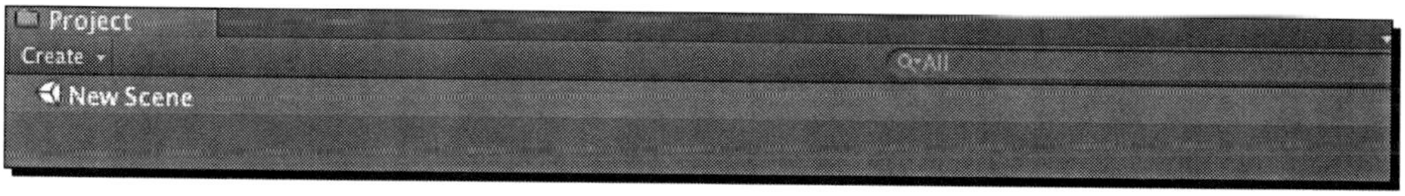

Once created and saved, a Scene will show up in the **Project** view and have a Unity icon next to it. If you're ever looking for your scene you can find it in the `Assets` folder of your project with a `.unity` extension.

Summary

In this chapter we learned to speak in the language of Unity. You now have knowledge of all the core concepts and how to use them so we can graduate from the newbie cube examples and take on more complex projects.

Now that we've learned about the core concepts, we're ready to build our first really complex application which will utilize all of the concepts that we have covered through scripting, which is the topic of the next chapter.

5

Scripting: Whose line is it anyway?

We have finally moved past the basics. As you may have observed, the tasks and even the assets we've been using have been getting more and more complicated along the way. Now that we have hit scripting, the rubber will meet the road. Scripting is how you breathe life into your creation and turn it into an actual game. Prior to this, the best we could do is move around a lifeless world by scripting the camera – now we get to play.

In this chapter we shall learn:

- How Unity handles scripting
- The specific scripting limitations and interfaces for iOS
- The basic iOS scripts that Unity provides
- Integrate with a web service to save our data

Scripting is possibly the most important thing that you need to know to interact with Unity effectively. While you can optimize your assets, build your scene efficiently, and take advantage of every feature on the device – if you don't get scripting right it won't do anything useful.

So let's get on with it...

Important preliminary points

This chapter assumes that you have a background in programming and that you know something about JavaScript, C#, or Boo. As these are the scripting languages supported by Unity, some understanding of their design is necessary.

Unity Scripting Primer

Unity has arguably the most flexible and complete scripting system of any engine at any price. Providing the ability for developers to use the languages Boo, Javascript, and C# – Unity covers the bases when it comes to supporting a variety of developers. While there is no specific support for Java within the system, C# is a mature language that provides a near peer to the language. In addition, through the .Net/Mono framework it is possible to roll your own support for Java, F#, or any other language that is supported by the .Net platform – including any new language that you create, though it's probably easier to just build a **domain specific language** (**DSL**) using Boo. The most important part is that each language is a first class citizen in Unity. With few exceptions, anything you want to do in Unity can be accomplished regardless of which language you choose.

The Unity Scripting system is at the heart of getting things done within Unity customizing the Unity editor and interacting with the runtime platform. Through scripts you have access to everything that you would want to change (and I do mean everything) including being able to extend the Unity compiler through the **Abstract Syntax Trees (AST)** themselves.

Oh no! You've got Mono!

When Microsoft originally created the .Net platform it created it principally for the Windows platform. However, Microsoft published the language specification to ECMA and shortly thereafter, the Mono open source project was created which brought the .Net platform to other platforms including OSX and Linux. At its core the Unity scripting system is built upon the .Net runtime and the benefits afforded it through the Mono project. While it was certainly possible that the Unity scripting system could have been based upon Java or some other system, .Net provided (out-of-the-box) a rich system for assemblies that made cross language functionality trivial to implement.

Common Language Infrastructure

Multiple scripting languages are possible in Unity due to the **Common Language Infrastructure (Cli)** of .Net. The purpose of the Common Language Infrastructure (CLI), is to provide a language-neutral platform for application development and execution, including functions for exception handling, garbage collection, security, and interoperability. By implementing the core aspects of the .NET Framework within the scope of the CLI, this functionality will not be tied to a single language, but will be available across the many languages supported by the framework. Microsoft's implementation of the CLI is called the **Common Language Runtime**, or **CLR**.

Boo- more than a ghost in mario

Boo is an object-oriented, statically typed programming language that seeks to make use of the Common Language Infrastructure's support for Unicode, internationalization and web-applications, while using a Python-inspired syntax and a special focus on language and compiler extensibility. Some features of note include type inference, generators, multimethods, optional duck typing, macros, true closures, currying, and first-class functions. Boo has been actively developed since 2003.

Boo is free software released under an MIT/BSD–style license. It is compatible with both the Microsoft .NET and Mono frameworks.

What does a Boo script look like?

```
import UnityEngine
import System.Collections

class example(MonoBehaviour):

    def Start():
        curTransform as Transform
        curTransform = gameObject.GetComponent[of Transform]()
        curTransform = gameObject.transform

    def Update():
        other as ScriptName = gameObject.GetComponent[of ScriptName]()
        other.DoSomething()
        other.someVariable = 5
```

Should I choose Boo?

If you're looking for a new and novel way to write code that doesn't have a lot of ceremony and doesn't waste your time with lots of curly braces, Boo is definitely a language you want to look into. While the idea of using whitespace as a delimiter is considered offensive by some, there is an elegance that comes from writing code in Boo. If you've written in traditional languages it's not difficult to understand and there are some functions of Unity (not the iOS version) which can only be accessed using Boo.

While Boo is a fine language, there are two reasons why you shouldn't choose it.

1. First, there are very few examples written in Boo and very little written about it in the community at large.
2. More importantly, Boo is not currently supported on the iOS platform as of this writing.

With that, our discussion of Boo within the context of iOS comes to an abrupt end.

UnityScript/JavaScript – Relevant beyond the web

JavaScript is an implementation of the ECMAScript language standard and is typically used to enable programmatic access to computational objects within a host environment. It can be characterized as a prototype-based object-oriented scripting language that is dynamic, weakly typed, and has first-class functions. It is also considered a functional programming language like Scheme and OCaml because it has closures and supports higher-order functions.

While UnityScript is, on the surface, syntactically similar to Javascript, the implementation used by Unity is not entirely ECMAScript compliant.

What does a JavaScript script look like?

```
function Start () {
  var curTransform : Transform;

  curTransform = gameObject.GetComponent(Transform);
  // This is equivalent to:
  curTransform = gameObject.transform;

}


function Update () {
  // To access public variables and functions
  // in another script attached to the same game object.
  // (ScriptName is the name of the javascript file)
```

```
    var other : ScriptName = gameObject.GetComponent(ScriptName);
    // Call the function DoSomething on the script
    other.DoSomething ();
    // set another variable in the other script instance
    other.someVariable = 5;
}
```

Should I choose JavaScript?

JavaScript is the defacto language in use by the Unity community and is prevalent across the web. Many people refer to Javascript as Unityscript. There are many people in the world who use it on a daily basis and if you're coming from a Flash background – this is as close to ActionScript porting ease as you're likely to get (until someone ports ActionScript over to Unity). One of the strong benefits of JavaScript is that there isn't a lot of ceremony involved with getting things done and in most cases you will find that you write a lot less boilerplate to build an application with JavaScript. There is no need to create class structures and there isn't much need in getting directly to the attributes of objects and using them.

JavaScript is available on all platforms including the iPhone, but as you begin building more complex examples with larger teams you may find that having more structure and typing will result in fewer defects. In addition, while JavaScript is the community choice today – most authors and developers are moving over to C# as their primary development language.

C# – The revenge of Microsoft

C# (pronounced "see sharp")[6] is a multi-paradigm programming language encompassing imperative, declarative, functional, generic, object-oriented (class-based), and component-oriented programming disciplines. It was developed by Microsoft within the .NET initiative and later approved as a standard by Ecma (ECMA-334) and ISO (ISO/IEC 23270). C# is one of the programming languages designed for the Common Language Infrastructure.

C# is intended to be a simple, modern, general-purpose, object-oriented programming language.

What does a C# script look like?

```
using UnityEngine;
using System.Collections;

public class example : MonoBehaviour {
  void Start() {
    Transform curTransform;
    curTransform = gameObject.GetComponent<Transform>();
    curTransform = gameObject.transform;

  }
```

```
    void Update() {
      ScriptName other = gameObject.GetComponent<ScriptName>();
      other.DoSomething();
      other.someVariable = 5;

    }

  }
```

Should I choose C#?

As a language, C# will be familiar to anyone who has done any modern object-oriented programming in the past 10 years. The syntax is very familiar for Java developers and reasonably easy for C++ developers to pick up.

There are a number of libraries that are available on the Internet that can be dropped right into your project to do things like XML parsing, connecting to social networks, loading pages, etc. In addition there is a critical mass of C# developers in the Unity community such that there is an increased emphasis on doing projects and documentation on C# going forward.

Finally, many of those that have published large numbers of iOS projects have stated that C# is an easier path to take for writing applications. If you're coming from a professional game development background or want a clean object-oriented Java/Pascal syntax – this is your best choice.

> For the rest of the book, we will be using C# as the language for scripts.

Time for action – Creating and organizing scripts

Creating a new C# script in Unity is similar to our approach for creating scripts using JavaScript or any of the other scripting languages.

1. Select **Assets | Create | C Sharp Script**. This will create a new C# script in the project:

> While the Boo Script does appear as an option, it is not usable for Unity iOS projects.

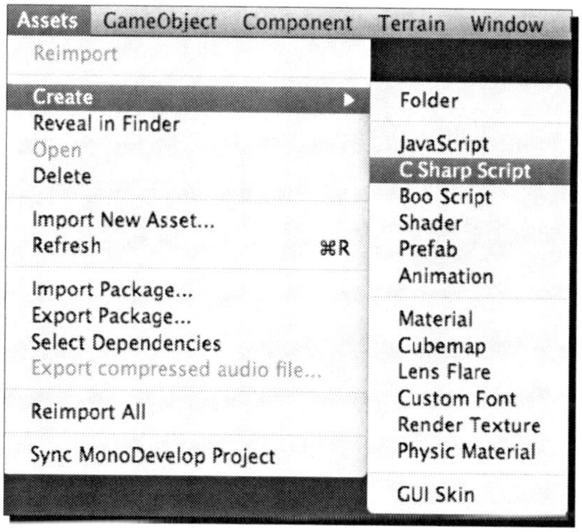

2. Once you have created the new script it will appear in the **Project** view with the name `NewBehaviourScript` with some stubs for the methods `Start()` and `Update()`:

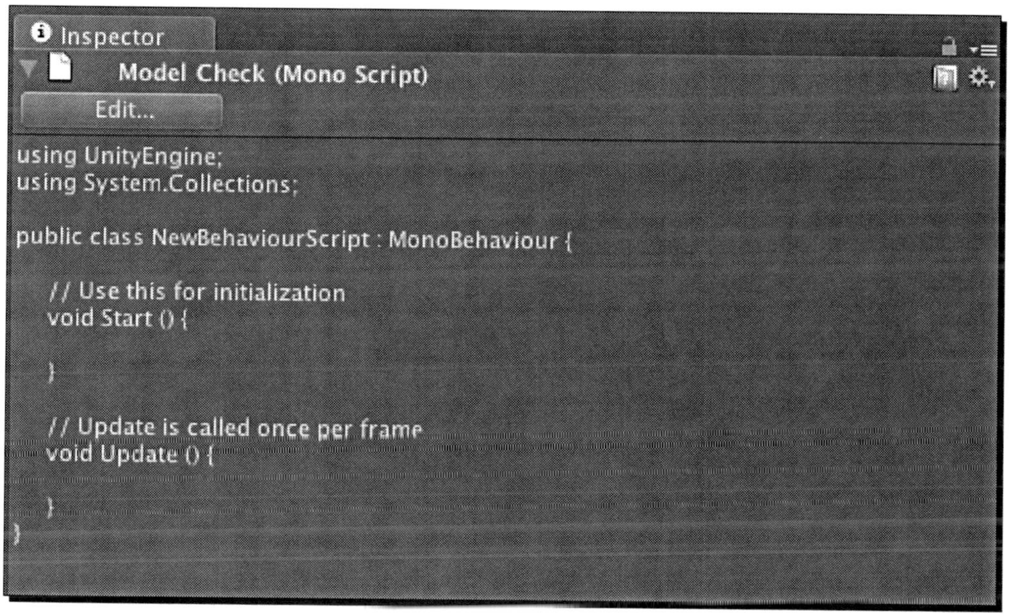

3. Create a folder named `Scripts` and then drag the newly created script into the Scripts directory.

What just happened?

A best practice for scripts is to put them in a folder in the project. What you call this folder doesn't really matter, as it is more for your own organizational purposes than it is for Unity. You may choose to put UI centric scripts in one directory and AI scripts in another. However you manage the scripts is up to you, but you will create a large number of scripts in the course of creating the average game so you want to organize them so that they aren't all sitting at the root of your game project.

Attaching scripts to Game Objects

As mentioned earlier, you can add a script to a **GameObject** by simply dragging the script onto the game object itself. What is important here, is that the **GameObject** is the owner of the script, if that game object is not participating in the scene – the methods in the script will never be called. For scripts that are global in nature, a common practice is to create an Empty Game Object in the scene and attach the global scripts to it. While it is common for people to associate these global scripts with the camera, you want to avoid this as many complex games will have many cameras – complicating the activation of the scripts as well as determining which object in the scene owns them.

Exposing variables in the Unity editor

Quite often you will find yourself in the position of having written a script providing some values for variables within your script. As you test your game you will find that you will want to expose some of these variables to the Unity Editor so that you can modify them in the editor without having to edit and recompile the scripts themselves.

This is particularly important since many times you will want to provide a default value within the script which you can override due to some specific game use case. Rather than coming up with some complex mechanism to do this, simply declare the variable as a public variable and it will show up in the Unity editor.

```
using UnityEngine;
using System.Collections;

public class SomeScript : MonoBehaviour {

  public int testExpose = 5;
  public String testStringExpose = "Test";


  // Update is called once per frame
  void Update () {

  }
}
```

Key scripting methods

Scripting inside Unity consists of attaching custom script objects called behaviors to game objects. Different functions inside the script objects are called on certain events. The most used ones being the following:

Method	Purpose
`Awake`	Called when the script object is being loaded but after all Game Objects have been initialized
`Start`	Called only one time – when the object this script is attached to is initially used in the scene
`Update`	This function is called before rendering a frame. This is where most game behavior code goes, except physics code.
`FixedUpdate`	This function is called once every physics time step. This is the place to do physics-based game behavior. Unlike Update, this method is not called every time, but at a specific interval. Use this for things that should be frame rate independent.
`LateUpdate`	This function is called after Update has been called. This is useful if you want to execute some functionality after all of the other objects in the scene have been updated.
`"Other Methods"`	Code outside functions is run when the object is loaded. This can be used to initialize the state of the script.

iPhoneSettings

While the iOS SDK promises to give you a single platform to all of the iOS devices, there are going to be times that you want to do device specific things. For example, you may want to load Retina Display compatible assets if you are on the iPhone4 or you may want to provide another networking interface other than Game Center if you find yourself on a 1G, 2G, or base 3G device. Further, you may want to determine where this device is located in the world. All of this is accomplished by gaining access to iPhoneSettings.

Screen orientation

iPhoneSettings provides an interface for getting the current screen orientation from the device and it will allow you to specify the orientation you want your content to be displayed in.

If you want to only operate in one mode, you can attach a script to the camera and in its `Start()` method define the orientation you want.

```
// Start in landscape mode
function Start () {
  iPhoneSettings.screenOrientation = iPhoneScreenOrientation.Landscape;
}
```

Later in the chapter we will build an example that illustrates how to move between the multiple modes that the device is capable of, as the user changes the device orientation.

Sleep mode

By default, any iOS portable device will follow power management settings and darken its screen after a certain amount of time to prevent draining the battery if the user isn't using it. The iOS power management system will reset its internal timers every time a touch event happens on the device. However, for games this may become a problem since you may not require the user to maintain contact with the device or through a Bluetooth keyboard during gameplay. Driving games and flight simulators come immediately to mind as two genres of games that may be impacted by this.

In these cases it makes sense to put the device in a state where the device will not be allowed to go to sleep. This can be accomplished by setting the `screenCanDarken` attribute of `iPhoneSettings` to `false`. It is important to review that statement again – the device will not be allowed to go to sleep – EVER. As long as your application is running, it will block the device from entering a sleep state. Consequently, it is your responsibility to make sure that if you leave the states of your game where users aren't touching the device that you flip the `screenCanDarken` attibute to `true` so that iOS can darken the screen.

Device information

Unity provides several useful fields to the developer that gives information about the device and its unique identification.

Field	Description
name	This is the name that the user has given to the device. Useful if you want to allow users to find one another across the wan or locally
model	Provides a simple text model name
systemName	This is simply the name of the OS running on the device
generation	This will tell you what generation this device belongs to. The values are enumerated in iPhoneGeneration and provide a reliable way to determine exactly what type of device the user has
uniqueIdentifier	This is the globally unique identifier that identifies this device specifically

Time for action – Identifying the type of iOS

Let's suppose that we have designed our application such that it is optimized for high definition (HD) on iPhone 4 and the iPad.

> If the player runs this version of our application we want to tell them that the application would perform better if they used the standard definition (SD) version of the game.

We will do this by detecting the device and either starting the application immediately or showing them a notice screen and then starting the application.

Let's walk through the steps that would be necessary for this application functionality.

1. Identify the type of device we are using.
2. Based on conditional logic display a splash screen.
3. Dismiss the splash screen.

Identify our device information

What we need to do is:

1. Add some device detection to the Start() script that we're attaching to our Camera.
2. What we're looking for are iOS generations that are older than the iPhone4 and the iPad. We can check for this by looking at the value of `iPhoneSettings.generation`.
3. We choose `iPhoneSettings.generation` as opposed to `iPhoneSettings.model` because generation will return us an enumerated type and since all of the models are represented – this will be less error prone than trying to compare strings.

```
void Start () {
  if ( ! ( ( iPhoneSettings.generation ==
              iPhoneGeneration.iPhone4 ) ||
  ( iPhoneSettings.generation == iPhoneGeneration.iPad1Gen ) ) )
  {
    // this device isn't an iPad or an iPhone4 and therefore
    // doesn't support HD.
  }


}
```

Conditionally show splash screen

Now that we know whether or not we have an HD "qualified" device, we have the ability to conditionally display a screen. In this example we have built out our SD display as a level all on its own. This was done so that we could compartmentalize this body of work by itself without it cluttering up the rest of the game.

1. To load this SD purchase suggestion level we make a call to the `Application.LoadLevel()` method and provide it the name of the level that we want to load – in this case it will be our `"SDAdvisory"` level.

```
Application.LoadLevel("SDAdvisory");
```

Unity will now load this level and display it on the screen. Since we've set its background to just be an image for displaying this information we need to provide a mechanism for this advisory to be dismissed.

Dismiss the splash screen

In our new scene we want to be able to acknowledge that we've seen the advisory that we should be using the SD version of the game, yet proceed to playing the game in high definition. If you aren't building universal binaries of your game (which you should!), you should check for the appropriateness of the version of the content the user is attempting to run.

To dismiss this level and load our regular game we need to display a button on the screen that the user can click on and we need to listen for activity on this button. UnityGUI provides a clean mechanism to do this quickly, albeit not with the best performance. Ways to improve this performance will be covered in the Performance and Optimization sections later in the book.

```
using System.Collections;
using UnityEngine;

public class SplashGUI : MonoBehaviour{

  void OnGUI(){
    if ( GUI.Button(new Rect(10,10,100,25), "I Understand") ) {
      Application.LoadLevel("MainGame");
    }
  }
}
```

Now when the user clicks on the button with the `I Understand` label, the application will load the level `MainGame` and our game will continue on without any further interruption.

What just happened?

When Unity started the player on our iOS device, it populated the `iPhoneSettings` class with the settings for our device. Since our script was attached to an object in the scene, our script had the ability to read these settings from the Unity player on the device. Based upon this we used a simple C# conditional if statement to determine if we were fine to start or needed to display a standard definition splash screen. We then presented a simple `UnityGUI` script that waited for the user to press a button which launched the main game.

Location services

The location services provide an interface to the cell tower triangulation and GPS functions of the device. You can get the status of the services through `iPhoneSettings`, and the location data will be available through `iPhoneInput.lastLocation`.

To start the service, access the `StartlocationServiceUpdates()` method and give it the accuracy that you desire, as well as the update distance, both in meters. The update distance is the amount that the device must move before it will update the `iPhoneInput.lastLocation`. If you are familiar with using CoreLocation, you are familiar with the location services for iOS as Unity provides a wrapper around the CoreLocation API and simply exposes the data updates through `iPhoneInput.lastLocation`.

It is important to note, however, that GPS satellite acquisition is not instantaneous and Unity will expose the state of CoreLocations's response in the `LocationServiceStatus` attribute. This will return one of several LocationServiceStatus states which can be polled until you achieve a `LocationServiceStatus`. Running in the field at which point you will have actual GPS data in `iPhoneInput.lastLocation`.

Time for action – Changing state according to player location

Location-based gaming is one area of innovation that has gone largely underutilized by the game development community. Let's suppose that we want to start a whole line of games that utilize the actual players location information to change some of the state in our game. For our purposes we will utilize the players location to determine the weather in their area, as well as the time of day so that we can have the player's game world match the world outside.

Let's walk through the steps that would be necessary for this application's functionality:

1. Start the location services on our device,
2. Poll the device location information,
3. Get the weather for this location,

Start the location services on our device

As this is something that we only need to do when our application first starts, we can perform all of our operations in the `Start()` method of our script. All we need to do is:

1. Call the `iPhoneSettings.StartLocationServiceUpdates()` method and Unity will start its interaction with the platform's CoreLocation services.

```
//Use this for initialization
void Start () {
  iPhoneSettings.StartLocationServiceUpdates();
}
```

2. Now that the location services have started, we need to wait for them to be available. Location services do not activate immediately and if the GPS is being utilized, the internal systems will have to acquire satellites to triangulate the device's location. If we try to acquire information from the device before this has completed, the resulting behavior is not defined.

3. In order to wait for the location services to start we need to enter a loop where we will check for the status of the location services and then enter a short wait state before checking again. We can do this by specifying an amount of time to wait that we configure in the Unity editor.

Expose variable to Unity editor

To expose a variable to the Unity editor we need to define it in such a way that it is public in our script. This will allow Unity to expose this variable to the rest of the IDE and we will be able to change the value for this variable without having to edit the script again.

1. In our example we want to expose the maximum amount of time we will wait before we assume that we won't get location services working.

```
using UnityEngine;
using System.Collections;

public class LocationBasedGaming : MonoBehaviour {

  public int retries = 20;

  // Use this for initialization
  void Start ()
  {
    iPhoneSettings.StartLocationServiceUpdates();
  }
  // Update is called once per frame
  void Update () {

  }
}
```

This will be represented inside of the Unity Editor in the **Inspector** when you examine the Game Object that this script is attached to. In our example, if you take a look at the Camera object that we've attached this script to you will see the variable and whatever value it currently has. If you change this value, you will be overriding the default value that the script is providing:

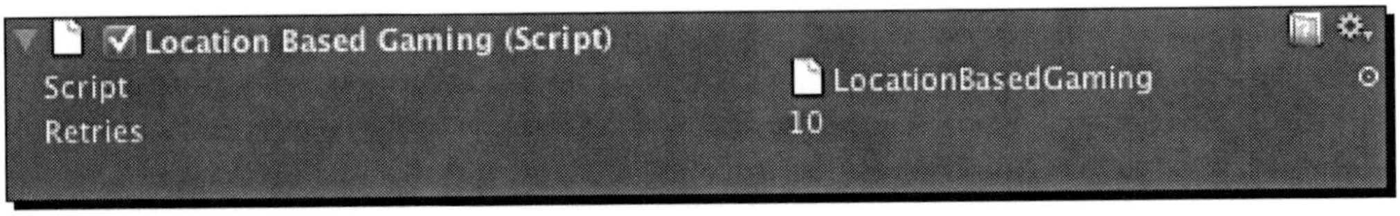

Unity provides an overridden method `WaitForSeconds`, which takes an amount of time to wait. In order for us to invoke this method, we must:

2. Perform a yield operation to tell Mono that our code needs to pause while this function runs. Normally one would simply add this as a single line of code, however, C# requires that the method which performs this yield has a different return type other than `void`. Thus, we cannot simply expose this in our `Start()` function. However, this is easily remedied by providing a secondary function which can handle this.

```
IEnumerator EnterWaitState( float time )
{
  yield return new WaitForSeconds( time );
}
```

3. Now we can invoke this method from inside our `Start()` function, wait for a certain amount of time and then check to see if the location services are available.

```
// Use this for initialization
void Start ()
{
  iPhoneSettings.StartLocationServiceUpdates();

  while( iPhoneSettings.locationServiceStatus ==
    LocationServiceStatus.Initializing && retries > 0 )
  {
    EnterWaitState( 2.0f );
    retries --;
  }

}
```

This code will check the status of the device, wait for 2 seconds and then check again. Each time it will reduce the number of retries remaining. When this reaches zero we can safely assume that either the user has chosen to not allow location services or there is something wrong which is preventing the location services from working (like Airplane Mode).

4. A second method that could be accomplished is to change the signature of the `Start()` method from one that returns `void` to one that returns `IEnumerator`.

```
IEnumerator Start ()
{
  iPhoneSettings.StartLocationServiceUpdates();

  while( iPhoneSettings.locationServiceStatus ==
    LocationServiceStatus.Initializing && retries > 0 )
  {
    yield return new WaitForSeconds ( 2.0f );
    retries --;
  }

}
```

Either mechanism is acceptable depending on what you intend to do and the style of development you're accustomed to. Both are included here for completeness.

Poll the device location information

Now that we know that the device is giving us location data, we can simply look in the `iPhoneInput.lastLocation` variable and extract the longitude and latitude. From these we can then integrate with a web service, which can tell us what the weather is where the device is located.

```
if (iPhoneSettings.locationServiceStatus ==
  LocationServiceStatus.Failed)
{
  Debug.Log("Unable to activate the location services.
    Device reports failure");
}
else
{
  // success path for location services - get information
  // from Google
  float latitude = iPhoneInput.lastLocation.latitude;
  float longitude = iPhoneInput.lastLocation.longitude;

}
```

Get the weather for this location

Now that we know the latitude and longitude for the device, we can get the weather at this location so that we can use it in our game. To accomplish this we will use Google's Weather API and parse the XML we receive.

```
public class GoogleWeather : MonoBehaviour {

  String city;
  String conditions;
  String tempC;
  String tempF;
  String humidity;
  String wind;

  // Use this for initialization
  void Start () {

  }

  // Update is called once per frame
  void Update () {

  }

  void forLocation( float lat, float lon )
  {

    String postLat = "" + lat * 1000000;
    String postLon = "" + lon * 1000000;

    XmlDocument   responseXML = new XmlDocument();
    responseXML.Load("http://www.google.com/ig/api?weather=,,," +
      postLat + "," + postLon );

    city = responseXML.SelectSingleNode("/xml_api_reply/weather/
      forecast_information/city").Attributes["data"].InnerText;
    conditions = responseXML.SelectSingleNode("/xml_api_reply/weather/
      current_conditions/condition").Attributes["data"].InnerText;
    tempC = responseXML.SelectSingleNode("/xml_api_reply/weather/
      current_conditions/temp_c").Attributes["data"].InnerText;
    tempF = responseXML.SelectSingleNode("/xml_api_reply/weather/
      current_conditions/temp_f").Attributes["data"].InnerText;
    humidity = responseXML.SelectSingleNode("/xml_api_reply/weather/
      current_conditions/humidity").Attributes["data"].InnerText;
```

```
        wind = responseXML.SelectSingleNode("/xml_api_reply/weather/
          current_conditions/wind_condition").Attributes["data"].InnerText;

    }
}
```

The code first starts by defining variables that will store the results of our weather query: city, conditions, tempC, tempF, humidity, and wind.

The `forLocation()` method takes latitude and longitude and converts them into the format that Google expects (the API doesn't support the decimal version of lat/lon – just an integer representation).

Next the API requests the XmlDocument from the Google servers by compositing the URL that will be passed to Google and telling the C# to load this data. Once it has returned we simply select the `current_conditions` for our location and we now have the weather for where our player is currently playing the game.

What just happened?

We activated the location services on our device and polled the device to determine where our device was located. We entered a wait loop to give the location services a chance to start and provide the user an opportunity to interact with the OS and give our application permission to use the gathered data. But, for our inability to launch this application remotely we just performed the same job as `FindMyiPhone`. Next we interfaced with a web service, which provided us the location that this lat/lon represents. With this information we accessed another web service that told us what the weather was in this location. By exposing this data to our environment script in the game we have created a game that uses real location data to function.

Screen manipulation

One of the great things about modern smart phones is that they enable the device to be operated from a horizontal or vertical orientation. Due to this, it has become expected behavior that games are able to work in whatever orientation the device is in. Fortunately, there are ways to detect the screen orientation and have Unity update our content as a result of the change in device orientation.

Time for action – Rotating the screen

One piece of functionality, that I felt an odd omission from the iOS Unity product, was that of "out of the box" rotation so that when a user flips the screen, the game flips orientation as well. Fortunately we can rectify that with a simple rotation script.

Let's walk through the steps that would be necessary for this application functionality:

1. Identifying that the screen orientation has changed.
2. Updating the player orientation.
3. Let's see how it is done.

Identifying that the screen orientation has changed

The first step in handling an orientation change is:

1. To actually realize that the orientation has changed.

   There are two ways we can do this:

   - We can either check when the game first starts up only, in which case we need to put our orientation detection in the `Start()` method as it is only called once.
   - If we want to check orientation changes as the user is playing the game then we need to check the state of the orientation on a frame-by-frame basis. We do this by putting our orientation code in the `Update()` method.

Method	Description
`Input.deviceOrientation`XE "Input. deviceOrientation method"	Returns the physical orientation of the device

2. We will use the `deviceOrientation` attribute of the `Input` class to determine what the orientation of the device is. This information comes directly from the OS in real time, so as the orientation changes, we will be notified and can respond to the change without having to interrupt gameplay.

```
using UnityEngine;
using System.Collections;

public class OrientationChange : MonoBehaviour {

  // Use this for initialization
  void Start () {
```

```
    }


    // Update is called once per frame
    void FixedUpdate () {
      if ( Input.deviceOrientation == DeviceOrientation.Portrait )
      {
      }
      else if ( Input.deviceOrientation ==
        DeviceOrientation.LandscapeLeft )
      {
      }
      else if ( Input.deviceOrientation ==
        DeviceOrientation.LandscapeRight )
      {
      }
      else if ( Input.deviceOrientation ==
        DeviceOrientation.PortraitUpsideDown )
      {
      }
    }
  }
```

Updating player orientation

Now that we know that the orientation has changed we need to update the Unity iOS player so that it displays our content with the proper orientation.

Method	Description
`iPhoneSettings.screenOrientation`	Sets the logical orientation of the screen.

```
void Update () {
  if ( Input.deviceOrientation == DeviceOrientation.Portrait )
  {
    iPhoneSettings.screenOrientation =
      iPhoneScreenOrientation.Portrait;
  }
  else if ( Input.deviceOrientation ==
    DeviceOrientation.LandscapeLeft )
  {
    iPhoneSettings.screenOrientation =
      iPhoneScreenOrientation.LandscapeLeft;
  }
```

```
    else if ( Input.deviceOrientation ==
      DeviceOrientation.LandscapeRight )
    {
      iPhoneSettings.screenOrientation =
        iPhoneScreenOrientation.LandscapeRight;
    }
    else if ( Input.deviceOrientation ==
      DeviceOrientation.PortraitUpsideDown )
    {
      iPhoneSettings.screenOrientation =
        iPhoneScreenOrientation.PortraitUpsideDown;
    }
  }
```

With `iPhoneSettings.screenOrientation` we can now tell the Unity player to change its orientation. You can set the orientation to any one of the `iPhoneScreenOrientations` available. It is recommended that you don't do anything that would be uncharacteristic to the way the iOS device is expected to operate as Apple may reject your application for that behavior.

What just happened?

By adding a script to our camera we get an `Update()` notification on a frame by frame basis. We can then look to see what the device orientation is and adjust our orientation accordingly. By updating the `iPhoneSettings` attributes we can quickly flip our scene to match whatever orientation we find ourselves in.

iPhoneUtils

`iPhoneUtils` is a set of simple utilities to perform some basic functions on the iOS device. There isn't much in `iPhoneUtils`, but it does provide functionality to determine if your application has been tampered with on the device, trigger vibration on the phone, and play movies.

Playing movies

There are two mechanisms for playing movies within iPhoneUtils: `PlayMovie` and `PlayMovieURL`. `PlayMovie` will play content that is on the phone in the `StreamingAssets` folder. Given that you have limited resources to move content if you want to perform over the air (OTA) distribution, `PlayMovie` may not be of use to you. `PlayMovie` is best suited to game cut scenes and your initial game intro movie since these will generally not be long.

`PlayMovieURL` is more practical for long running movies, dynamic content that you want to deliver to the user (episodic), or content that is simply too large to reasonably be distributed within your application. Remember, these are still mobile devices and they have bandwidth constraints. If you make your app large enough that it cannot be downloaded over the air, you are placing a limitation on your possible audience and hurting your customer's experience.

Is my application genuine?

While not the end all in determining whether or not someone has stolen your application, `isApplicationGenuine` provides a mechanism through which you can detect if the application has been tampered with. It won't catch every pirate out there, but it is a useful function. Don't depend on this function exclusively for combating piracy!

Time for action – Yarr! There be pirates!

Reality check – people are going to steal your game. For whatever reason they do it, you probably want to do something in response. Let's suppose that we want to detect whether or not someone has pirated our application and if they have stream them an advertisement movie from the web before continuing to a demo version of our application.

Let's walk through the steps that would be necessary for this application functionality:

1. The first step in this process is to create a demo scene.
2. In this scene put all of your assets that you want to comprise this scene. In my case I'll create a simple scene that displays a simple puppy sitting by some rocks. You can control the puppy and move him around the scene.
3. Now let's create a demo version of the scene. For demo purposes I'll use the same puppy, but I will just set him up in a sleep animation loop in this scene. Whenever a user enters the demo world, all the puppies that they find will be asleep.
4. Based on conditional logic, display the demo scene.

```
void Start ()
{
  if ( iPhoneUtils.isApplicationGenuine )
  {
    Application.LoadLevel("RegularGame");
  }
  else
  {
    Application.LoadLevel("DemoLevel");
  }
}
```

We can determine if our application hasn't been signed by Apple by checking the `iPhoneUtils.isApplicationGenuine` property. It is important to note that when you're building the application on your local machine it will return `false`. It will not return `true` until it has been signed by Apple and is on its way to the AppStore. Therefore, you do not want to simply check to see if the application is genuine and then refuse to load if it isn't as the reviewer may determine that your app doesn't work and then reject it accordingly.

What just happened?

When the unity player starts we check to see if this is an authentic version of our application. If Unity detects that the application has been tampered with it will send the user to an ad and a demo version of the game.

But let's stop for a second. Pirates will STILL be able to get around this and they will be able to write a specific patch for your application. At this time there is no fool-proof mechanism for detecting or preventing piracy of any iOS application. As long as an iOS device can be jailbroken, people can get around any mechanism you put in place to prevent piracy. I put this example in here so that you will have some idea about creative ways to work with the reality of the situation, but don't expect that this alone will prevent piracy of your app.

Accessing the camera

At the time of this writing Unity iOS did not have functionality to access the camera for taking pictures or streaming video. While there is certainly a gap there, this is a functionality which is generally not used in games. However, if you do want to gain access to the camera you have two choices; write a native code plugin for the camera or license the Prime31 Etcetera plugin (`http://www.prime31.com`).

Summary

In this chapter we learned about the different Unity scripting languages at a high-level and gained some insight into C# as a scripting language, which we will continue to use throughout the remainder of the book. In addition, we spent some time looking at the iPhone specific scripting interfaces and building a number of real-world examples, which utilize the functions available to you in the Unity iOS player.

With this specific iOS scripting under our belt and our demo project updated, we can continue and begin integrating with the iOS input system – the keyboard, the touchscreen, and the accelerometer.

6

Our Game: Battle Cry!

We've spent some time talking about the basics of getting to know Unity iOS and we've looked at some examples of how to use some of its basic functions, but we need to bring it all together to build a game for the iOS market. While we could dream up any game concept we want, we need to be aware of our platform and the user expectations of the platform. Just because something worked well on a Nintendo DS or a PC with a keyboard and mouse, that doesn't mean that the game is appropriate for players whose primary interface is touching the screen and moving the device.

In this chapter we shall:

- Walk through the design decisions for building an iOS game
- Organize our project
- Determine the project asset budget
- Import and optimize assets for our project

Game Concept

As this is the first game we're going to be building for the app store, we will start with something that is fun, but relatively basic in concept and implementation—a third person perspective dungeon crawler. The design inspiration for the game will be the arcade classic Gauntlet. We will take advantage of common services used for mobile games through plugins and third party services to exploit some of the iOS functions available in Unity.

Story

Every game needs a story and this one is no different. A story doesn't have to be a grand epic, but it should explain to the player why they are doing what they are doing and give them the motivation to play the game – and its sequel. For Battle Cry, which is a fairly simple third person shooter game, we will go with a fairly simple story.

The planet of Vosh is the ancestral home of your people. The planet has one special resource – heavy water that, unbeknownst to the people of Vosh, is highly sought after by other intelligent species in the universe as it is used in their fusion power reactors. The people of Vosh have been filtering the heavy water into a special type of beverage for the royal family of the planet.

One day an alien craft appears in orbit above Vosh carrying aliens that have determined that they need the heavy water and start an invasion of the planet. You are a soldier that is based at one of the filtering factories and responsible for defending the facility. Your commanding officers have called out for support, as your weaponry is limited. All you need to do is hold out and keep the facility in good repair.

With this simple story we can drive the player through our scene and easily incorporate elements of multiplayer gameplay.

Interface

The interface for this game can be relatively rudimentary and that is important as our gameplay has relatively straightforward gameplay considerations. We need a way to move our character through the world, a way to have them attack enemies, a display for health, and a way to keep score:

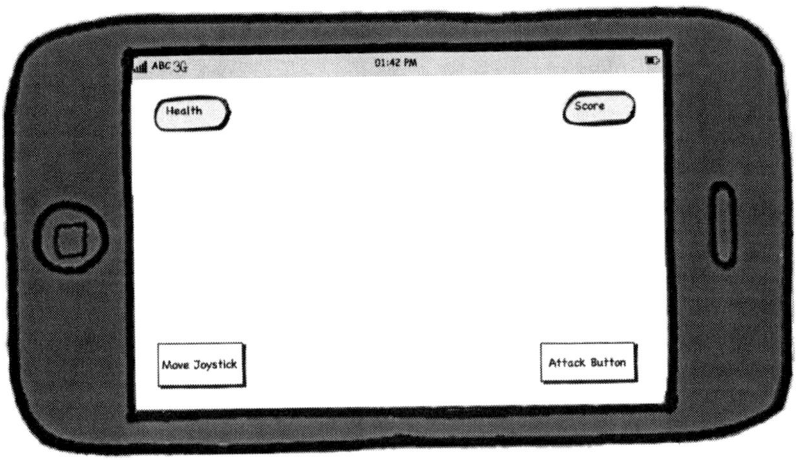

This mockup represents the interface that we will need to construct for our game. The game design requires touch with the device and up to this point there is no reason for us to process voice, shake the device, or anything else. If there is no reason for these features, there is no reason to add them. Good game design is a matter of following the KISS principle (Keep It Simple Stupid).

Control

Control is one of the more difficult things to get right on a touch screen device and it's usually because you're dealing with a device that is designed to be held. Given this you have two general orientations of the device that you need to prepare for.

The first use case is that the user is holding the device in the hands. In this case the primary user interaction is going to be their thumbs – a relatively low precision touch instrument and one that does not lend it self to rapid movement.

The second use case is that the user has positioned the device on a table and is looking down at it. In this case the user is more likely to be using a pointing finger, which is higher precision and capable of more rapid movement.

Why is this important, you may ask? If the user is working with a lower precision control instrument and a slower moving finger, to remove an element of frustration for a wide variety of genres of game, you need to make your control area larger and you need to make your game more responsive to its movement and vice versa. Given this, we need to give the user two sets of controls to reflect the different user hand sizes and we need to allow those controls to have variable sensitivity – preferably configurable by the user in the game's settings.

Audio

Audio is usually an after thought in game design when it really should be thought about in great detail early in the design, so that it feels part of the game. If you feel that the audio of your game isn't nearly as important as the graphic element I offer you two challenges: listen to your favorite movie with the sound off, do a search on the Internet for video game music. Sound and music done properly will elicit an emotional response in the user and allow for a deeper emotional attachment to the rest of the game.

We will want to have sounds for a variety of user interactions – the grunts of enemies, the battle cry of the champions of the city, the sounds of arrows in flight, the cries of the slain, and so on. Additionally, we will want to have several sets of music that will reflect the different moods of the game. Most importantly, we want all of this sound to actually fit on the device. We could make a design decision and allow the user to access their iTunes music library for music, but it isn't appropriate in this context.

Time for action – Project setup

It is now time for us to create the project for our game that will be used for the rest of the text. While we have walked through this at a high-level before, there are particular details that we want to include with this new project that require review.

1. Create a new Unity Project.

   Our project will use some of the unitypackages that come with Unity to provide some of the core functions without us having to write a large amount of code.

2. Enter a directory name for the project.

3. Select the **Character Controller**, **Skyboxes**, **Standard Assets (Mobile)**, and **Terrain Assets** packages in the **Project Wizard**:

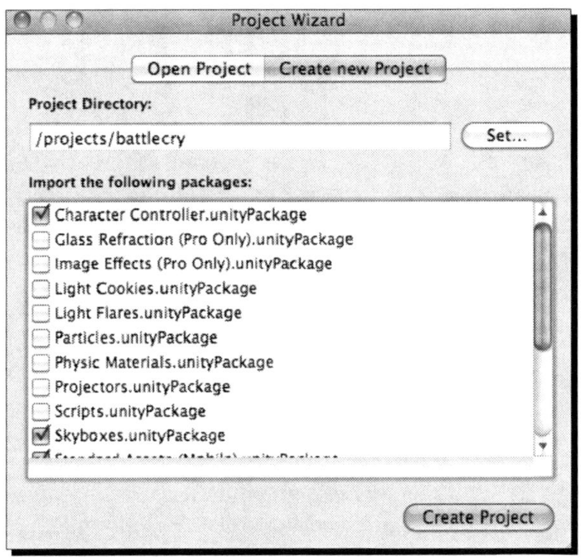

   - **Character Controller** will allow us to move our character around the level without having to deal with a lot of scripting.
   - **Skyboxes** are useful for being able to draw the sky for our world. We will be able to put up a simple texture to represent the sky or ceiling for our dungeons.
   - **Standard Assets (Mobile)** will contain a lot of interface and optimized prefabs specifically for the iPhone.
   - **Terrain Assets** will give us the basics for being able to paint on our terrain without having to go off and search for other assets.

4. As we've done previously, we need to create a new **App ID** and provisioning profile on the Apple Developer Center's provisioning portal.

5. Download and import the provisioning profile into XCode.

6. In the **Player Settings** change the **Product Name** to **Battlecry**. This is the name that the application will display when it is installed on the device.

7. Set our **Bundle Identifier** to that which we have from the provisioning portal. Here I have inserted `com.sojournermobile.battlecry` to mimic what is stored in the provisioning profile.

8. As we're targeting both the iPhone and the iPad we must set the **Target Device** to **iPhone + iPad** so that we will end up with a universal binary:

9. Provide an image for the game so that it will display with a real icon when it starts. In the assets there is an "icon_57_57.png" file. Import that and drag it in to the Default Icon field:

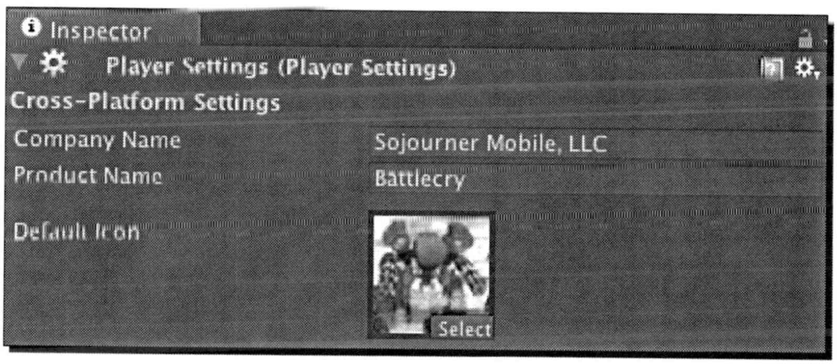

10. To ensure that we're linking to the latest SDK, and have access to all of the functions of iOS available to us, select iOS Latest as the SDK version:

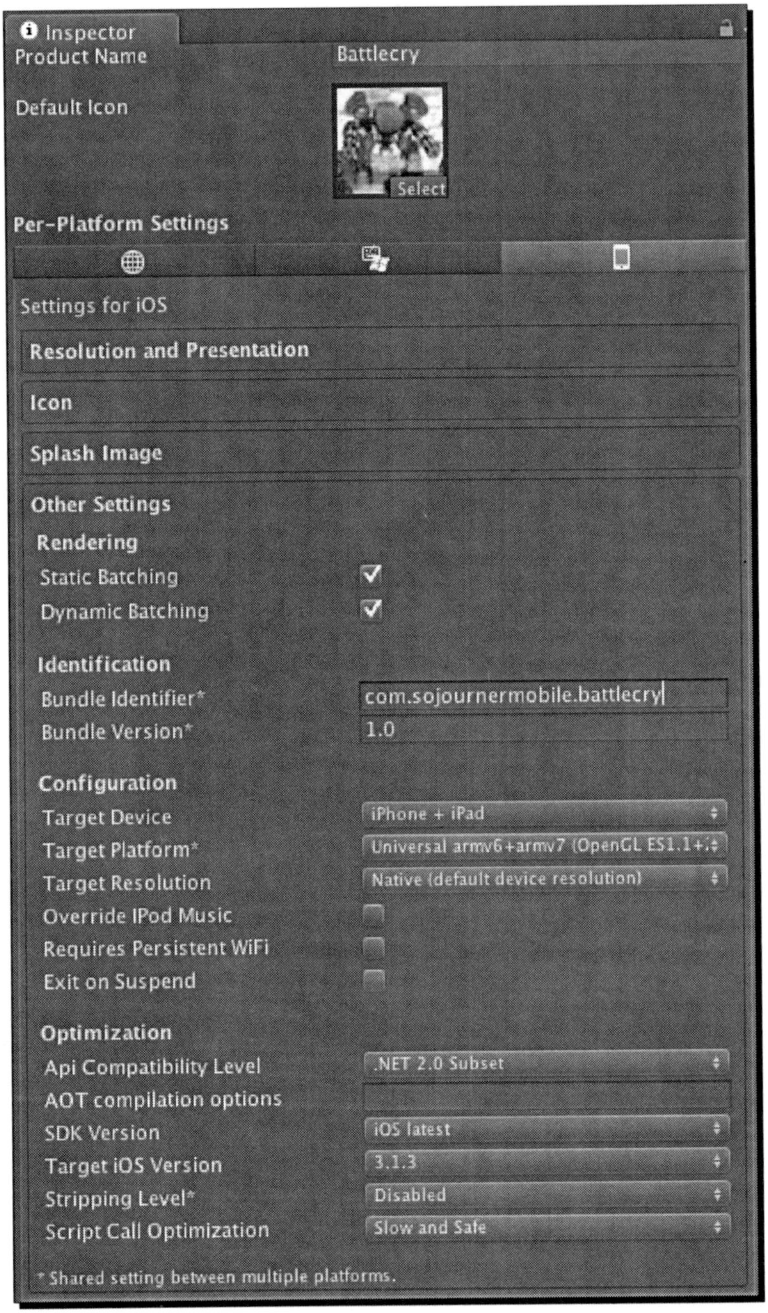

11. Save the scene in the project. You will need to do this before you can include the scene in the build:

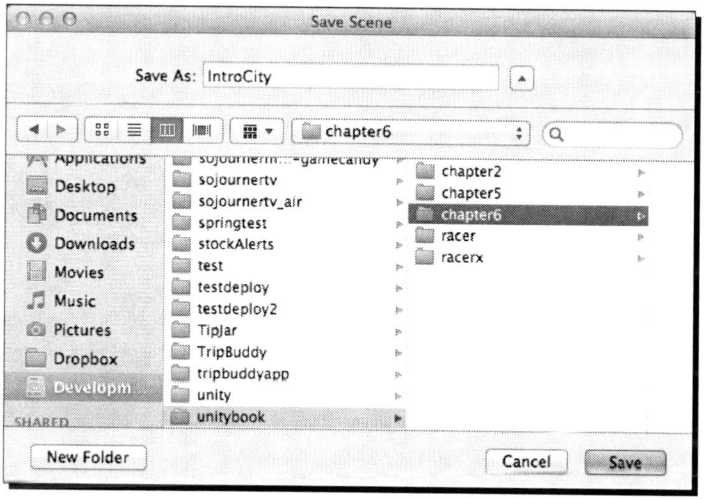

12. Open the **Build Settings** and check our scene:

[If the scene isn't showing up, make sure you have saved it.]

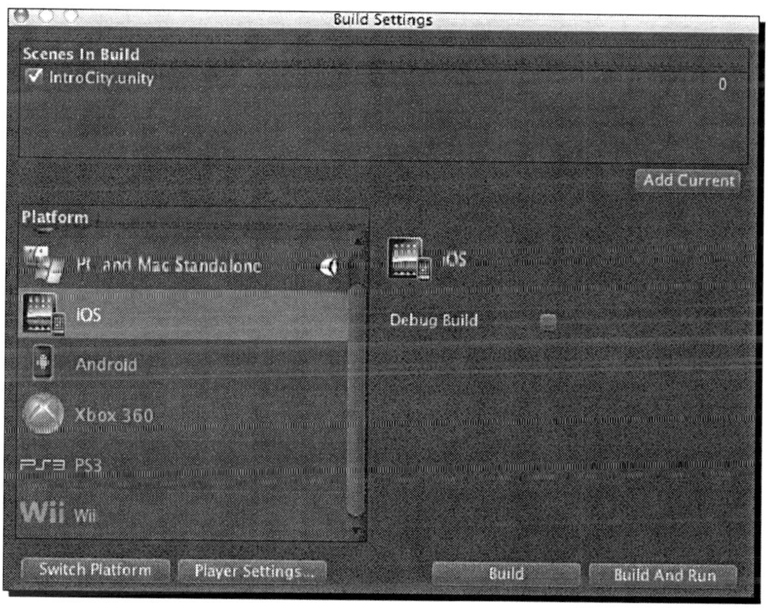

13. Select the **Build & Run** function from the **File** menu. If everything is okay you should see your iOS device start and display the Unity logo.

What just happened?

We have setup the project structure and produced our first build of the game. With this done we can begin to focus on importing assets into our project to begin building a real scene.

Time for action – Building a game world

There are a number of sites that we can reach out to to get assets for the game, but as of Unity 3.1 there has been an integrated store through which you can acquire assets for your project. This interface is so easy to use that it's worth examining for building our level. While we won't find everything here, this is a good start.

One word of advice is that sometimes assets within the Asset Store can be purchased cheaper through other means so be sure to shop around.

Unity Asset Store

The Unity Asset Store is a tool built right into the Unity environment through which you can purchase prefab and integrate them right into your project without ever having to leave the tool. The prefabs in the asset store cover models, scripts, and even functionality that will plug into the Unity IDE itself.

1. Open the store by selecting **Asset Store** in the **Window** menu:

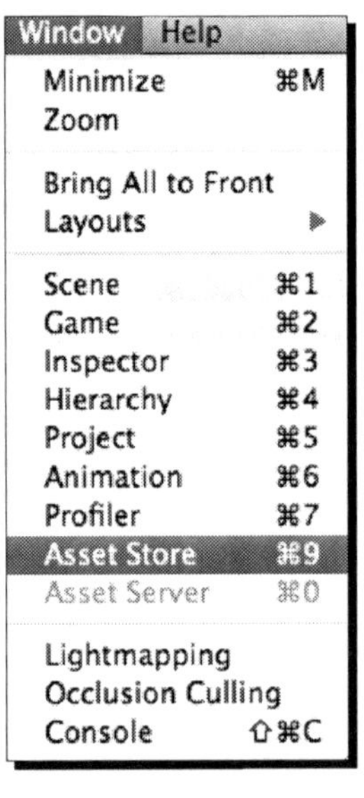

2. Authenticate with the **Asset Store** by creating an account if you have not already done so:

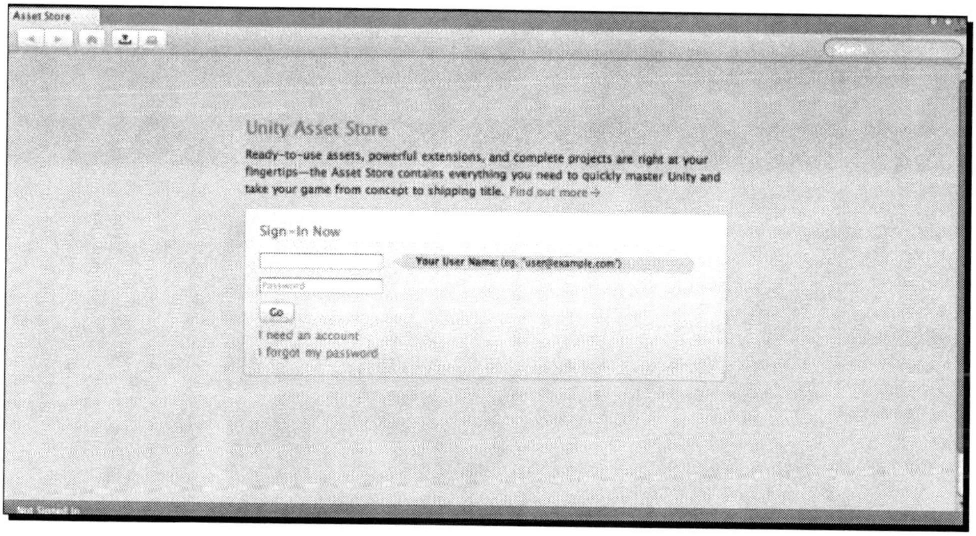

3. Next, you will be greeted by the main menu of the store where you can shop for various types of Unity compatible assets, sounds, prefabs, scripts, and so on:

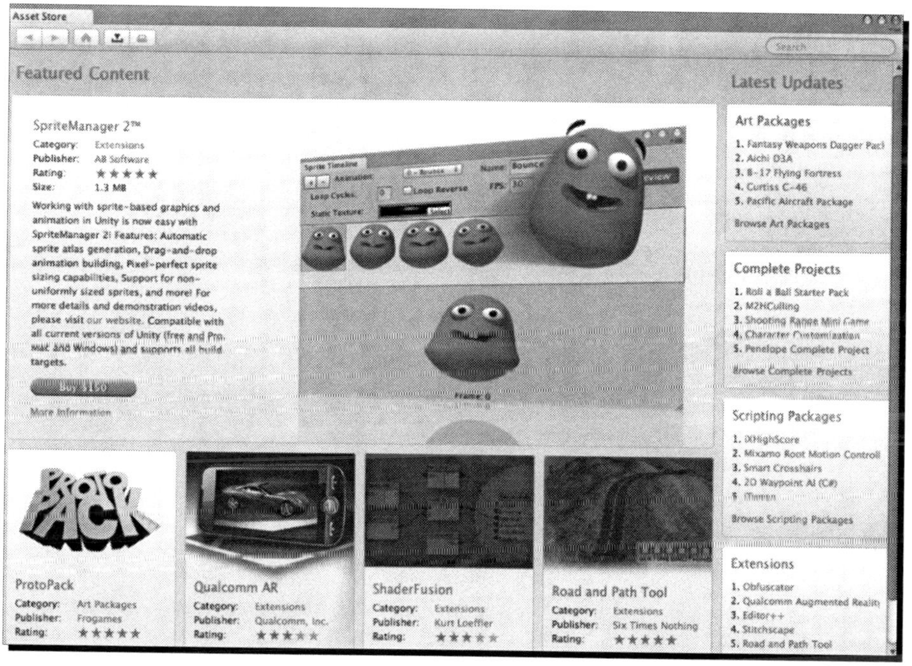

4. Create the ground plane for our scene with **Game Object | Create Other | Plane**.
5. Insert a light into the scene with **Game Object | Create Other | Point Light**.
6. In the Unity **Asset Store** window enter **Allegorithmic** and select the **18 FREE Substances** package:

7. Download the package and import the assets into the project:

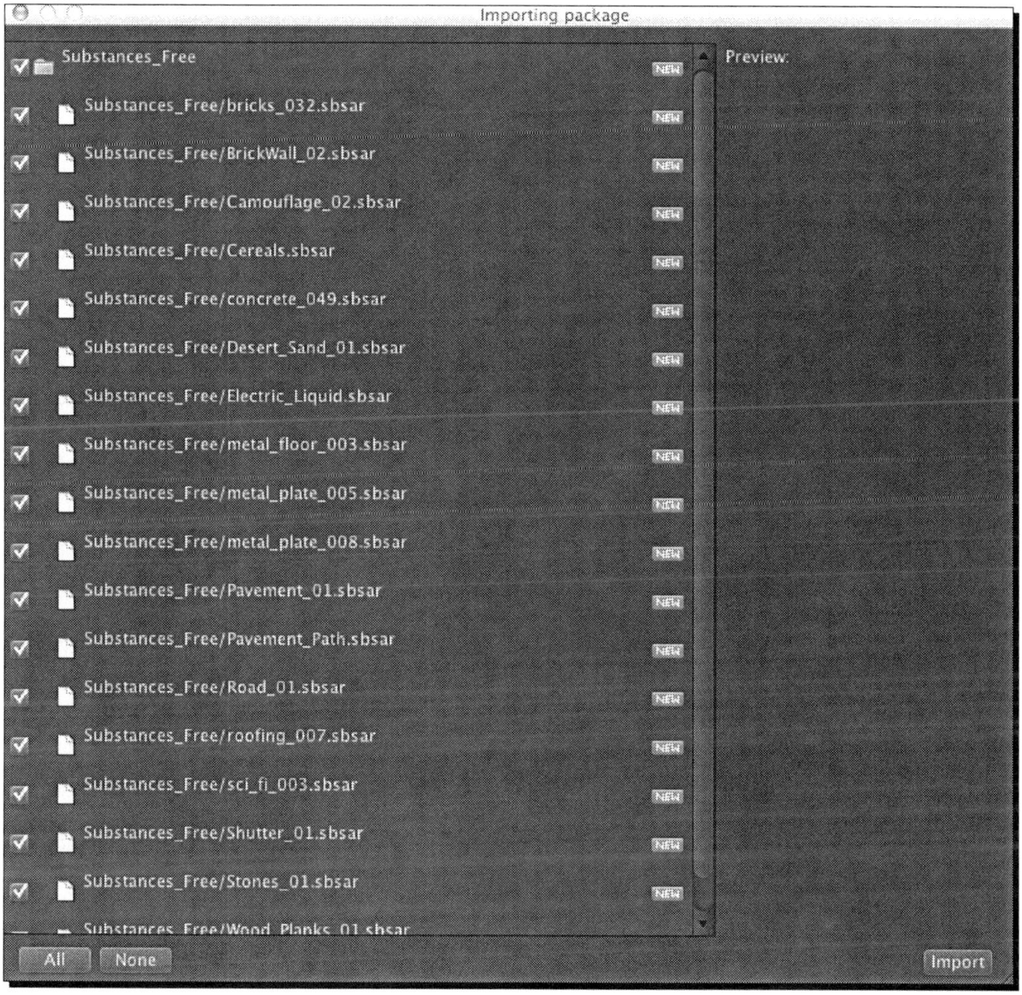

8. Expand the `Substances_Free` directory in your project.

9. Expand the **Desert_Sand_01** package.

10. Drag the **Desert_Sand_01** material onto the plane:

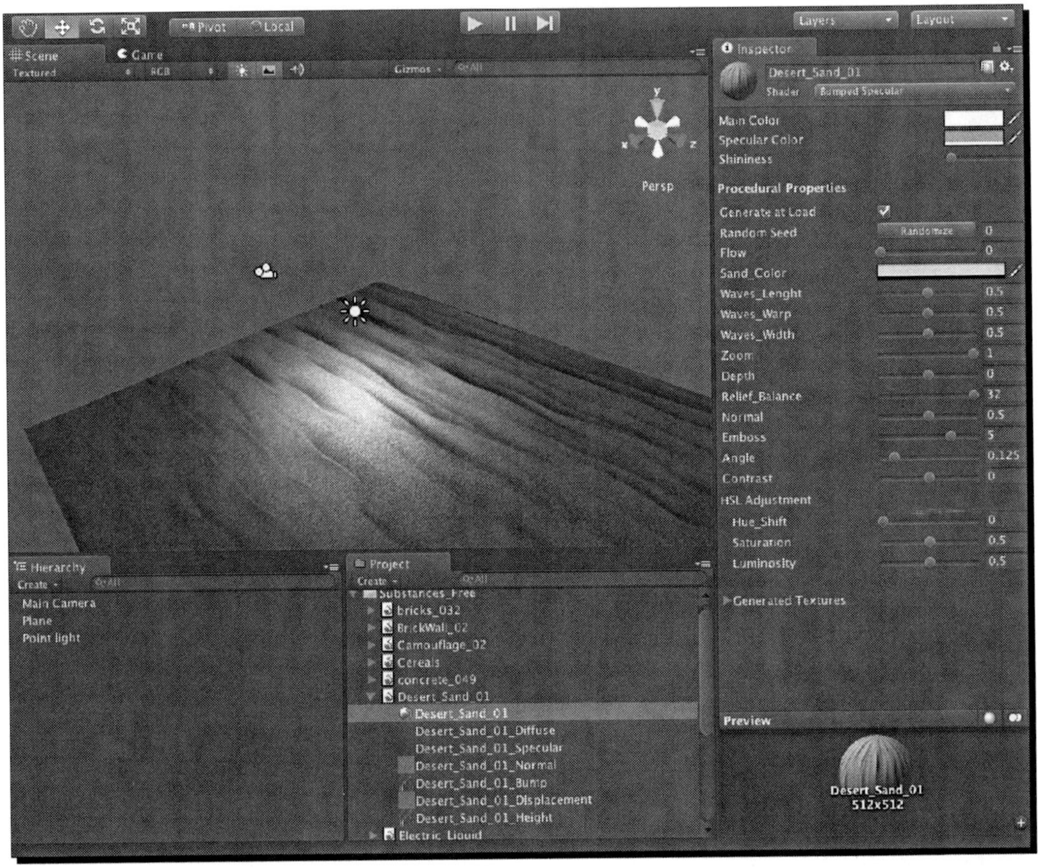

11. Enter **Soldiers Pack** into the search area:

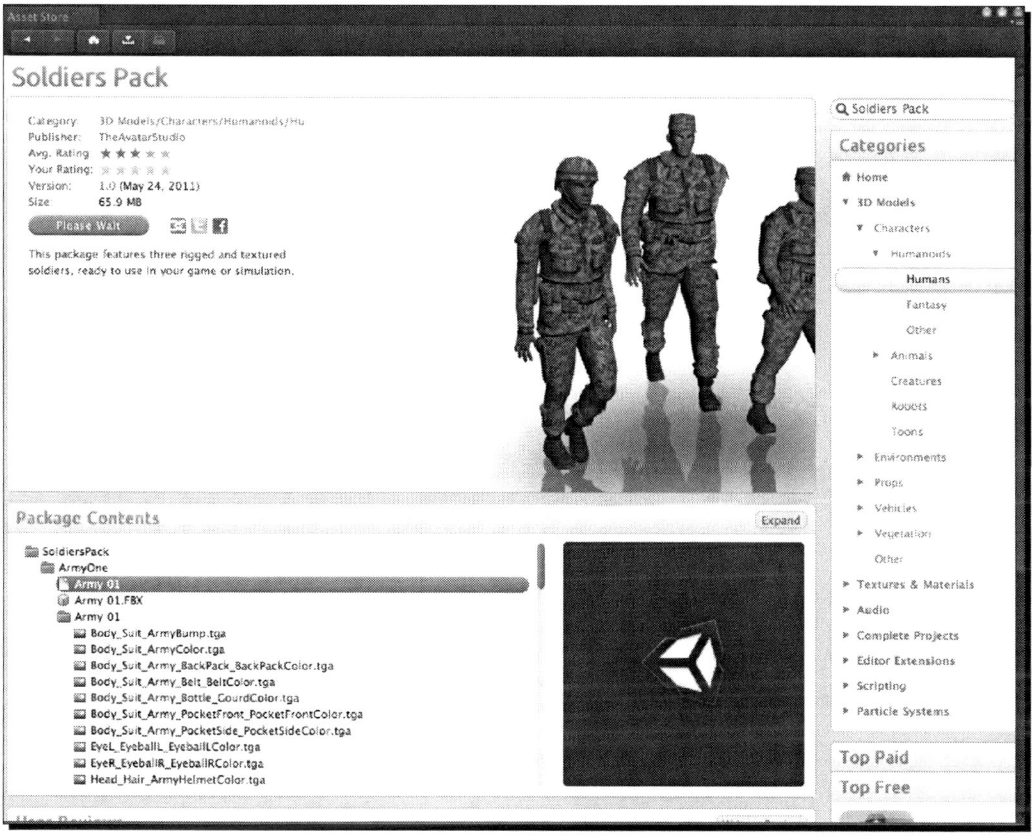

12. Import the **Soldiers Pack** by **TheAvatarStudioi** into the project:

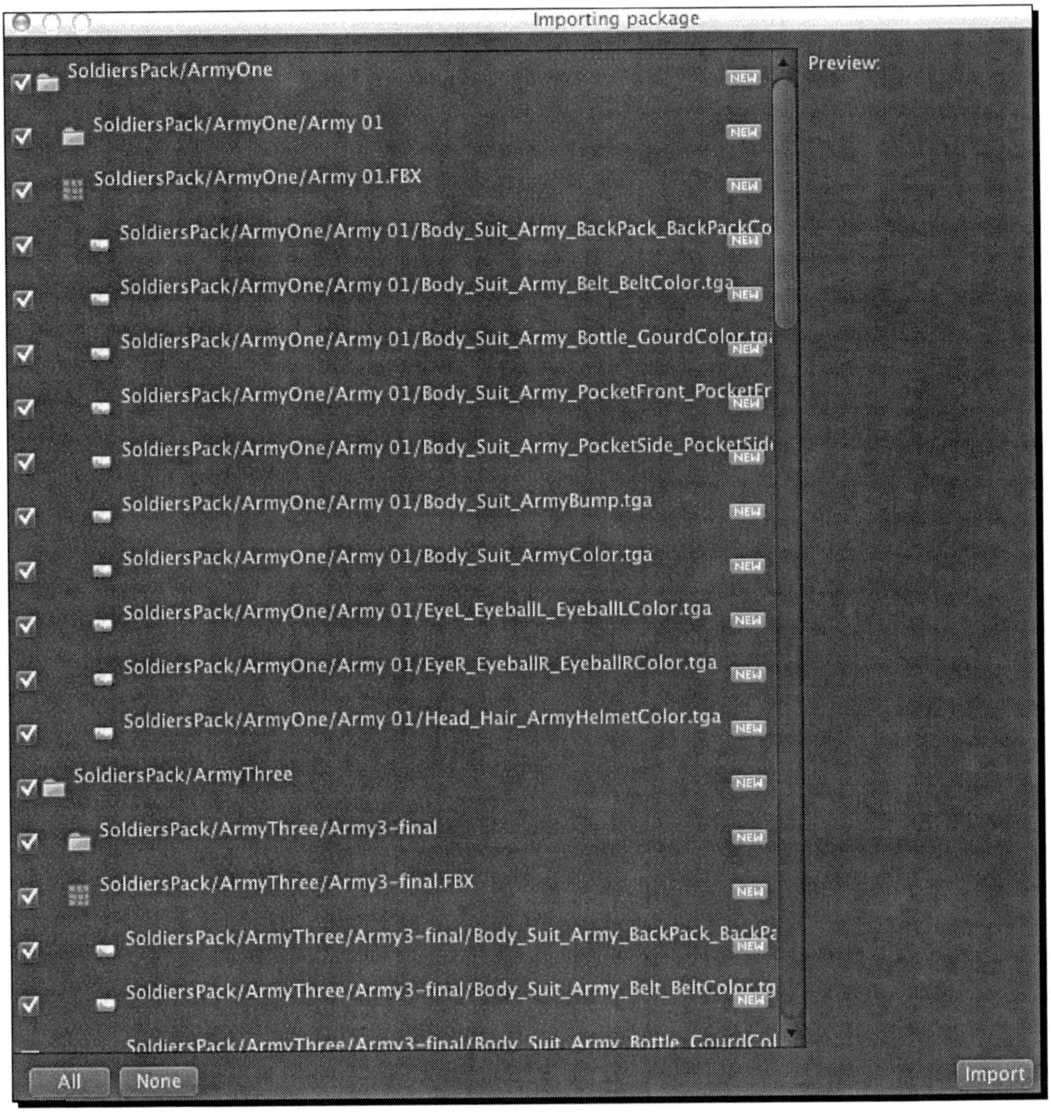

13. Expand the `SoldiersPack` folder in the **Project** view.

14. Expand the `ArmyOne` folder located beneath `SoldiersPack`.

15. Drag the **Army 01** prefab object to the scene:

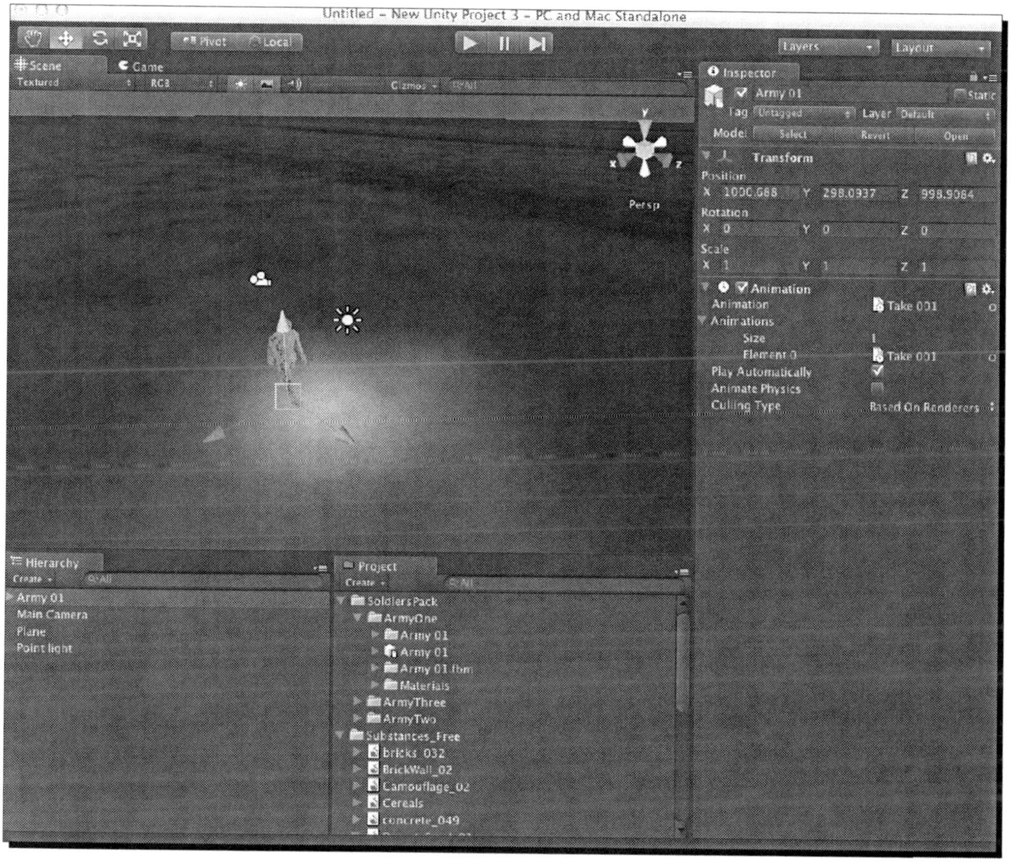

16. Enter **Stone** into the search field:

17. Import the Stone assets from the Universal Image into the project.

18. Expand the `Stone` folder in the project.

19. Drag the stone prefab into the scene.

20. Scale the Stone prefab by **10** units along each axis:

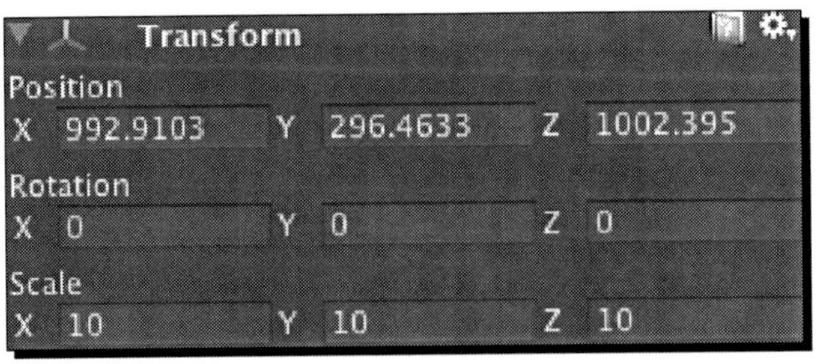

21. Position the enlarged stones in the scene to make some basic scenery:

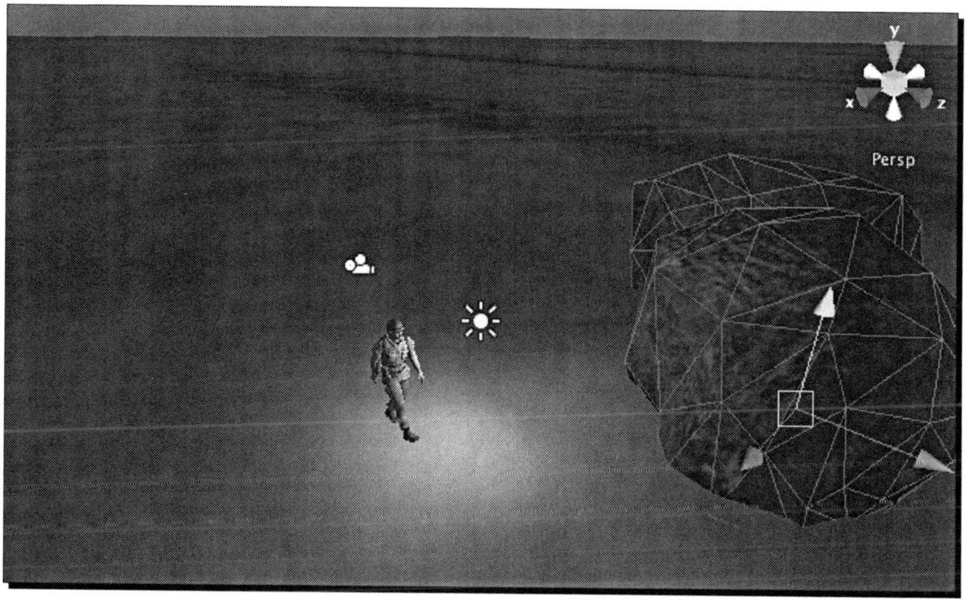

22. Save the scene.

What just happened?

We have laid out the stage where all the action will take place in our game by importing assets from the **Asset Store**. While we have some basic animation ready for actors in the scene, we don't have a player character that can be controlled by the player. What we are missing are actors to participate in the game. We need to build a controller for our player character that will work with our game design.

Summary

In this chapter we discussed the design of our game and set up our project. Along the way we have setup version control, imported assets from a wide variety of sources including the Unity asset store, and produced the first build for our device. We are now ready to move onto the first hurdle that is to move our player character through the scene.

7

Input: Let's Get Moving!

Up to this point we've done some basic moving around a scene, but nothing like we'll need if we're going to build commercial games for iOS devices. One thing that is often overlooked when writing games for iOS is that while iPads, iPhones, etc. can perform many of the same functions as their desktop cousins – there are very specific techniques you need to be aware of when moving from the keyboard mouse world to that of touchscreens and accelerometers. In this chapter we're going to spend some time getting into the nitty gritty of what those details are.

In this chapter we shall:

- Learn about the iOS touch screen interface
- Learn about accelerometers and how they work
- Create an interface on the touch screen for moving through an environment
- Learn how to process gestures

This may not sound like a lot, but with iOS development there are many things that you can do incorrectly, which will lead to difficulties when working with Unity. Rather than assume that you'll get it all right we're going to talk through it step by step to make sure that you can spend your time building games and not trying to decipher mysterious error messages.

So let's get on with it...

Input Capabilities

The iPhone is a collection of a wide variety of technologies that can be used to detect input from the user. The two most important technologies, from the perspective of a game developer, are the touch screen and the accelerometer. With these two input mechanisms nearly every game available to date has been constructed, so we will perform an in-depth analysis of how they work and how we can use their capabilities to determine the intent of the user within our game.

The technology of touch

A touch screen is a display device that can detect the presence and location of one or more touches within the display area. While early touch devices relied on passive instruments, such as a stylus to detect interactions with the touch surface, modern touch devices detect physical contact with the device.

While it may not seem the case, there are a variety of technologies used to drive touch interaction with devices. The decision on which technology is chosen depends upon a multitude of factors such as cost, durability, scalability, and versatility. It is very easy for one to suggest that one touch technology is superior to others, but a technology that works well for one particular application may be entirely inappropriate for another. For example, the technology used in the iPhone requires a person to make physical contact with the surface for a touch to be registered. However, if you're building a kiosk, you may desire that users are able to interact with the device with gloved hands. This seemingly innocent choice has radical implications on the technology chosen as well as the design of the device itself.

There are several common types of touch surfaces that are common in devices today: resistive, capacitive, and infrared. While the mechanics of their implementations vary, they all follow the same basic recipe – when you place your finger or stylus on the screen, there is some change in state on the surface that is then sent to a processor, which determines where that touch took place. It is how that change in state is measured which separates the technologies from one another.

While all of today's iOS devices utilize a particular surface type – capacitive, it is foreseeable that Apple may change technologies at some point in the future as they expand the platform to cover new types of devices. In addition, it is important to understand the other types of surfaces that you may encounter as you port your content to other platforms.

Resistive technology

A resistive screen is comprised of layers of conductive and resistive material. When pressure is placed on the screen, the pressure from the finger or stylus causes the resistive and conductive material to come into contact – resulting in a change in the electrical field. At this point, measuring the resistance on the circuits connected to the conductive material will denote the location of the touch.

Given that any pressure can cause the contact to occur, a resistive screen works well when you want to have a passive implement such as a stylus as a possible touch instrument. In addition, you can keep your gloves on with this technology, as a gloved hand will work just as well as a naked one. As resistive technology has been around for a lot longer it tends to be cheaper to produce and is the technology most commonly found at the lower end of the cost spectrum.

Capacitive technology

A capacitive screen uses a layer of capacitive material that holds an electrical charge. When touched, this material registers a difference in the amount of charge at a specific location on the surface at the point of contact. This information is then passed onto the processors which can determine precisely where the touch takes place. The iOS devices simplify this process by arranging the capacitors in a grid such that every point on the screen generates its own signal when touched. This has the added benefit of producing a very high resolution of touch data that can be processed by the processor.

As the capacitive approach relies on having capacitive material in order to function, it requires that something that can conduct electricity performs the touching. Since the human body conducts electricity this works fine, but it rules out the stylus approach, or more specifically it requires that a special capacitive stylus be used.

Infrared technology

An infrared screen uses an array of infrared or LED light beams, which it projects beneath the protective glass, or more commonly, acrylic surface. A camera will then peer up at this grid of beams and look for any interruption of the signal, similar to the grid approach used by iOS devices – just with an infrared camera and beams of light. This approach is refined and deployed with the Microsoft Surface and has some particular unexpected benefits. Since a camera is used to determine the touch location, that camera can also look at the object at that location. If that object is a marker, it can then extract information from that marker as well. This is used to good effect with the Microsoft Surface.

The obvious downside to the Infrared approach is that it requires a fair amount of space to work its magic. Due to the nature of the optics, the further you are away from the surface the more resolution you are able to gain on that surface. This makes the technology impractical for the typical iPhone application.

Accelerometer

An accelerometer is a device that measures the acceleration of motion on a structure. In iOS devices the accelerometer is a 3-axis system such that it can determine acceleration along the various axes of the device (x,y,z). When at rest, an accelerometer would be measuring the force of gravity (1g). As the device moves, the device will be able to measure the movements of the device based upon these accelerations along the various axes and determine the orientation of the new device. Without getting into the associated math, the only thing that you really need to know is that no matter what orientation you put the device in, the device is aware of that orientation:

Gyroscope

A gyroscope is a device for measuring the orientation of a device. Unlike an accelerometer, the orientation of a device can be derived without the device actually moving. Currently only available on a subset of the iOS devices, the gyroscope enables a much more refined detection of movement in the device. The 3-axis gyro in the iOS devices work in tandem with the built-in accelerometer to produce a complete 6-axis sensitivity for motion gestures. At the time of this writing there is no support within Unity for the Gyroscope so we will not focus on its use within the context of our game.

Touch screen

Our game design calls for having a set of joysticks at the bottom on the screen that we can use to move around the world and manipulate the camera. The control scheme mirrors what a player would expect if they were familiar with an Xbox style controller.

We also need to perform actions with the right button. Similar to the Xbox controller we want to be able to invoke actions by tapping down on the right joystick as an action.

The next feature we want to plan for is the ability to perform gestures on the surface so that we can avoid having to fill our interface with extraneous buttons. There are several gestures that we want to support in our gameplay.

Gesture	Meaning
Swipe Up	Throw Grenade
Swipe Left/Right	Dodge Left/Right
Swipe Down	Guard/Take Cover

Accelerometer/Gyroscope

Our game design doesn't call for the use of the accelerometer, but for the sake of instruction we will use the accelerometer as an additional mechanism for manipulating the camera and provide a shake command that we will use if the character is ever knocked down and needs to heal.

Motion	Meaning
Shake	Heal
Turn Left/Right	Rotate Camera

Implementing Joysticks

Our game design sketch calls for playing this game while the device is in landscape orientation so we need to start off the application in landscape.

Time for action – Getting oriented

From our previous applications we know that we can accomplish this by performing a quick orientation change within the `Awake()` method of our application:

```
function Awake()
{
  iPhoneSettings.screenOrientation =
    iPhoneScreenOrientation.Landscape;
}
```

In previous examples we put our functions in the `Start()` method, but we are putting this call in the `Awake()` method. The reason for this is that we want this script, and the orientation settings, to be processed as soon as the scene is loaded, but before the joystick script tries to determine where to put the joysticks. If we didn't do this the position of the joysticks would be too close together as their positions would have been derived from the portrait orientation.

If you were to run your application now you would find that the application will hold to a single screen orientation, however, when you rotated you would get a black outline that rotates with the screen. This black outline represents the iOS keyboard interface rotating with the device. To prevent this from happening you need to lock the keyboard so that it is in the same orientation with the application.

Key Class/Methods	Description
iPhoneSettings.`screenOrientation`	Gets/Sets the orientation of the device
`iPhoneScreenOrientation`	Enumerated type of the possible device orientations
`iPhoneKeyboard.autorotateXXXX`	Sets whether or not the iPhoneKeyboard will rotate to a particular orientation when the device changes orientation

```
void Awake()
{
  iPhoneSettings.screenOrientation =
    iPhoneScreenOrientation.Landscape;
  iPhoneKeyboard.autorotateToPortrait = false;
  iPhoneKeyboard.autorotateToPortraitUpsideDown = false;
}
```

What just Happened?

We have configured the game so that it will default to landscape orientation when it starts. In addition, the game will do what the users expect and you won't have the graphical glitch of the iOS keyboard trying to adjust for the device orientation.

Next, our design calls for a touch interface with two joystick areas with the one on the left acting as the movement stick and the one on the right acting as the rotation joystick. We will use these to capture user interactions and drive our character around the game world.

Time for action – Implementing the joysticks

1. Expand the Standard Assets (Mobile) unitypackage that we added to the project initially in one part of our solution. Inside of the `Prefabs` folder there is a `Dual Joysticks` prefab:

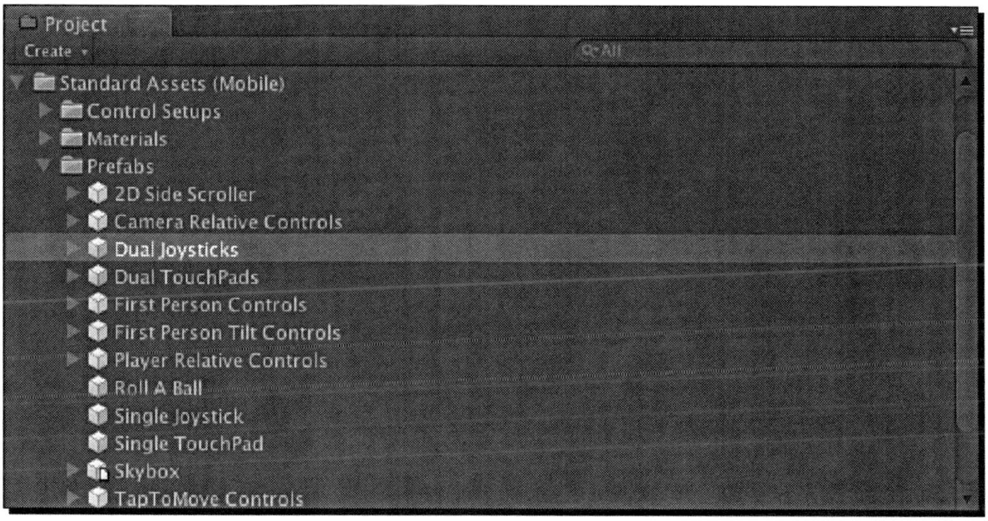

2. Since this is going to be moving with the user interface plane of our camera we can simply make it a child of the camera:

3. Set the **Game** view to display in iPhone Wide by selecting the dropdown in the upper left of the Game view. This will result in a more accurate depiction of how the game will look at startup. Now, when we take a look at the Game view we can see exactly what our camera will see when our game starts:

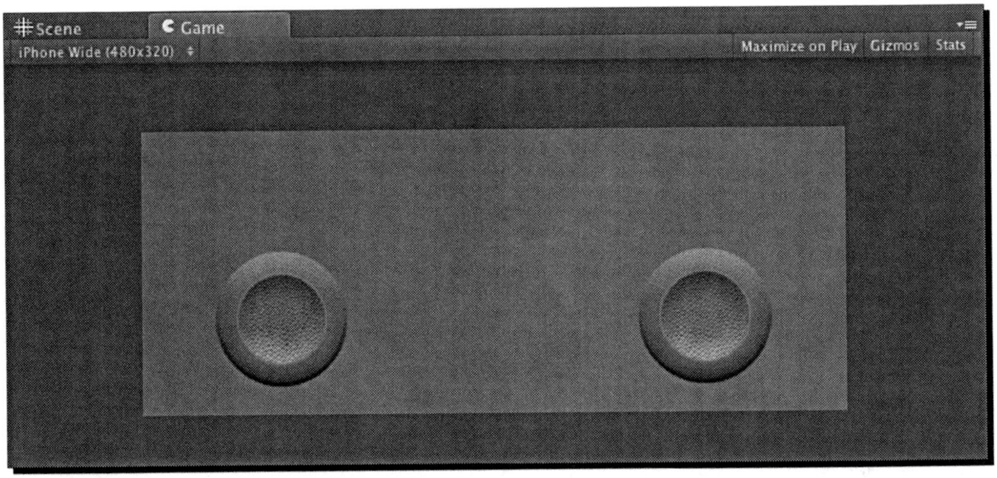

This figure represents what we expect to see – our two Joystick nubs in the user interface ready for user interaction. If you start your application on your iOS device you will see that as you place your fingers over the joystick nubs, they will move around as your fingers manipulate them during a touch. When you remove your finger from the nub it will snap back to the center position. This information is captured by the Prefab and passed off to the built-in Joystick script.

To pass the input to some other script, simply alter the script that the Prefab is pointing to. Note that each Joystick can have its own script so you can have two entirely different behaviors per joystick.

You can also change the texture that the joystick uses by updating the **Texture** field on the **GUITexture** which represents the joystick:

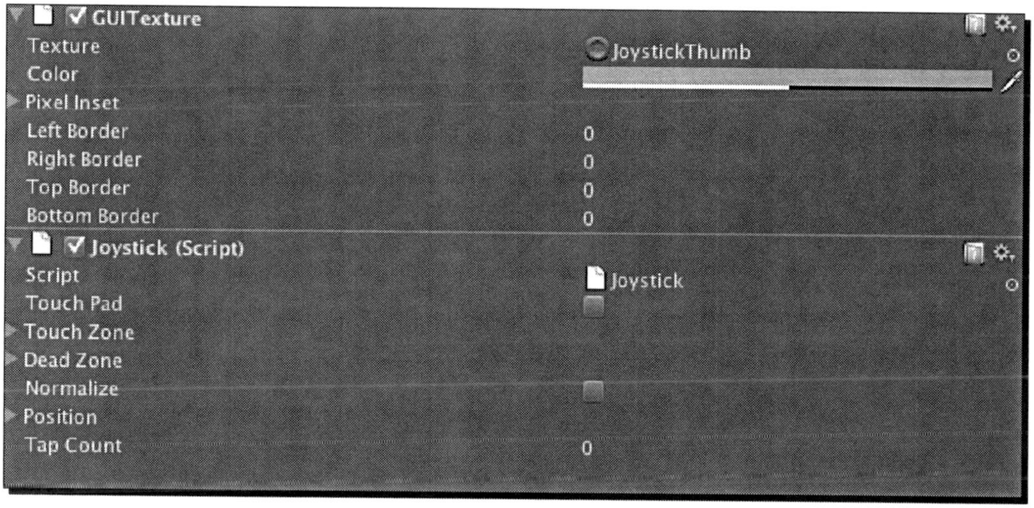

What just happened?

We have just implemented the primary means of input for our game – the dual joystick nubs. As we move these joysticks around they relay data to the Joystick script. While this is interesting, it still doesn't move our character around the scene. If all we needed were some basic joystick processing we'd be done, but we need to control a character and move our camera around the scene. Fortunately, there's a prefab for that.

Moving around

Now that we have an interface which is ready to accept input we need to process the touches from that interface and move our character around the scene. Our plain joystick is one part of the plan, but now we need to handle the rest.

Time for action – Implementing the camera control

1. The first thing we need to do is delete our Main Camera and the Dual Joysticks from the previous scene. Don't be concerned that we've deleted the Main Camera as we will be adding a new camera to the scene.

2. Perform a search for the **Camera Relative Controls** in the **Project** window:

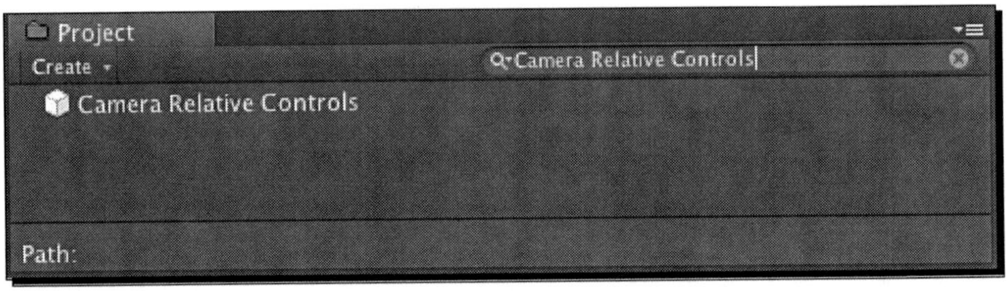

3. Drag the Camera Relative Controls prefab into the **Hierarchy** view. When you drag this prefab into your **Hierarchy** view you will find that it consists of both the Dual Joysticks that we were using earlier, as well as something called **Camera Relative Controls**. Beneath the **Camera Relative Controls** you will find the camera pivot and the player objects.

   The **camera pivot** as the name suggests is the point in space around which the camera will pivot. When you move the right joystick to rotate the camera in 3D space, its actions are relative to this point.

   The other object is the Player which hosts our Character Controller object and has an aptly named child "`ReplaceWithRealCharacter`". When we have our real character we will insert it here:

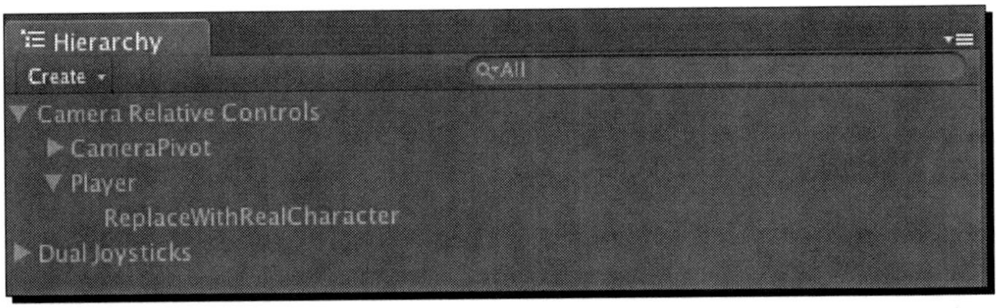

4. Switch to the **Game** view and we will see what this scene represents at runtime:

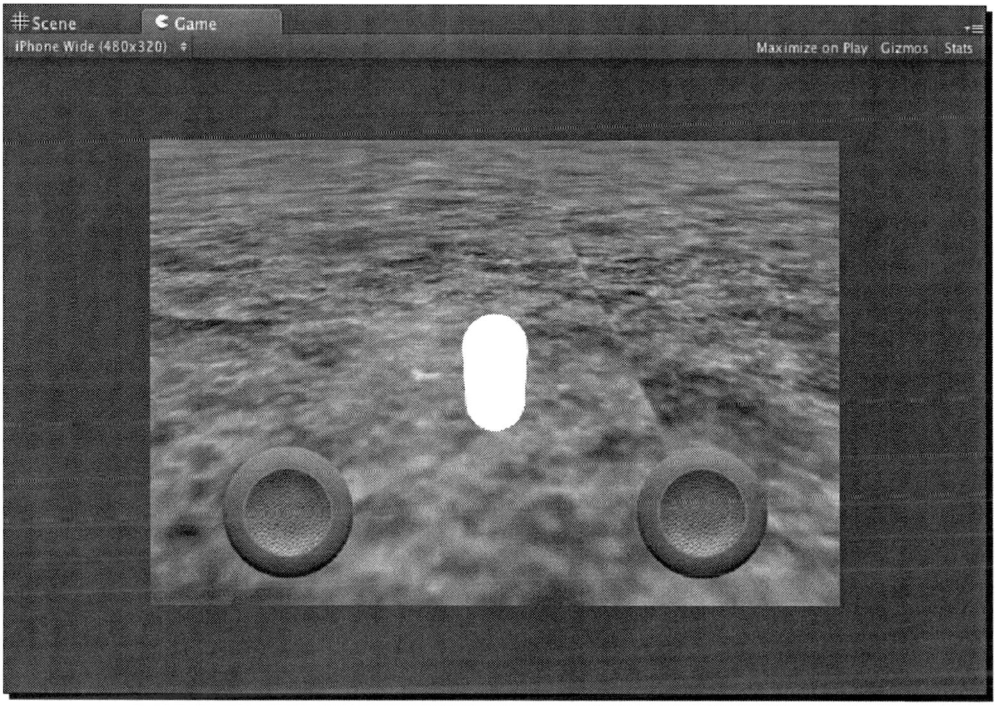

As you can see, the joysticks are in place and the white capsule represents the Character Controller and Player Game Objects. If you deploy this project to your iOS device now you will see that you will be able to move around the scene with the Joysticks, the left moving you around the scene and the right one rotating the camera.

5. Next let's import our player's character. Open the **Asset Store** and perform a search for the **Solder Character Pack**:

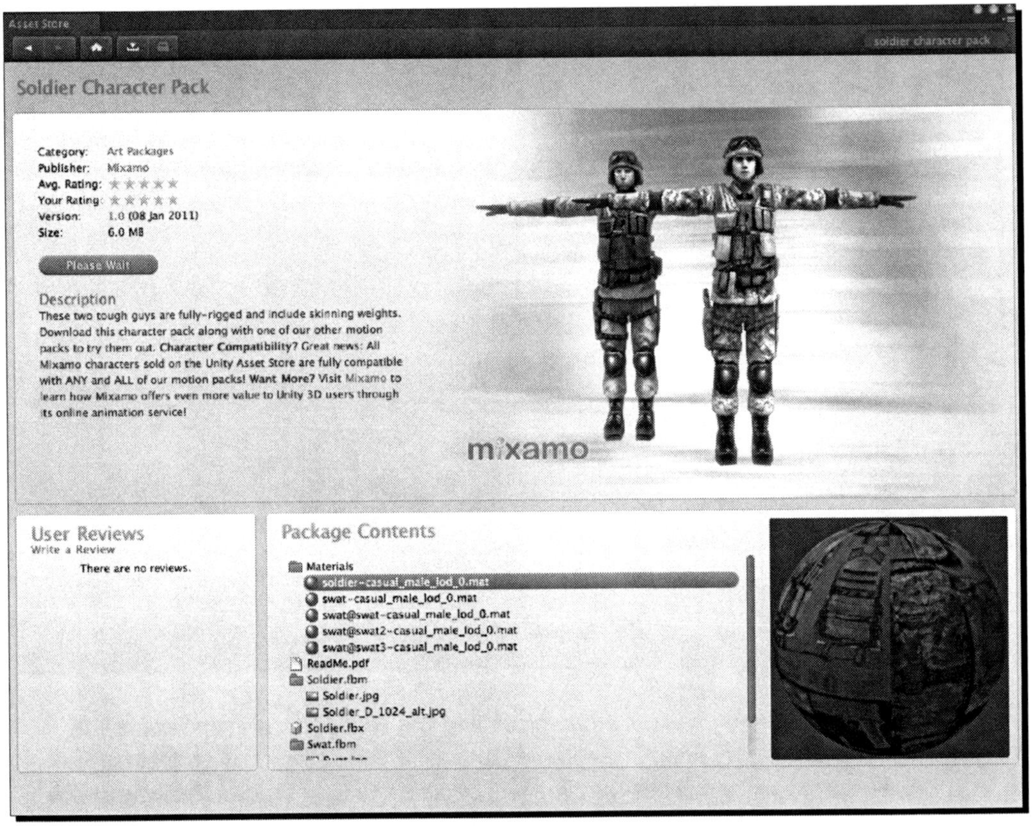

This pack contains a fully rigged character that we can use with our game.

6. After importing the character pack, drag the **Solider** prefab over to the **Camera Relative Controls**, Player node as a child. This will break the prefab link, but this is not a problem as we need to sever that link to add our own geometry to the game.

7. Now delete the `ReplaceWithReachCharacter` child of the Player node and you will have a soldier in your game ready to be used. This soldier isn't the most efficient model we could use for our application, but it is freely available on the asset store and will work just fine for our purposes:

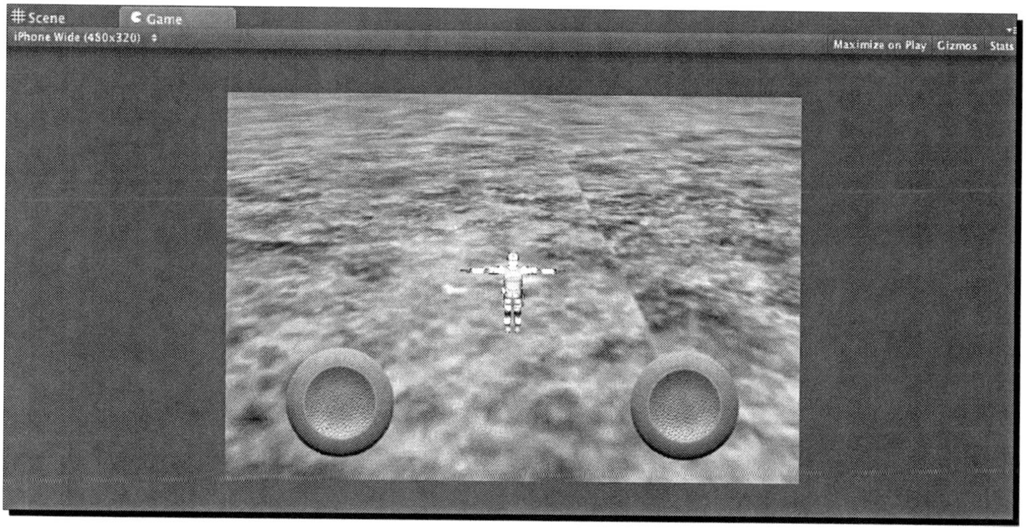

8. Deploy this application to your iOS device and use the joysticks and you will find, that for your limited effort, you have a character in the world that will navigate the world with the left joystick and that you are able to manipulate the camera with the right joystick. We're starting to get something that looks more like a game, except that the player doesn't animate. We need a way to put some animations on this character and have the person walk around, move through the attack animations, take damage, and die if we're going to have a real game.

What just happened?

We have extended the functionality of the existing application to include controls to move around our world, along with camera controls for our player character. Now that we have imported a character for our character controller, we need to animate this character based on user input.

Time for action – Animating the player character

The character that we imported is what is known as a rigged character. A rigged character is one that has all of its bones for animation. These bones are what drive the movement of the mesh itself during animation. Let's disable the rendering of the mesh so we can see the bones themselves..

1. Select the Soldier mesh in the **Hierarchy** view.
2. In the **Inspector** view, scroll down to the Mesh Render component and click its check box. This will disable rendering of the mesh in Unity and in the Game:

3. Open the **Scene** view of the project and select the mesh in the Hierarchy. You should only see the bones for the soldier character we imported:

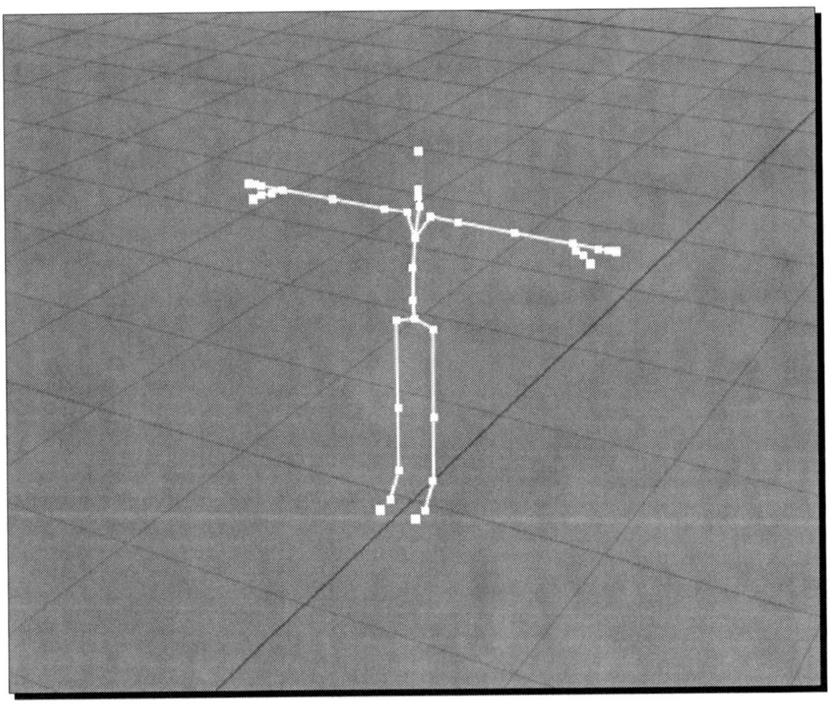

As mentioned earlier, Unity's animation system is fairly robust and has an easily scriptable animation blending system built right into it. As a consequence, we can deal with simple animations such as walk, run, use weapon, and so on, and we can have Unity blend between the animations to allow us to walk while using the weapon.

Importing an animation

The next step is to associate an animation with this rigging so that we can 'drive' our character around the scene. There are a number of ways that you can animate a character, such as motion capture or animating by hand. Unity supports two approaches for importing this content into our game: animation splitting and multiple animation files.

Animation splitting

There are times when you will receive an asset which already has multiple animations baked onto a model. In many content-purchasing scenarios this is quite a common practice. In these situations, when you import the model you will have to tell Unity how to split the single large animation into multiple distinct animations. You will do this in the **FBXImporter** that appears when you bring the model into the Unity IDE:

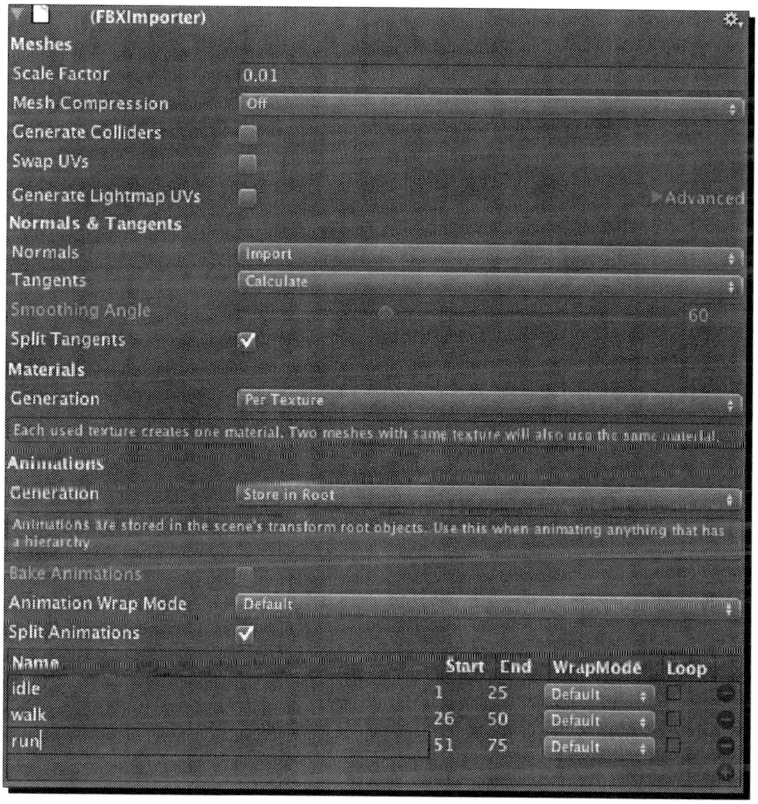

By selecting the option to **Split Animations**, Unity will enable a table that will allow you to specify each animation that is present. For example in this scenario there is an animation called **idle** which runs from frame **1** through frame **25**, a **walk** that plays from frame **26** through frame **50**, and so on. Once you have imported the animations you can reference them by the names that you have given them in the table for all animation actions. We will discuss this in more detail shortly.

Multiple files

The preferred way to import animations is to use multiple animation files. To do this you create a separate model file for your animation data using the naming convention 'model'@'animation name'.fbx and simply drag this `.fbx` file into Unity, the same as you would any other asset.

Through this you can import your animations distinctly for each character and it becomes much easier in your workflow to modify these animations, without having to worry about which frames changed or ending up with extra frames in your animation data, to allow for potential changes. It is important to note that these files contain only animation data – not the actual model geometry. Further, it is important to note that Unity will not attempt to enforce the mapping of the model name to the name of your models:

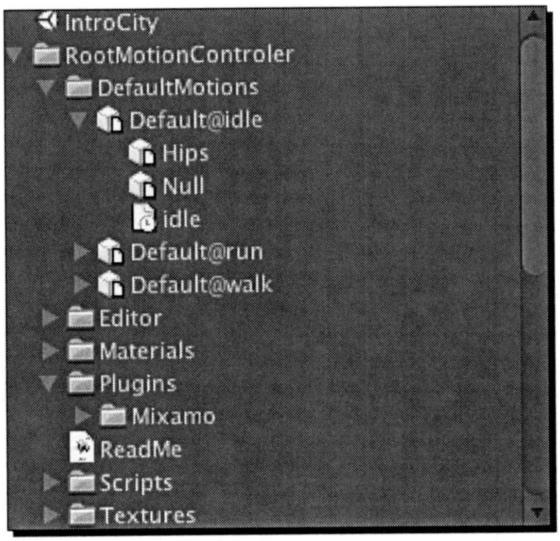

For example, here we have imported some animations in an FBX file. There is no default model in our scene, but we can still use these animations since the bone hierarchy of these animations matches that of the character we already have in the game.

To use this animation within our game we need to select our character and in the **Inspector** expand the animation settings:

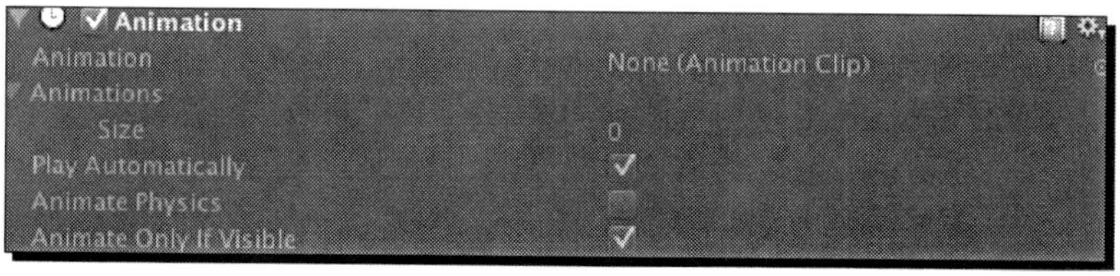

Here we see that our character has 0 animations specified. In addition in the **Animation** element we see that there is no animation scheduled to play. We can easily fix this by increasing the animation count to **3** to match the three animations we have imported:

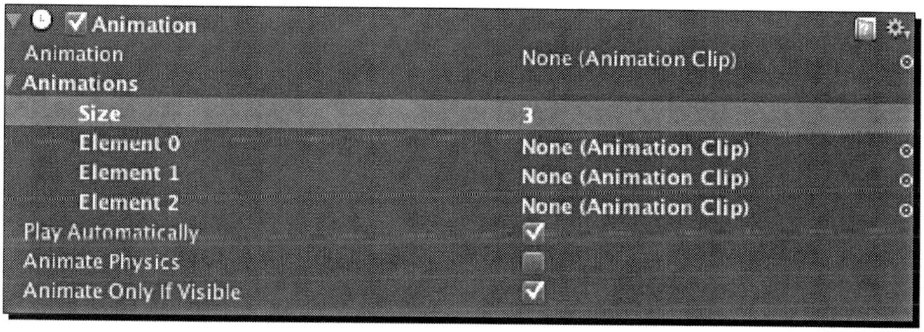

These slots can all hold the animations that we have imported. The animation itself being represented by a document icon with a clock on it which, coincidentally, has the same name as the animation itself. Simply drag the animations onto these slots and you will have set up animations for the character:

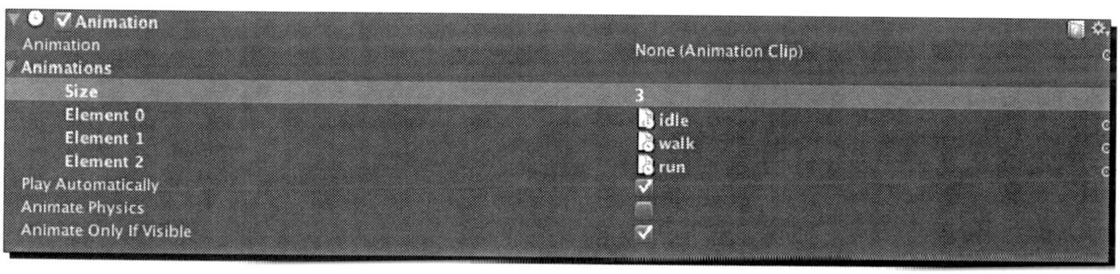

If you want to set up a default animation for the character you can drag an animation onto the **Animation** slot. I have chosen to select the idle animation in this case:

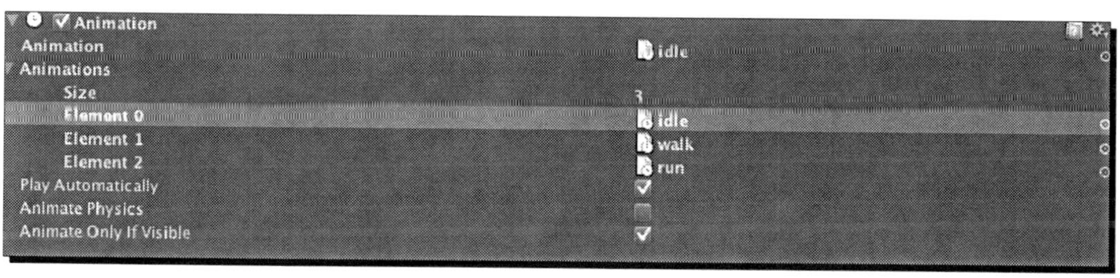

Now your character is all setup and ready to animate. If you run the game in the editor you will see that your character moves from his default T position to the idle animation and plays through it:

What just happened?

We just took our rigged character from the asset store and added animations to it using the two approaches of animation splitting and unique FBX animation importing. Now our character can have emotion, driven by animation data.

Importing an animation

There may be times when you don't have animation data readily available, or you simply want to cut down your development time by integrating an existing animation. One service that is well integrated with Unity is the animation service from Mixamo. Mixamo provides this functionality, not only for their characters, but also for any rigged character that we can find.

Time for action – Importing from Mixamo

We can get started by going to the `http://www.mixamo.com/` website (there is a plugin that is integrated into the latest versions of Unity as well) and browsing through their library of animations:

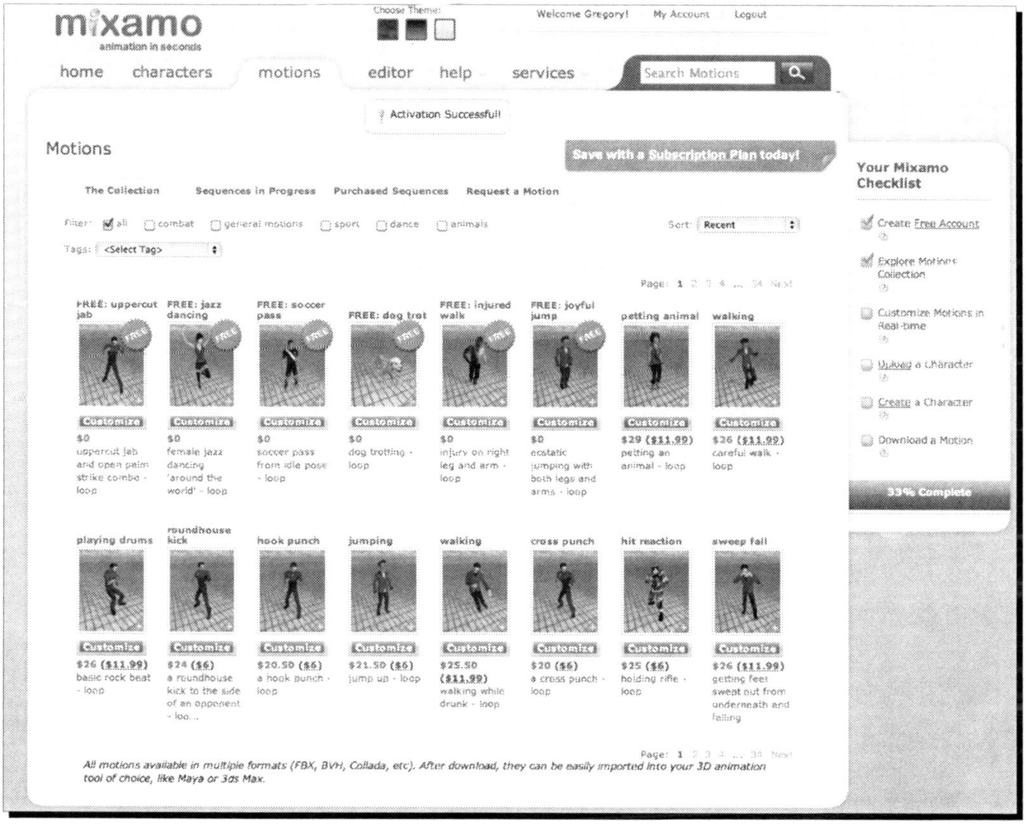

Since we want to ensure that the animation will work properly with our character we can upload our character to Mixamo and see the animation being played on our character:

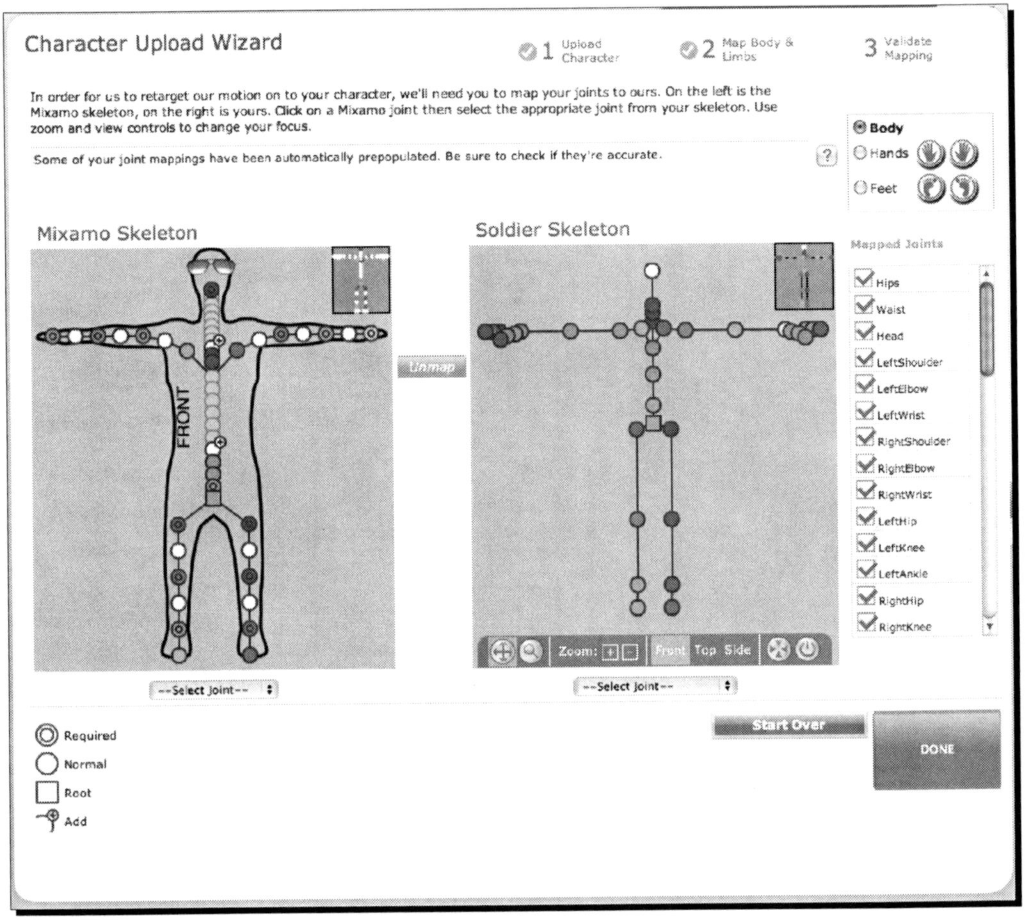

We have the opportunity to tweak any of the bones in our character to fit those that Mixamo has defined in their default skeleton. This will help ensure that our animation plays properly. In most cases Mixamo will map to the right bones by itself, but if you need to help it out because of some special mapping that you've done – all the tools are there:

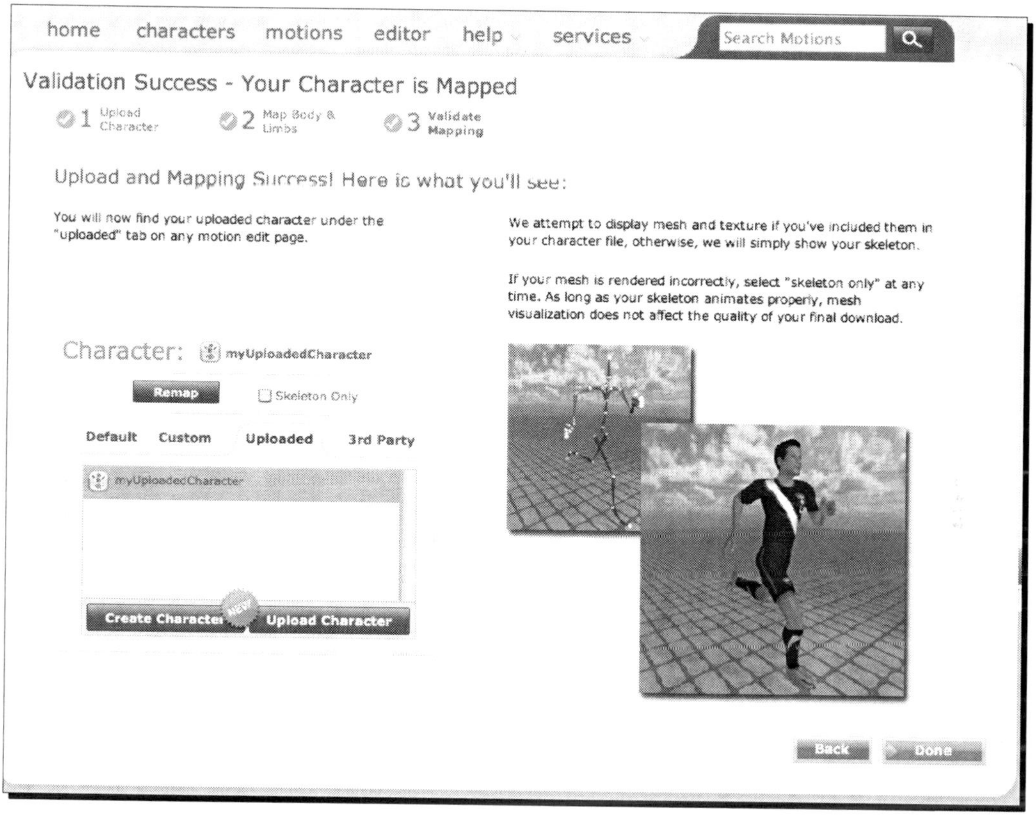

Once mapped, we can reference this uploaded character as we browse through the catalog of animations in the Mixamo library when we create our own custom animations using the service. Now that our model is here we can look at exactly how the animation will perform, as Mixamo has an integrated Unity player on the website where we can preview and customize the animation as necessary.

We can adjust the sliders to customize our character motions in real time and get them precisely the way we want them. Once we've done that we can download our animation in the appropriate Unity animation format.

If we already have an animation that we want to import into Unity, we can use this same approach to import those animations as well. Unity supports two approaches for importing this content into our game: animation splitting and multiple animation files.

What just happened?

We just took our rigged character from the asset store and added animations to it using the Mixamo animation service. Using these animations we're able to have our character move around the scene in sync with animations. Now that we can move around let's deal with the other part of our input requirements – being able to attack enemies or perform other actions on command.

Driving our character

The last thing that we need to do with our character is drive him around the scene. This is the one area that will either make or break our game because it needs to be fluid with user interaction. This is important because the main character is likely to be one of the most used things in the game so it should be well made.

As the character moves around, our character needs to move through the animation and change position in the scene as well. In addition, we need to seamlessly blend between different animations that the character is doing. We can't have the player stop walking, then swing, then start walking again.

Time for action – Driving our character

If you deployed the application after the last step you would have observed that our current controls could already move the character around the scene. We can use the left joystick and the player will glide over the ground while going through the idle animation:

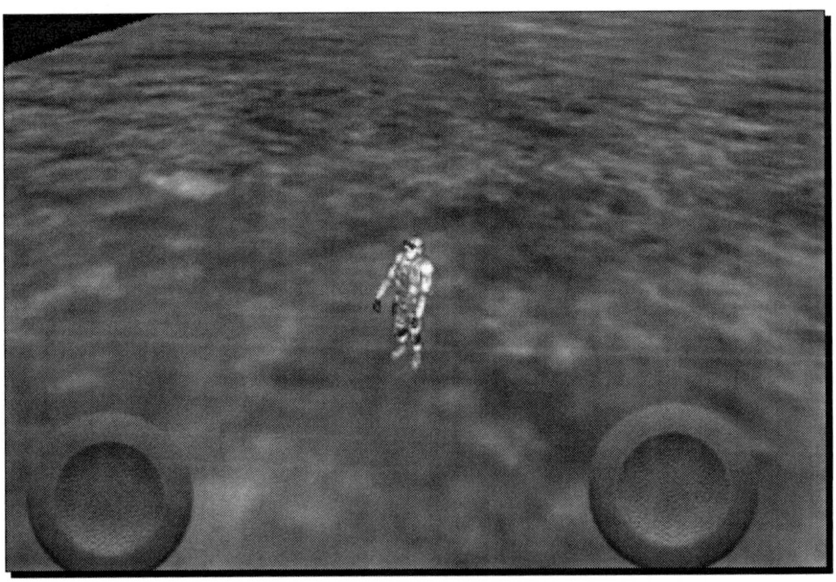

We want our character to walk when the player is moving the joystick so we can make a very simple change to the `CameraRelativeControl` script for this to happen. You can locate this script by taking a look at the **Player** object in the **Hierarchy** view:

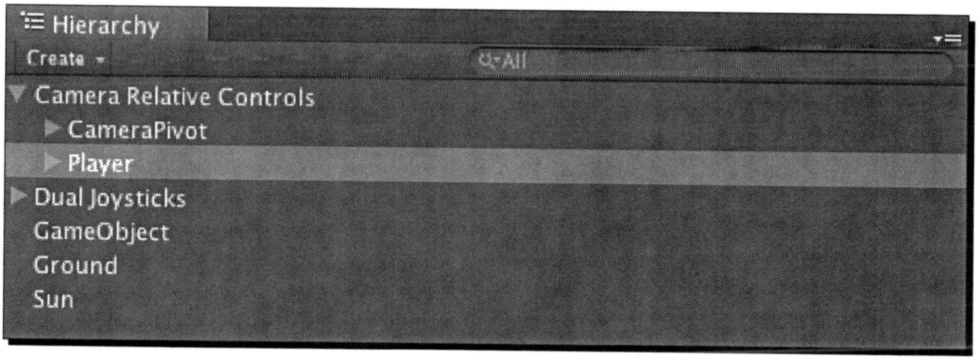

Now look at the Inspector and you will see all of the scripts that are driving this object. Keep track of this, as we will change some of this later:

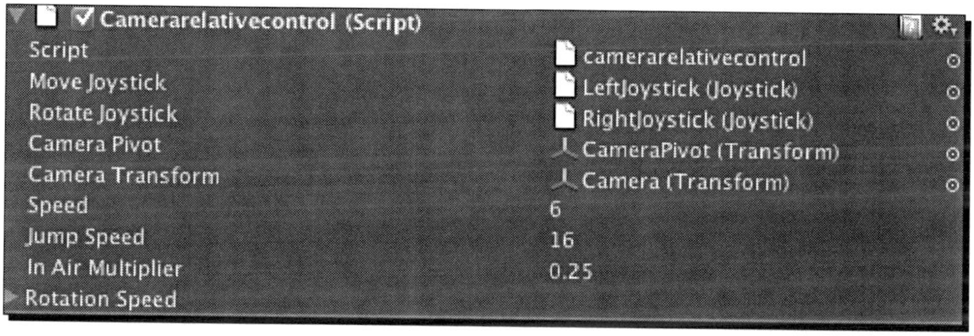

First let's add a variable to the script so we can gain access to our soldier GameObject. You will note here that I am defining the type in this script, as opposed to just declaring it as var. In Unity iOS you must define the types of all objects, dynamic typing is not allowed for performance reasons:

```
private var thisTransform : Transform;
private var character : CharacterController;
private var velocity : Vector3;  //Used for continuing momentum
while in air
private var canJump = true;
private var soldier : GameObject;
```

```
function Start()
{
// Cache component lookup at startup instead of doing this every
frame
   thisTransform = GetComponent( Transform );
   character = GetComponent( CharacterController );
```

Now we need to just look for some change in velocity in our character, which is conveniently managed by the Character Controller, and change the animation accordingly.

```
   if ( soldier )
   {
      if ( ( movement.x != 0 ) || ( movement.z != 0 ) )
      {
         soldier.animation.Play("walk");
      }
      else
      {
         soldier.animation.Play("idle");
      }
   }
```

Now, if you go back and run the application you will find that the player moves into a walk animation when we move the joystick around whenever the player reaches a certain speed:

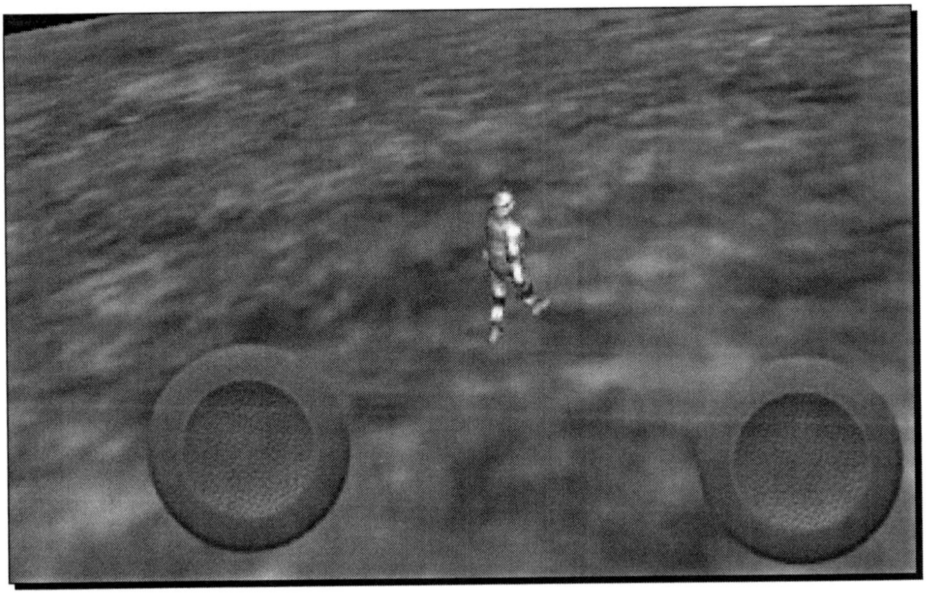

What just happened?

We have just added in functionality to drive our player around the world using the joystick numbs and the standard locomotion system employed by Unity. However, there are a number of limitations to our approach when we want to employ multiple animations.

We could certainly put in some code to look for when the player is beyond a certain velocity and have them move into a run animation with some simple conditional logic changes, but if you play around with the application you will find something very wrong with this picture. The player animates from the local origin and then snaps back to the origin when they reach the end of the animation. In addition when physics is applied to this character there will be a disconnect between the animation and the character hierarchy.

You could certainly fix some of this by having the animator perform the animations in place, but then you would lose the ability to really see how the animation will look. Seeing the gait, stride, and swing of the character is only really possible when the character is actually in motion.

To fix all of this, however, we need another solution. What we really need to do is track where the character is during their animation so that when they are at the end of the animation we can start playing the animation again at that position and orientation. This will become increasingly important as we try to have our player walk on steps, or collide with objects. In other words we need to drive the character's motion with the animation itself, and we can't do that by simply changing the character's location and telling them to play an animation.

Time for action – Getting a driver's license with Root Motion Controller

Fortunately, there is a prebuilt solution that, unsurprisingly, is available from Mixamo that will solve this problem for us with very little impact to our application code - the Root Motion Controller:

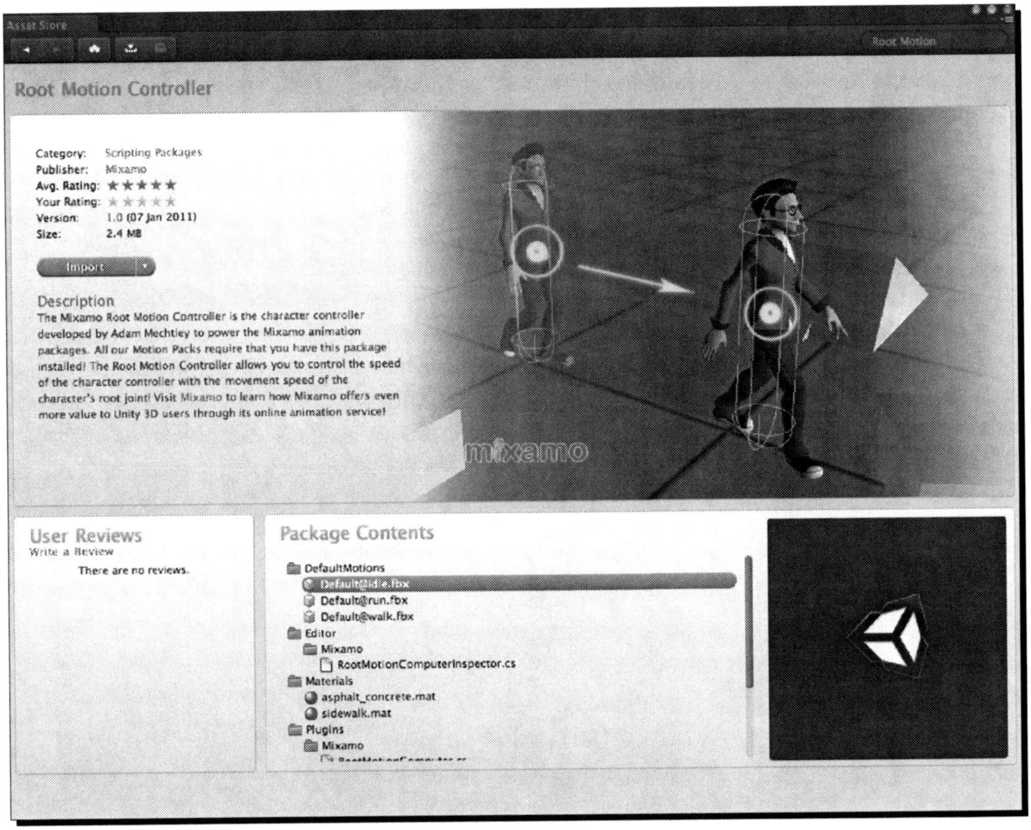

1. First, go back to the **Asset Store** and search for a package known as the **Root Motion Controller**. This package from Mixamo, and developed by Adam Mechtley, has all of the functionality necessary for us to drive our character using the animation data – we need only configure it:

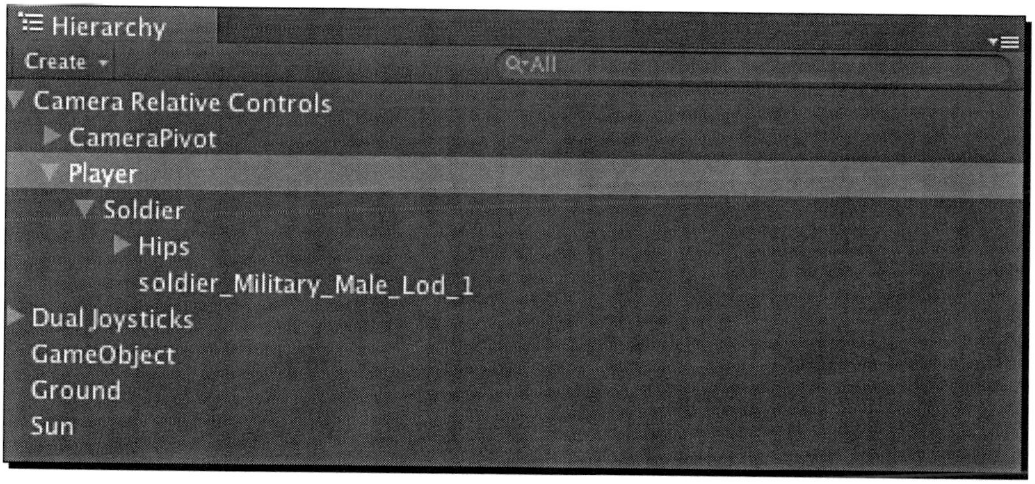

2. Next we need to select the **Player** model from our hierarchy, since this is the component of the hierarchy that we want to control with our new controller. When adding this to a similar project, just be sure to add this to the same node that contains the Character Controller, as you want movements from the Root Motion Computer to result in motion on everything at this level of the Hierarchy:

> If you were to attach the **Root Motion Computer** to the Soldier node, for example, the **Camera Relative Controls** would not be aware that the player has actually moved.

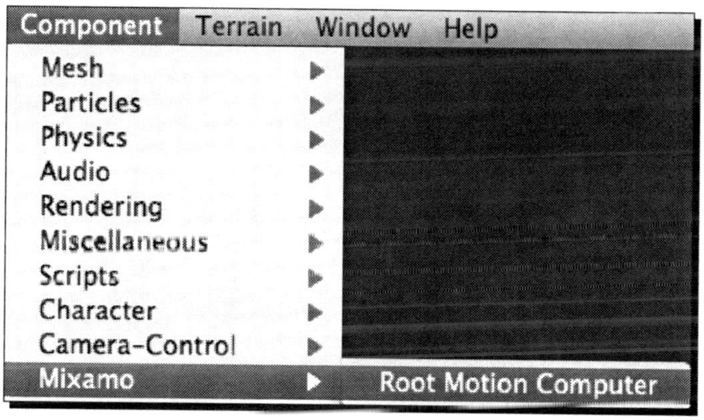

3. Now that we have the right node in the hierarchy selected we can add the **Root Motion Computer** component by selecting the **Mixamo** menu item:

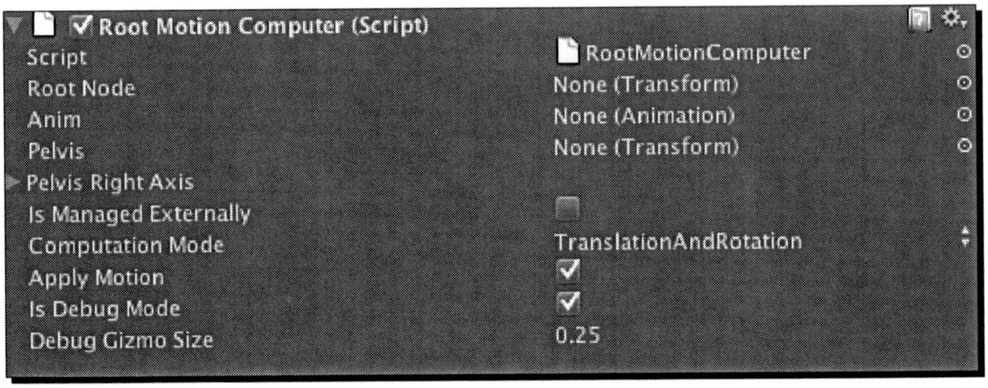

4. In the **Inspector** view you will see the **Root Motion Computer** component added to our Game Object. And with that we're actually done with the vast majority of the work that needs to be done. So let's take it out for a test drive:

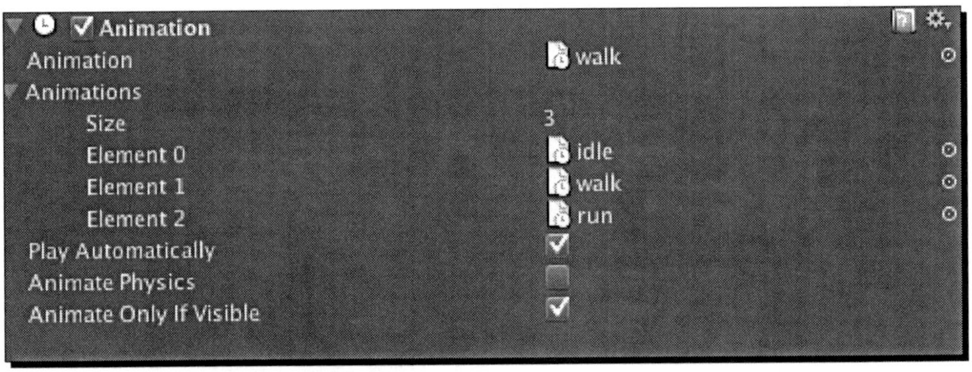

5. Change the settings of the animations for the character, so that the default animation is set to **walk**:

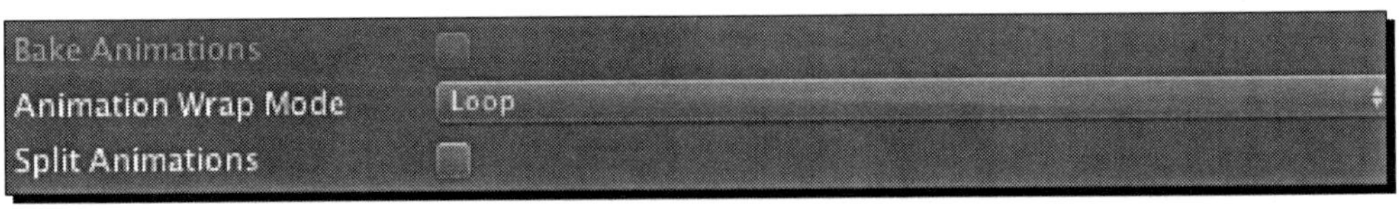

6. Next, set the **Animation Wrap Mode** for the animation to **Loop** so that it will play repeatedly. Now when you run the application the player will walk repeatedly forward until they walk off the world.

What just happened?

We've just accomplished a significant step! Not only have we imported animations, but we are also using the animations to drive the character around the scene. With all of our animations synchronized with the location and orientation of the player in the scene and controlled with the joysticks we can turn our attention to the gameplay elements.

Rotation via Accelerometer

The next thing we need to handle is rotating the camera based upon the user tilting the device. In our design we said that this would represent rotation of the camera so we need to detect these motions and adjust our camera based upon the user's intent.

Time for action – Updating upon device tilt

As discussed earlier, iOS devices have a defined access that allows us to determine changes in the device's orientation. We can detect this as changes in the x, y, or z values in Input. acceleration:

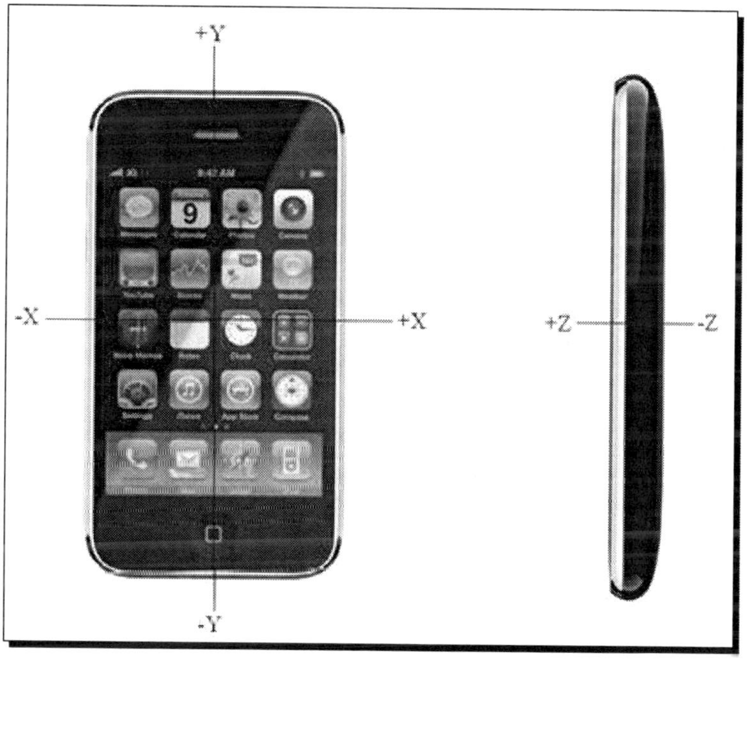

Since our game design requires us to manipulate the camera based upon the tilt, the only step we need is to check for the direction of the orientation change and then rotate the camera accordingly. To accomplish this we can attach a script to a GameObject in whose `Update()` method we examine the `Input.acceleration` attributes and determine how the device has changed. Remember also that we have specified that our application be designed to run in landscape mode so we are looking for rotations along the device's Z-axis.

Key Method	Description
`Input.acceleration`	Returns the accelerometer readings of the device

```
using UnityEngine;
using System.Collections;

public class CameraRotate : MonoBehaviour {
   public float speed = 10.0f;

   // Use this for initialization
   void Start () {

   }

   // Update is called once per frame
   void Update () {
      Vector3 direction = Vector3.zero;
      direction.x = - Input.acceleration.y;
      direction.z = Input.acceleration.x;

      if ( direction.sqrMagnitude > 1 )
      {
         direction.Normalize();
      }

      direction *= Time.deltaTime;

      transform.Translate( direction * speed );
   }
}
```

With `iPhoneSettings.screenOrientation` we can now tell the Unity player to change its orientation. You can set the orientation to any one of the `iPhoneScreenOrientations` available. It is recommended that you don't do anything that would be uncharacteristic to the way the iOS device is expected to operate as Apple may reject your application for that behavior.

What just happened?

By adding a script to our camera we get an `Update()` notification on a frame by frame basis. We can then look to see what the device orientation is and adjust our orientation accordingly. By updating the `iPhoneSettings` attributes we can quickly flip our scene to match whatever orientation we find ourselves in.

Shaking the device to perform a healing action

The last thing we need to do is detect when the user has chosen to shake the device as our design specifies that we will use this as an indication that the user will perform a healing action.

Time for action – Detecting a shake

1. The first step in handling an orientation change is to actually realize that the orientation has changed. There are two ways we can do this – we can either check when the game first starts up only, in which case we need to put our orientation detection in the `Start()` method as it is only called once. If we want to check orientation changes as the user is playing the game then we need to check the state of the orientation on a frame-by-frame basis. We do this by putting our orientation code in the `Update()` method.

Key Methods	Description
`Input.acceleration`	Returns the accelerometer readings of the device

We will use the `deviceOrientation` attribute of the Input class to determine what the orientation of the device is. This information comes directly from the OS in real time so as the orientation changes, we will be notified and can respond to the change without having to interrupt gameplay.

```
using UnityEngine;
using System.Collections;
public class DetectShake : MonoBehaviour {
   public float shakeThreshold = 2.0f;
```

```
    // Update is called once per frame
    void Update () {
       Vector3 accel = Input.acceleration;

       float x = accel.x;
       float y = accel.y;
       float z = accel.z;

       float shakeStrength = Mathf.Sqrt( x * x + y * y + z * z );

       if ( shakeStrength >= shakeThreshold )
       {
          // do the shake action
       }


    }
}
```

Physician heal thyself

Now that we know that a device shake has taken place we can perform the specific action that we want associated with the shake.

In our `player` class we have a simple representation of the player's health as an integer within our `Player` class:

```
public class Player {

   public static int MAX_HEALTH = 100;

   private int health = 0;


   public Player()
   {
   }

   public int getHealth()
   {
      return health;
   }

   public void heal()
```

```
        {
            health = health + 10;

            if ( health > MAX_HEALTH )
            {
                health = MAX_HEALTH;
            }
        }
    }
```

In our `Player` class is a simple heal method that we call whenever we detect that a shake of the device has happened.

What just happened?

We have implemented the last input features for the game by detecting shakes of the device. Based upon this shake we have changed the user's state and taken an action. While shaking isn't a common action in games today, and I encourage you to use it sparingly, there are certainly times when it represents the best input option available.

Summary

In this chapter we discussed the primary sensors used for input on iOS, namely the touch screen, gyroscope, and accelerometer. With this task covered we can provide a touch screen interface from our player which they can interact with, as well as gather information from movement and orientation of the iOS device.

Specifically, we covered:

- The different types of touch technologies, their strengths and weaknesses
- How to build a touchable user interface for the user on the device and gather input from it
- How to import existing animations and how to import Mixamo animations
- How to detect gestures and determine the user's intent
- How to detect movement of the device and orientation changes
- How to use this information to move an on-screen character through a 3D world
- How to drive a character from animation data as opposed to programmatically

Now we have a character that we can control through our 3D world and we can animate this character based on input from the user. We have the beginnings of an actual game now, but the world is very quiet and the game is without flair. In the next chapter, Multimedia, we will explore how to add sound, music, and video to our game to give it some sex appeal.

8
Multimedia

Now that we have spent some time exploring the gameplay components of our game and building systems for control, we need to spend some time examining the components of the game that deal with video and audio. Things such as background music, the sounds of enemies, and playing movies are important parts that our game needs.

In this chapter we shall:

- Learn to play background music
- Learn how to add ambient sounds
- Learn how to play movies that are embedded in the application
- Learn how to stream movies from remote locations

So let's get on with it...

Important preliminary points

This chapter assumes that you have some understanding of compressed audio formats such as MP3 and OGG, as well as video formats such as MP4. Further, it assumes that you know how to create this content using your favorite tools.

Audio capabilities

Our game is very quiet right now. Even though we can see the actions of our player, we cannot hear what the player is doing – nor do we have a feel for the environment itself. We want to add some sounds that will exist in the environment and we want to provide some feedback when things happen in the game.

Playing sounds

As discussed in the Unity Fundamentals, all audio that is played is done so from the perspective of the AudioListener. So, if we want to have something in our game make noise, we simply need to add an AudioSource to that GameObject and we will get a sound. In our design we call for having ambient sounds in the environment.

Time for action – Adding ambient sounds

While we're in our town we want it to sound like a town that is in the middle of the forest. To accomplish this we should have some ambient sound that is low volume that just blends in to the environment. A good source of Creative Commons licensed sounds is The Freesound Project which can be found at `http://www.freesound.org`. There are a number of good candidates on the site and I have picked up one from user reinsamba for this test. You will find a copy of it in the assets folder of the project called `evening in the forest.wav`.

1. To keep your assets organized create an `Ambient Audio` folder in your project.
2. Simply drag the asset, an `evening in the forest.wav` file in this case, into the project and Unity will perform the necessary conversion:

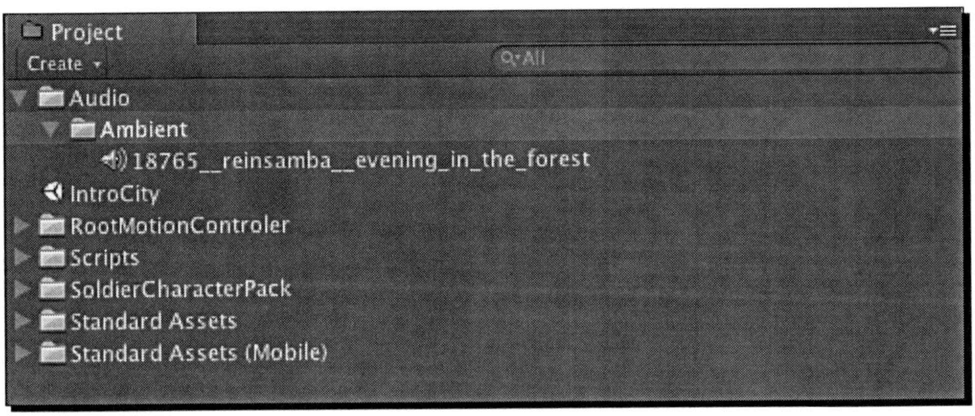

Now you have a usable AudioSource that can be added to other GameObjects in the scene. But remember, Unity will not distort the assets unless we tell it to by changing some properties of the original audio file. We brought in a fairly sizable AudioSource as a `.wav` file.

3. Tell Unity to compress this asset by selecting **Compressed** from the **Audio Format** option so that the file doesn't take up as much space. Also, check the **Hardware decoding** checkbox so that Unity will use the iOS hardware built into an iOS device:

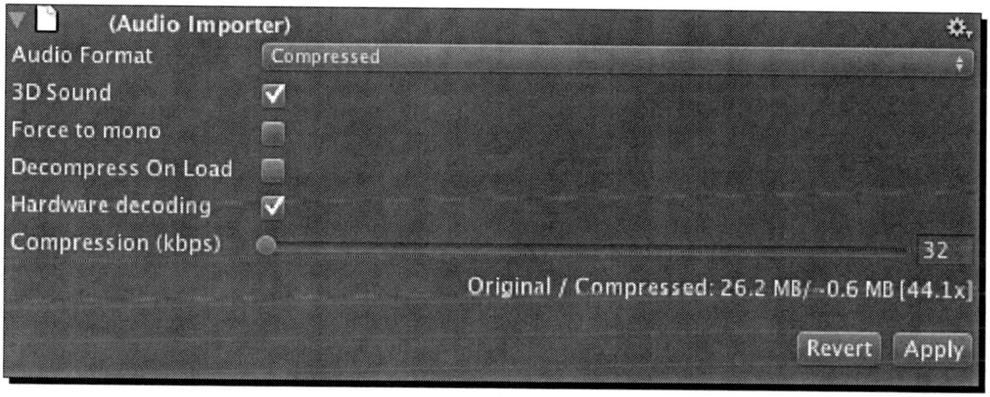

If hardware isn't available, Unity will automatically fall back to software decoding. In our case here we are going from a 26.2MB Wav file to a 0.6MB compressed MP3 file. If you want a higher quality sample you can adjust the Compression slider to a higher value, but in our case this is simple ambient noise so we don't need an excessive amount of fidelity.

Now that we have created the AudioSource we need to attach it to a GameObject so that it will play. Since this is the sound of the environment, we can attach this to the ground that the player will walk around on.

4. Simply drag the Audio source onto the ground in the **Scene** view, or drag it over to the ground in the **Hierarchy** view. Either will result in an AudioSource Component being added to the ground.

5. Ensure that the audio continues to play by selecting the **Loop** option from the **Audio Source properties** in the **Inspector**:

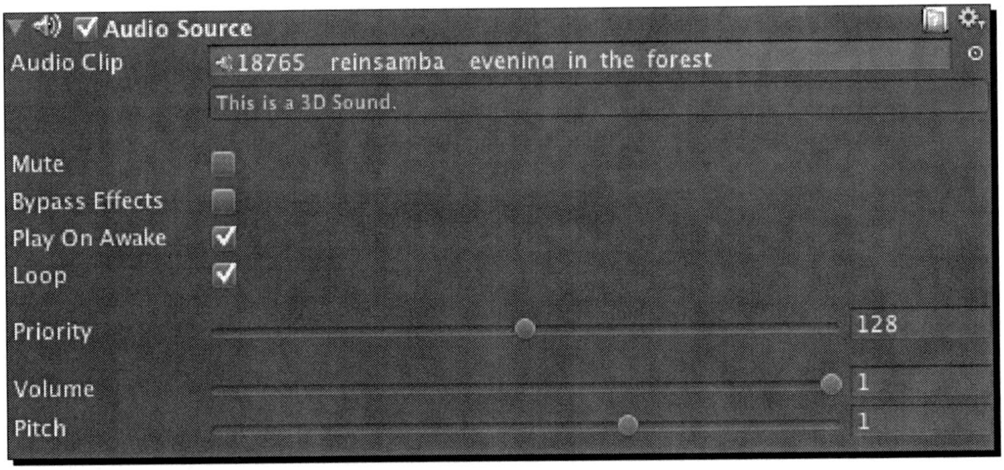

We have told this AudioSource to loop its audio so we should hear this audio clip for the duration of the game while we're on this ground GameObject. One special note about compressed audio in iOS is that the compression process may tweak the beginning or end of your audio data, so you will want to listen to it after compressing it to make sure that it still loops properly.

We didn't necessarily have to attach the sound to the ground, we could have attached it to a different object. For example, if we wanted to give a marketplace the sounds of marketplace chatter we could attach that directly to the GameObject that represents the marketplace and when the player walks away from it, the sound would diminish.

What just happened?

We just created an ambient sound track for our world. By importing a `.wav` file and compressing it we have integrated an asset that is suitable for use on our mobile platform and can use the iOS device hardware to decompress the audio stream. Since we've attached this AudioSource to the ground of our world, we can be certain that it will be audible as we move through our environment. With this we have created some atmosphere for our world and given this area of the world a personality.

Time for action – Adding sounds to actions

While we have created some background ambient sounds, we still don't have any sounds for actions that take place in the game. For example, if we use our ranged attack swipe gesture and throw something, our player should make some sound as he is going through the throw animation and the thrown object should make a sound if it hits the ground – or some other object.

Let's import a simple sound that we will play when the player is going to throw something for their range attack. Once again I have utilized a Creative Commons Licensed sound from `www.freesound.org`. The author of this sound is Sruddi1 and I have sampled the sound to contain a single grunt that will be the sound our character makes when they perform a ranged attack. I have compressed this sound similar to the steps used when importing our ambient sound:

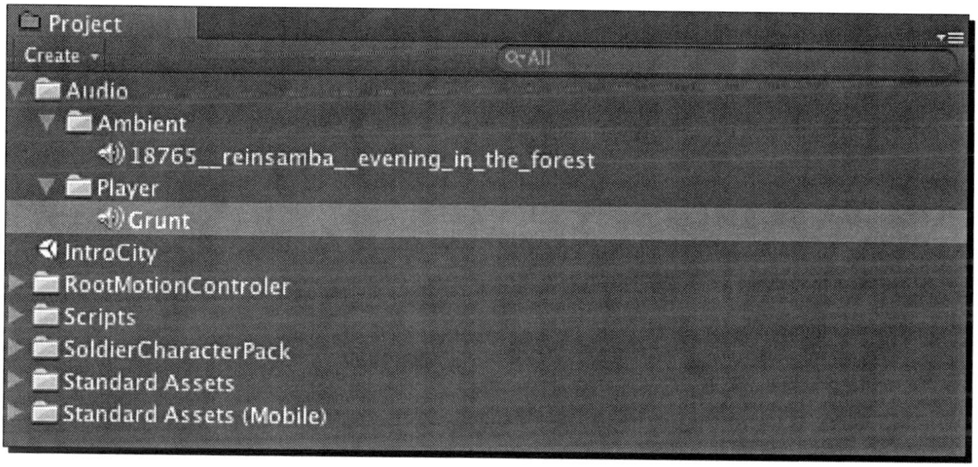

Now all we need to do is associate this grunt sound with a scripted action that would be the user throwing something. Accomplishing this is a simple extension of some of the skills we learned earlier in the book. Remember, from the scripting section that we can pass variables to scripts and those objects can be references to things from Unity. We need to create a simple script that represents the action and expose a variable that will contain the sound.

```
using UnityEngine;
using System.Collections;
public class ThrowSomething : MonoBehavior {
```

```
    public AudioClip         audioClip;
    // Update is called once per frame
    void Update () {
        // perform the animation for throwing
        animation.Play("throw", AnimationPlayMode.Mix);
        // play the audio clip one time
        //
        audio.PlayOneShot( audioClip );
    }
}
```

This script will now play the desired `AudioClip` whenever it is invoked. All you have to do is drag an `AudioClip` onto the component that you've attached this script to and that is what will be played:

It is important to note that you don't necessarily have to attach an `AudioClip` to an in-game object in order to play a sound. You can create a `GameObject` on the fly when you want to play an `AudioClip`. In fact, this is very useful if you want to create sounds on the fly as a result of detecting some event.

```
using UnityEngine;
using System.Collections;

public class AudioEngine
{
    public AudioEngine ()
    {
    }

    public AudioSource Play( AudioClip clip, Transform position )
    {
        return Play( clip, position, 1f, 1f );
    }


    public AudioSource Play(AudioClip clip, Vector3 point, float
volume, float pitch)
     {
         //Create an empty game object
```

```
        GameObject go = new GameObject("Audio: " + clip.name);
        go.transform.position = point;
        //Create the source
      //
        AudioSource source = go.AddComponent<AudioSource>();
        source.clip = clip;
        source.volume = volume;
        source.pitch = pitch;
        source.Play();

        Destroy(go, clip.length);
        return source;

    }

}
```

So if we have installed this AudioEngine to a GameObject in the scene we can simply reference it and tell it to play the specific AudioClip that we want to play and tell it where we want it to sound like it is positioned.

What just happened?

We have created a sound that will play whenever a user performs the ranged attack gesture. By updating our script which animates a player when the ranged attack gesture is detected, we have specified a new AudioClip that we can play in our script by performing a simple scripting call. We can perform similar actions now when a player swings a sword, hits an enemy, and so on. We only need to expose an AudioClip variable in those scripts and pass along the sound that we want to play.

Playing music

Playing music in Unity has some particular nuances to get it working properly. While it is true that music is just like any other sound, just that it has a relationship to the player's position in the scene.

Time for action – The sound of music

In our application we want to have music playing constantly. We can accomplish this by attaching a `GameObject` to the player or camera object and having the music play from there. If you attempt this, your sound system will play music just fine until the scene changes. As such, the primary difference between playing sound and building a music system is making sure that the music keeps playing.

1. Create a folder called `Music`.
2. Import your favorite `.mp3` file into the game project. In the project's sample files you will find the track Orc March by basematic. You can find other creative commons music at `http://www.ccmixter.org/`:

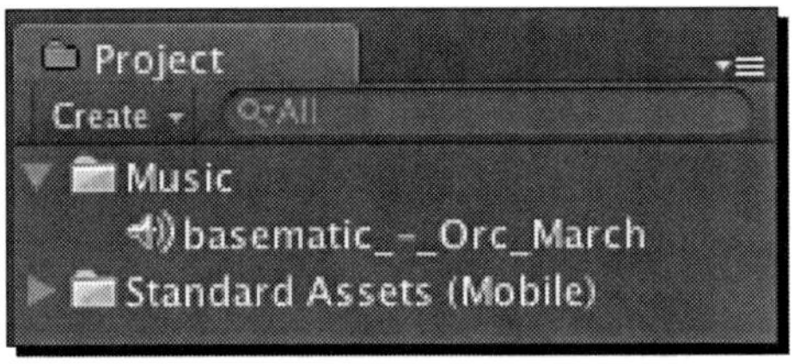

3. Create an empty Game Object called **MusicPlayer** and make it the child of the **Main Camera**:

4. Add an **Audio Source** component to the **MusicPlayer** Game Object.
5. Next, we need to ensure that our **MusicPlayer** object does not get destroyed as we move between scenes, by creating a script in Unity that is attached to the next scene. To do this create a second scene in the game called `scene_2`.

6. Create a script called `MusicPreserver` and fill it with the following code:

```
function Awake()
{
  // find the music player object
  var musicObject : GameObject =
    GameObject.Find("MusicPlayer");

  // make sure we survive going to different scenes
  DontDestroyOnLoad(musicObject);
}
```

7. Attach the MusicPreserver script to the new scene.

What just happened?

We can now play music in our game and have that music active as we move across scenes. This will give us the ability to set moods for areas of our game, yet give the flexibility of being able to change the scene data while the music continues to play.

By default, when Unity loads a new level or scene, all of the objects in the previous scene are destroyed (which would normally stop our music). The key to preserving the music is the `DontDestroyOnLoad` method which will tell Unity to leave this Game Object alone when it is disposing of objects from the original scene. Now we can have real music sound tracks that span our entire game.

Video capabilities

iOS devices have standard hardware accelerated playback for H.264 encoded video. Apple exposes interfaces to play this content using the `MPMoviePlayerController` class in the SDK. This class permits one to play a movie that is located on the device, or to stream one that is located at some arbitrary URL on the Internet. Unity exposes both of these methods in `iPhoneUtils` using the `PlayMovie` or `PlayMovieURL` methods.

iOS device video encoding is very specific, regardless of whether you are streaming video in the WebKit web browser using a UIWebView or doing it in Unity. The video must be compressed using the following compression standards:

- H.264 Baseline Profile Level 3.0 video
- Support resolutions up to 640x480 at 30fps
- B Frames are not supported in the Baseline Profile
- MPEG-4 Part 2 video (Simple Profile)

If you need some tools to help you create video that will work with iOS devices, you can examine the Quicktime Player itself and its video export options, as well as Handbrake. Handbrake (`http://www.handbrake.fr`) has specific profiles for encoding video for the iOS platform devices.

Time for action – Playing embedded video

For our application design we are supposed to play an introduction movie when the application first starts. This video is normally some animated logo or similar and in our case it will be the Sojourner Mobile intro movie (sometimes referred to as an interstitial).

I'm going to assume that you aren't a video engineer and don't know a lot about MPEG-4, H.264, or B Frames, but you have some content that you want to get into your iOS project. This is one thing that gives a lot of new developers trouble and results in video not displaying on the device.

We can avoid all of this drama by simply using a tool that was designed for producing content for iOS devices. One such tool that you can use for this is iMovie. It has functionality for exporting iOS device compliant video that you can use with your projects.

1. Import your content into iMovie and export it using the **Share** menu:

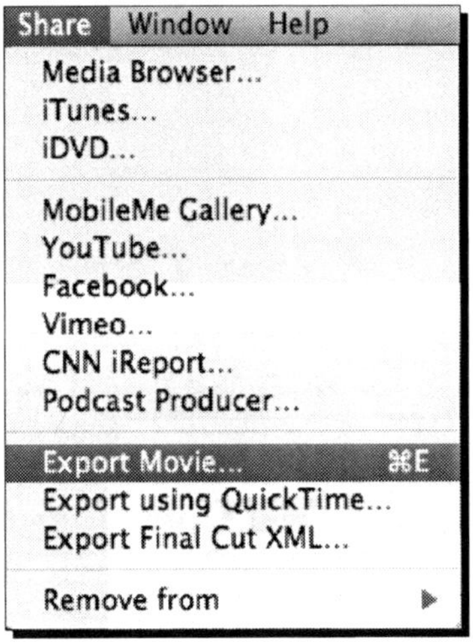

2. When prompted for the video type that you want to export to, choose the Mobile size and press the **Export** button:

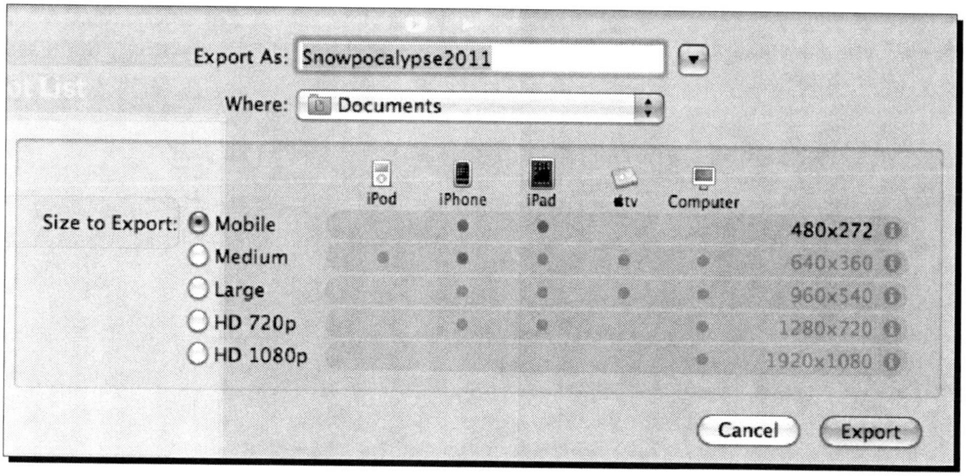

Note that you can choose the Medium size as well, but since this is media that is being embedded into our game, and will count against our maximum application size, it is best to keep this content as small as possible so that you can keep it for other things such as game assets.

3. Next we need to move the video into a special Unity assets folder called `StreamingAssets`. Unity will copy the files in this directory into our application bundle and put them in the appropriate location on the device so we can play them back at runtime:

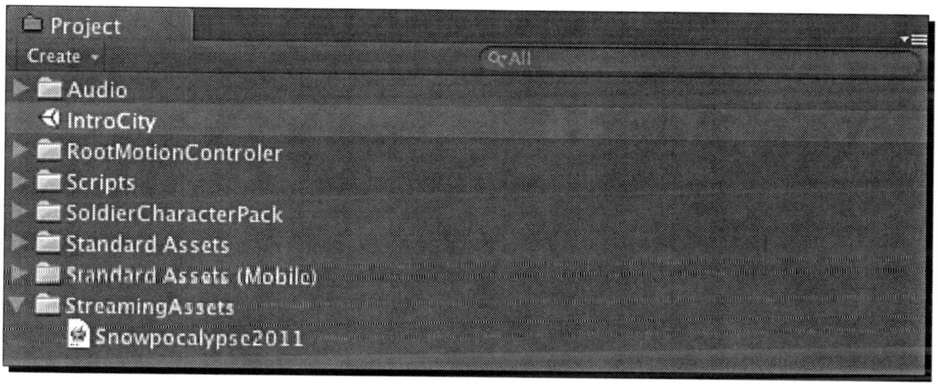

Now that we have our asset in the game we need to play it. The best way to do this is to have a single scene that does nothing other than display our movie and then loads the IntroCity scene.

4. Let's create a new scene called **GameIntro** that will serve this purpose:

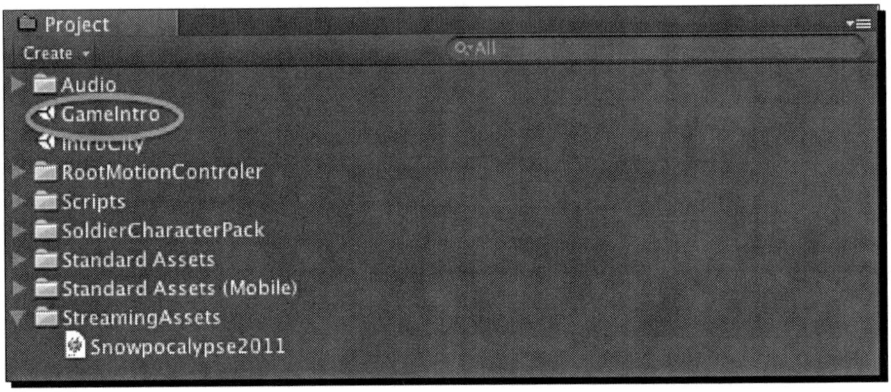

5. Now that we have our **GameIntro** scene we can create an empty **GameObject** and attach a script to it that will play our movie and load the next level after it's over.

6. Now, all we need is a simple script that we can attach to this **GameObject** and have start in the `Start()` of the script. We need to use the C# co-routine version of the `Start()` method as opposed to our normal version.

```
using UnityEngine;
using System.Collections;

public class PlayIntroMovie : MonoBehaviour {

  // Use this for initialization
  IEnumerator Start () {

    iPhoneUtils.PlayMovie("Snowpocalypse2011.m4v",
      Color.black, iPhoneMovieControlMode.
      CancelOnTouch, iPhoneMovieScalingMode.AspectFill );


    yield return null;


    Application.LoadLevel("IntroCity");
  }
}
```

7. With this script attached to our empty **GameObject** we now have a complete intro movie system and when we start the game we will be greeted with the Interstitial of our company.

What just happened?

We have just finished our introduction scene by playing a movie to display our studio intro movie and then loading the level that we had been working on, which is the beginning town-level. Now our content is beginning to feel like the content that we would find on the App Store.

Time for action – Streaming video

The first thing we need to do is make sure that an Internet connection is available. Once we know that the Internet is available we can start to stream our video. We need to check for a network connection because we want to respect the fact that our user may deactivate the network connection for Airplane Mode, trying to preserve battery life, or because our device may not be in an area of network connectivity.

We can determine whether or not the iOS device can reach the network by using the iPhoneSettings' `internetReachability` class variable. This will be updated as the network status changes and will also tell you what type of Internet connection you have available. For our purposes we simply need to check whether or not there is a connection of any kind. We can resolve this with a simple condition check:

```
if ( iPhoneSettings.internetReachability !=
iPhoneNetworkReachability.NotReachable )
{
}
```

It is very important that you perform this check for Internet connectivity. If your application tries to reach out to the Internet and fails and you do not deal with this gracefully, by either showing an error that is visible to the user or not performing the functionality that requires network access, Apple will reject the application. You should be prepared to test your game in Airplane Mode exclusively to know whether or not it is going to behave properly if there is no network connectivity.

Now we know that we can reach the Internet, we want to stream some video to the device. I have stored a video online that the iOS device can stream from our server:

```
if ( iPhoneSettings.internetReachability !=
iPhoneNetworkReachability.NotReachable )
{
iPhoneUtils.PlayMovieURL(http://www.sojournermobile.com/assets/
unitybook/commercial.m4v, Color.black, iPhoneMovieControlMode.
Hidden )
}
```

As you can see this isn't much different from playing back content that is stored on the device. As we want this to behave like a commercial we want to remove the player's ability to cancel this video or skip through it so we use the `iPhoneMovieControlMode.Hidden` enumeration to ensure that the player will have to watch the movie.

What just happened?

We have performed network detection to determine whether or not an Internet connection is available. After ensuring that a network connection was available we connected to a stream on the Internet and began playing our commercial.

Summary

In this chapter we performed all of the steps necessary to handle multimedia in our project. We've given more of a soul to our game by providing the expected environmental cues of video and audio that people have come to expect in games, to make our games as professionally built as those already in the App Store.

Specifically, we covered:

- How to add ambient sound to the environment
- How to add background music to the game
- How to play sound based upon actions in a script
- How to play video embedded in the Unity project
- How to detect whether or not our network connection is active
- How to play video hosted on an external website

Now that we've learned about these and formed the core of our game, it's time to take a step back and begin looking at how we can check for performance issues and debug our application.

9
User Interface

While it may seem that we have created the bulk of our game, there is one very important thing that is still missing – the **User Interface** *(UI). Creating UIs is very important, as this is the real look and feel that your game will have for your users. If you have a generic interface, no matter how your models look, the game will feel generic. There are many ways that you can design a UI in Unity, but most of those are designed for desktop applications and will perform poorly on mobile devices. We will examine the standard Unity library facility for building our UI and we will build a UI with the Prime31 UIToolkit.*

In this chapter we shall:

- Use the native Unity interface system
- Explore the popular third-party Prime31 UIToolkit approach for generating interfaces

After we finish this chapter we will have all of the tools at our disposal to create almost any type of game we want to create.

So lets get on with it...

Important preliminary points

This chapter assumes that you understand the basic concepts of tools such as GIMP and Photoshop including layers, masks, and fills. While the screens in the chapter will be focussed primarily on Photoshop, all of the concepts utilized here are easily transferrable to other software.

Translating the design

The design sketch of Battlecry's user interface design should be able to display some simple assets for displaying the player's current health, the score of the game, a joystick, and an action button.

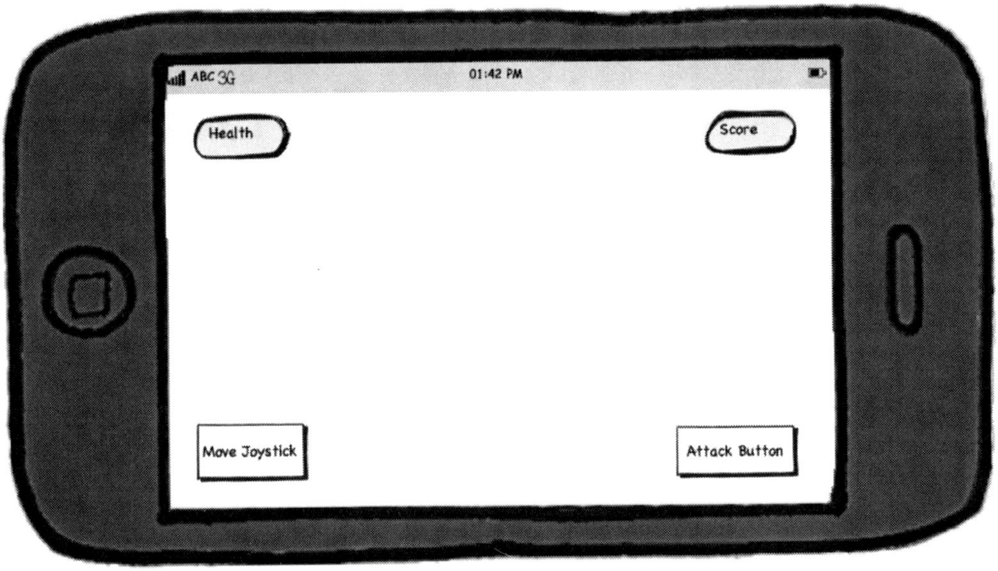

We covered the joystick and action button in the Input chapter so we can focus on the health display and showing the score. We need a nice font for displaying text and some images to show the health. In addition, we will want to build a main menu for the game that will consist of a button to start the game and one that will show the credits.

Immediate mode game user interfaces

The Unity game engine provides developers with a complete integrated system for game user interface (GUI) development. These GUIs are built using an immediate mode approach to defining the GUI and responding to its events. For most games this will not be an issue and will be one of the easiest ways for you to put a HUD and simple controls on the screen. However, as it is an immediate mode API, the developer is very close to the mechanics of how the UI operates.

As an example, we can look at how to construct a simple GUI that displays a button on the screen. As you might have guessed, since there are no tools, and as we're in immediate mode, we have to manually specify the layout for the components on the screen.

```
function OnGUI () {
   if (GUI.Button (Rect (10,10,150,100), "I am a button")) {
      print ("You clicked the button!");
   }
}
```

Despite how different this may feel from hopping into Flash, Photoshop, Objective-C, or your favorite GUI framework, immediate mode GUIs are nothing new. In a traditional GUI framework, you setup your GUI components in a variety of classes and then setup callbacks and messaging systems so that the event loop can relay data from the components to the actual application logic that will handle the events. So what's wrong with this, you may ask. At the end of the day you will find that you have code all over your application – especially if you're really trying to be object-oriented and are designing your application for reuse.

While this is something that makes sense for a complex business application that may have to change its layout dynamically based on user-type, screen resolution, or the data being used, that is not the problem that we're trying to solve with our game. You will find that an immediate mode GUI is very compact, with all of the logic that makes your game work generally in a small number of places. Any state data necessary for the UI is made available to all of the interface components without the need for querying or passing data. This makes the application easier to follow and is very performance friendly.

Time for action – Creating the menu background

The first thing we need to do is create a background for the main menu of our game. This will give us a chance to see how to setup Unity GUI components. To keep things simple, initially we will start with the main menu.

1. Create a new scene called **MainMenu**.
2. As this is a military style game we can use a simple camouflage texture for the background of our main menu.

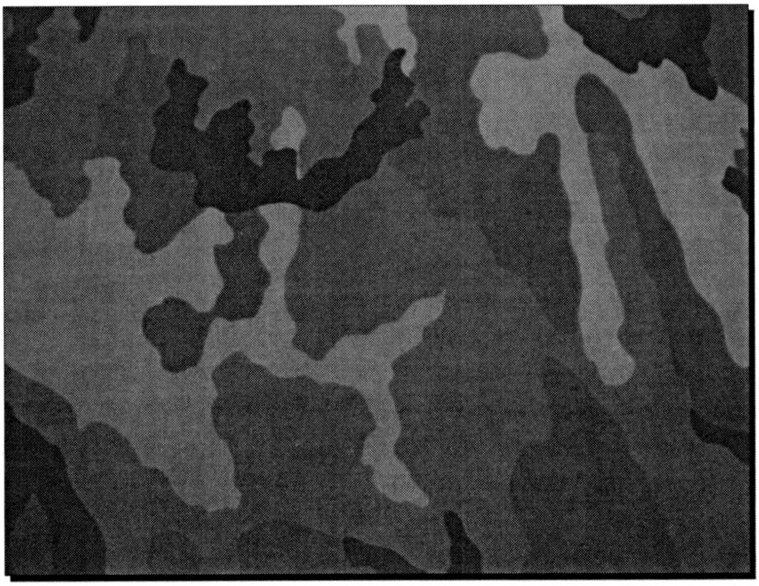

On top of this we will display the buttons for our game. While it is possible for us to modify our existing **GameIntro** scene to handle a main menu, it is better from a design perspective to create a standalone scene for the main menu. This will aid the development workflow as content creators can work on this scene in isolation.

3. After adding our **MainMenu** scene we need to make a change to our `PlayIntroMovie` script to have it load the **MainMenu** scene instead of just dropping directly into the game.

```
using UnityEngine;
using System.Collections;

public class PlayIntroMovie : MonoBehaviour {

  // Use this for initialization
  IEnumerator Start () {
    iPhoneUtils.PlayMovie("Snowpocalypse2011.m4v", Color.black,
    iPhoneMovieControlMode.CancelOnTouch,
    iPhoneMovieScalingMode.AspectFill );

    yield return null;

    Application.LoadLevel("MainMenu");

  }

}
```

4. The next step is to import the texture that we will be using for the background. In the project folder for this chapter you will find the asset `army_camo.jpg`. If you drag this into Unity it will be imported and ready for use. However, there are a few settings we want to change for our iOS release. If you display the **Inspector** settings for the asset you will find that it is imported at 1024x1024. However, for our iOS game, we don't want such a large texture simply as a background.

5. Override the settings for this texture for our iOS device by selecting the iPhone icon and checking the box to override the settings for iPhone. Set the **Max Size** for this texture to **512** and click on the **Apply** button.

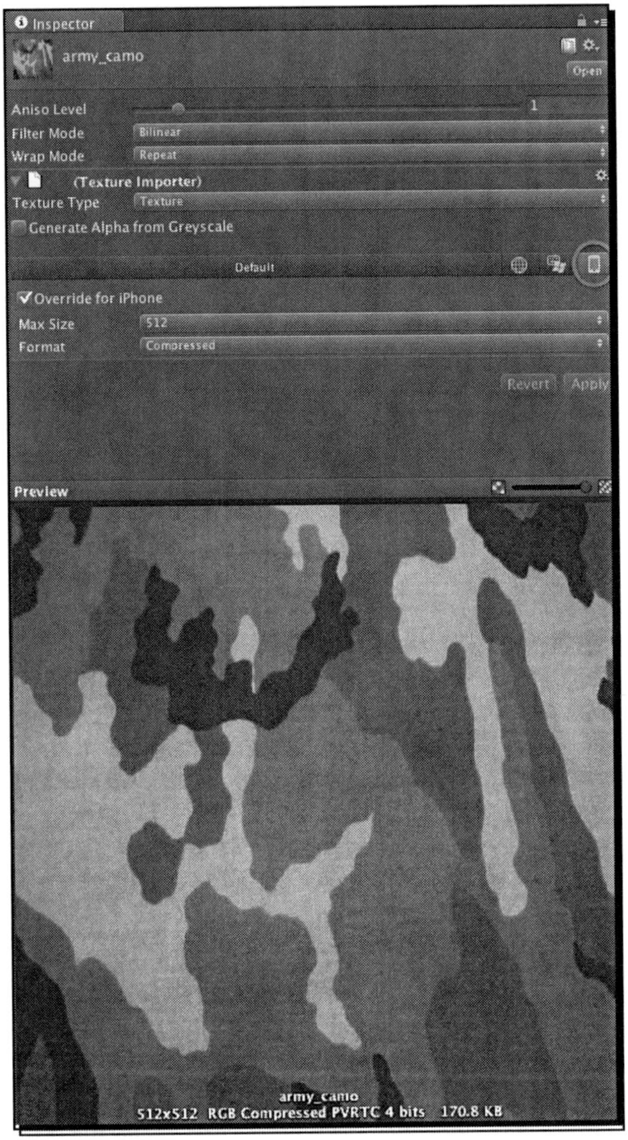

Now our texture for iOS will only be 512x512, while it can be 1024x1024 for other platforms. From a workflow perspective this is important, as you will want to override your assets for the platform you're deploying to, while not creating entirely new assets for each platform.

6. Our next step is to make this image the background of the scene. Select the texture that we just imported in the **Project** view and create a **GUI Texture**.

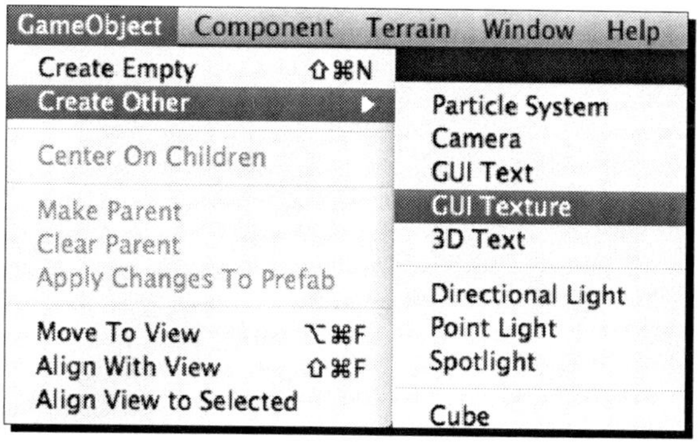

7. Change the scale of our background texture to (1,1,1) so that it is scaled to fill the screen. Since a **GUITexture** is a Unity UI construct specifically for UI elements, all of its position and scale is done in screen space as opposed to world space. By setting this to **1** in all dimensions. We're telling Unity to fill the screen with our **GUITexture**. The Z-axis in this case is the same as for prior chapters. If you need to draw other items in front of the background, they simply need to have a lower Z value than the background.

> We did not have to make the **GUITexture** a child of the camera for this to happen.

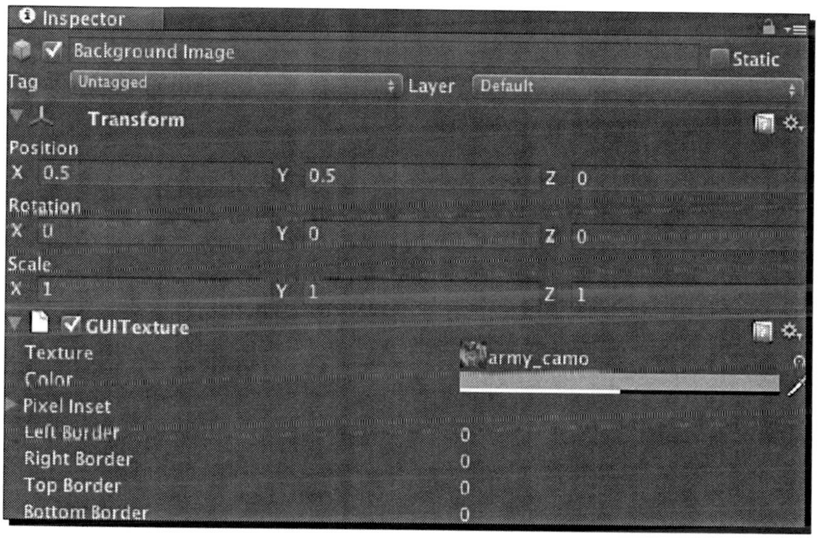

8. Run the project and you will see a camouflage texture that fills the entire screen.

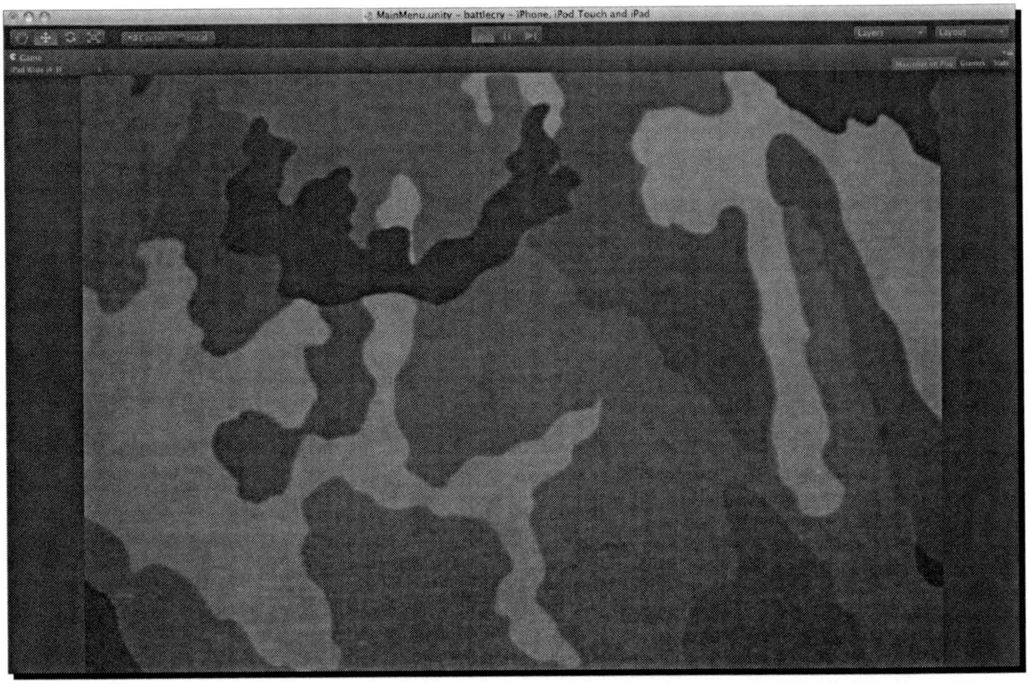

What just happened?

We have just created a background for our main menu scene. As you have noticed, this item is not parented to any part of the scene and will display without respect to any other items in the scene. Now we can move on to adding buttons to our menu.

Putting the menu on the screen

To make the immediate mode GUI work with Unity we simply need to provide one function in a script, `OnGUI`. Like any other script we will attach our UI script to a **GameObject** that is located in the scene and Unity will call it every frame to ensure that any GUI events that have happened during that frame are processed. One obvious warning is that this means that your GUI loops should be tight loops and highly optimized; you shouldn't be performing complex time-consuming computations inside the GUI code.

If we look back at our main menu example we know that we have two simple buttons that need to perform very specific actions when clicked. Thus, from a pseudo code perspective, we know that our application simply needs a basic if/else condition to examine the two controls that we're using.

```
// Use this for initialization
if ( MainMenuButton( control_x, control_y, width, height) )
{
  loadMainGameScene();
}
else if ( CreditsMenuButton( control_x, control_y, width, height)  )
{
  loadCreditsScreen();
}
```

In this example `MainMenuButton` and `CreditsMenuButton` represent two GUI controls that we will define in our script that will cause the main scene or credits scene to be opened respectively.

Time for action – Adding buttons to the GUI

1. Import the two textures from the assets folder `BTN_StartGame` and `BTN_Credits`. These will be used to build our main menu.

   You will also notice that these textures are somewhat larger than the buttons they contain. This was done because by default Unity will expect that your textures are some power of 2. We will address this limitation later.

2. Create an empty game object called **Menu Object**.

   Going back to our original foray into scripting, we know that we need some game object in our scene in order for our script to run. Since this object doesn't need to be displayed, or have any particular game functionality, we can simply insert an empty game object into the scene and attach our script to that.

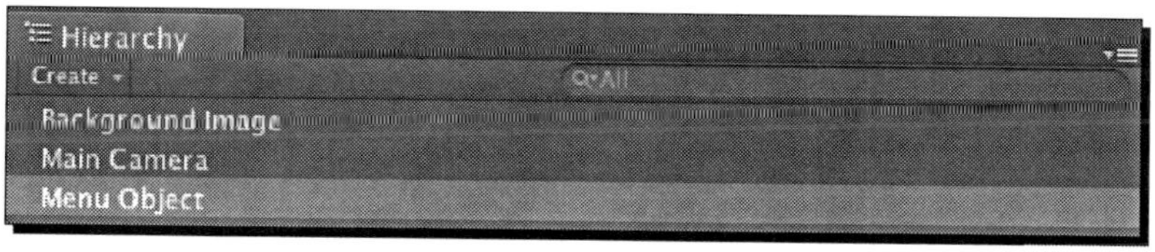

3. As we are going to be building an immediate mode GUI, it follows that we're going to have some script that drives the display of our GUI. Create a script called `MainMenu` and attach it to the **MenuObject** game object.

4. Define two public variables in the `MainMenu` script, which will allow us to specify the button textures for the main menu commands.

   When we originally imported the textures for our buttons Unity imported them as Texture2Ds. If we configure our script to take in Texture2Ds we can use the Unity GUI to configure the textures we want to display as opposed to having to hard code this value in our code. We can accomplish this by defining public attributes on the class which defines our script.

   ```
   public Texture2D   mainMenuButton;
   public Texture2D   creditsMenuButton;
   ```

5. Next we need to update our `OnGUI` method to display the buttons for the main menu. We want the Texture2Ds we imported earlier to show up as buttons in our interface so we need to use the Unity GUI system to render them as buttons.

   Unity has an easy to use `GUI.Button` class that performs this function. `GUI.Button` allows us to create a button on the interface with coordinates that are in screen space. We do this by defining a rectangle (`Rect`) with the position on the screen where this button will be drawn as the first two arguments and the width and height as the second two components.

   ```
   Rect( x, y, width, height )
   ```

   When combined with the normal `GUI.Button()` method call we get the following:

   ```
   void OnGUI()
   {
      GUI.Button( new Rect ( 0, 0, 256, 256 ), mainMenuButton );
   }
   ```

   Here we are creating a new button at the upper left corner of the screen with a size of 256x256 and defining the `mainMenuButton` as the Texture2D that should be drawn in this button.

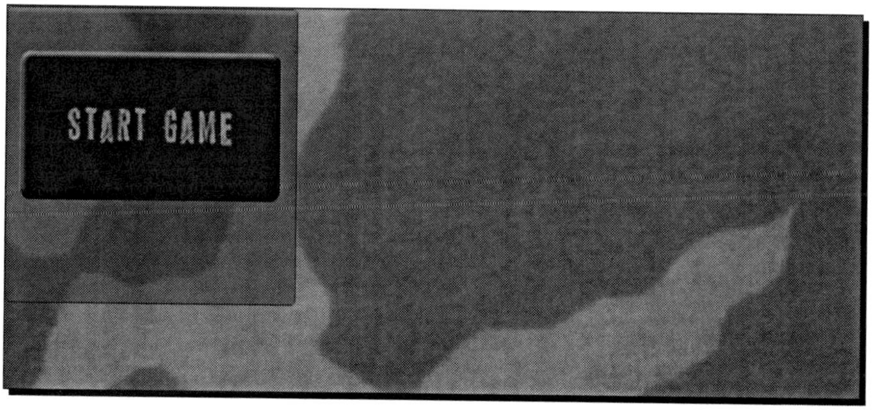

6. Next we need to tell the Unity GUI to perform an action in response to someone pressing that button. As in the pseudo code, this involves wrapping the button with an if statement – which will be evaluated in the `OnGUI`.

7. Add the `creditsMenuButton` and center the buttons on the screen by updating the Rects for the original `GUI.Buttons`.

```
using UnityEngine;
using System.Collections;

public class MainMenu : MonoBehaviour {

  public Texture2D   mainMenuButton;
  public Texture2D   creditsMenuButton;

  // Process the GUI
  void OnGUI () {

    int componentWidth = 256;
    int componentHeight = 256;
    int interfaceOrigin = 0;

    if (GUI.Button( new Rect ( Screen.width / 2 -
    componentWidth/2, interfaceOrigin,
    componentWidth, componentHeight ), mainMenuButton) )
    {
      Debug.Log("You clicked the start button ");
    }

    else if (GUI.Button( new Rect ( Screen.width / 2
    - componentWidth/2, interfaceOrigin + componentHeight,
    componentWidth, componentHeight ), creditsMenuButton) )
```

```
        {
          Debug.Log("You clicked the credits button ");
        }
      }
    }
```

While there are other ways to do this in Unity using GUI Groups, this will suit our purposes better as an instructional tool. If we render our scene now, we will find two buttons which contain our button textures:

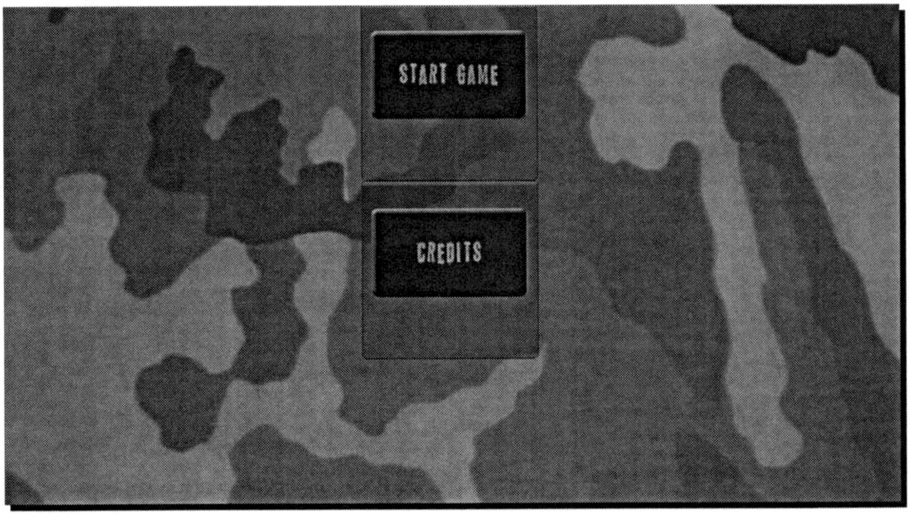

Pressing these buttons will show some debug text in the console:

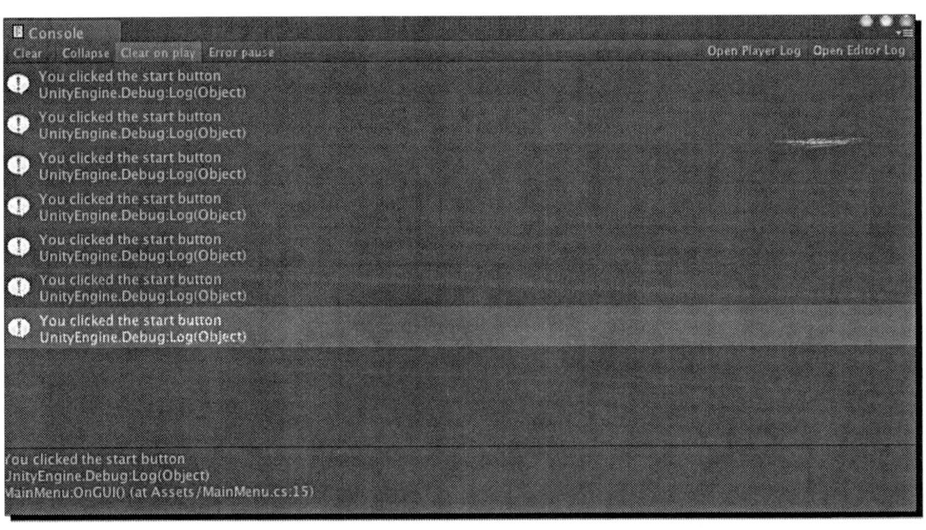

While this allows our buttons to be rendered, there is more GUI Button being rendered than we want. The Unity GUI has its own style engine defined in `GUIStyle`, which determines how a button should be drawn. As we have baked the look and feel of our buttons into the textures themselves, we don't need Unity to display any of this style.

8. Update the `GUIStyle` of the `GUI.Buttons` so that they have no associated style.

   `GUIStyle` defines a `GUIStyle.none` which allows us to turn off Unity drawing any of the GUI skin that it is currently drawing.

```
if (GUI.Button( new Rect ( Screen.width / 2 - componentWidth/2,
interfaceOrigin, componentWidth, componentHeight ), startButton,
GUIStyle.none) )
{
  Debug.Log("You clicked the start button ");
}
```

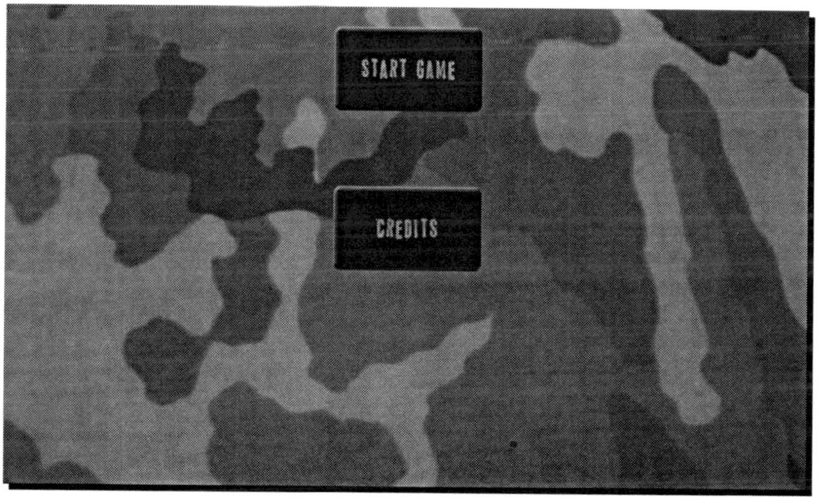

By making this simple change we will get the GUI rendered exactly how we intended.

9. Update the script to load the Unity levels when the buttons are pressed.

```
if (GUI.Button( new Rect ( Screen.width / 2 - componentWidth/2,
interfaceOrigin, componentWidth, componentHeight ), startButton,
GUIStyle.none) ))
{
  Debug.Log("You clicked the start button ");
  Application.LoadLevel("IntroCity");
}
```

By making the call to `Application.LoadLevel` as we have previously, we now have a mechanism for pressing a button in the interface and having Unity load a particular scene.

What just happened?

We have just constructed a simple immediate mode GUI to display the main menu for our game. We have accomplished this by using the Unity GUI system and building a script which renders our GUI. Under the covers, what Unity is doing is drawing our scene every frame, based upon the script. It is important to note that if you were to change the script so that, programmatically, it were to display certain things based upon some setting or every third frame, Unity will do that because it is processing the UI script each and every frame. Accordingly it is important to not perform any extremely complex operations in the `OnGUI` method as it could result in a substantial performance slowdown.

A better way – UIToolkit

One of the issues with the current implementation of the Unity GUI library is that it was designed for PC users and doesn't take into account any of the limitations of mobile devices. While it performs well enough in some situations, in most situations the number of draw calls it generates are enough to wreck the performance of your game.

In our previous example it is not possible to really see the impact of the performance slowdown because we aren't doing any rendering that is intense enough to impact the frame rate. As our scene is pretty static, one wouldn't be able to visually measure the result. However, if we look at our statistics we can see that even for this very modest GUI we're utilizing three draw calls – one for each GUI component.

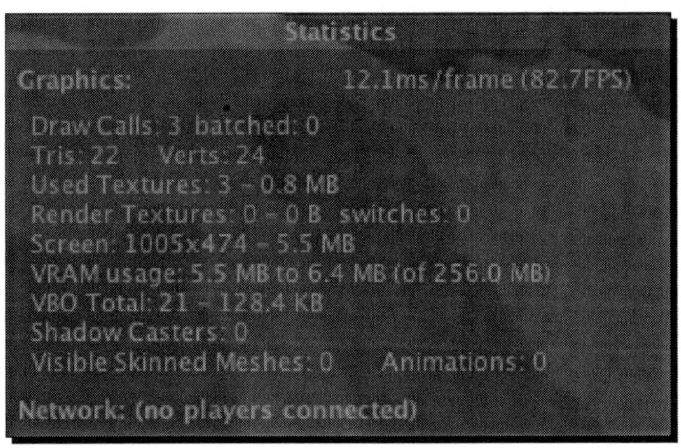

This may not seem like much now, but as you learn more in the chapter on optimization, this is a substantial amount of work that the iOS device is doing. So what if we could accomplish the same amount of work within a single draw call? What if we could have only one draw call regardless of the number of GUI elements we're drawing? Enter Prime31's UIToolkit.

Time for action – Prime31 UIToolkit

1. Download **code'n'web TexturePackerPro** essentials by visiting the website:

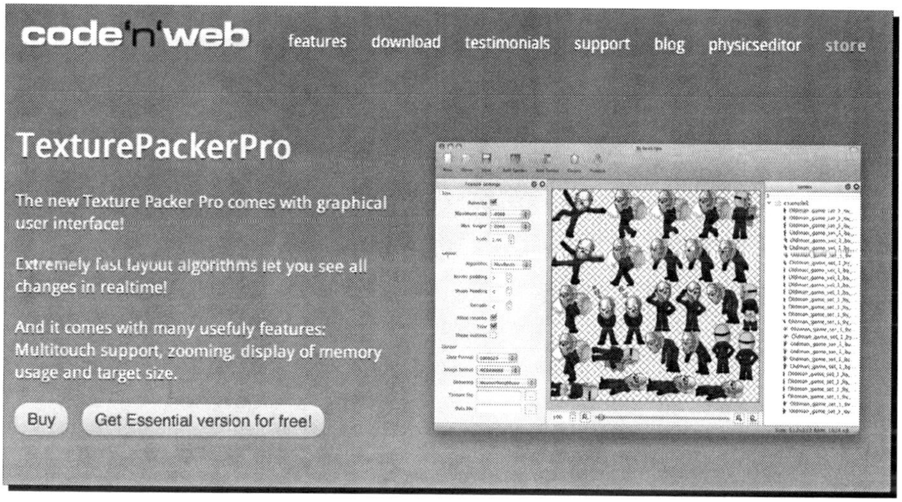

2. Select the latest available version of TexturePacker from the download list and install TexturePacker:

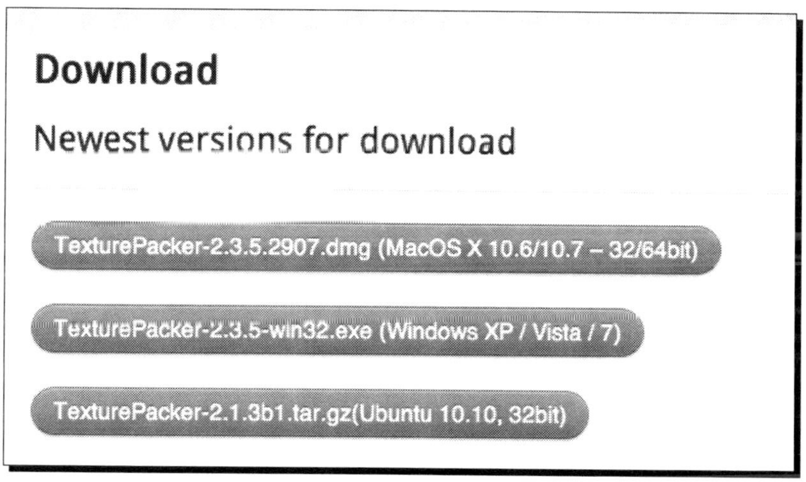

3. Next, drag the UI buttons for the credits menu and the start game menu into the interface. You can do this by dragging the images into the Sprites menu on the right-hand side of the interface:

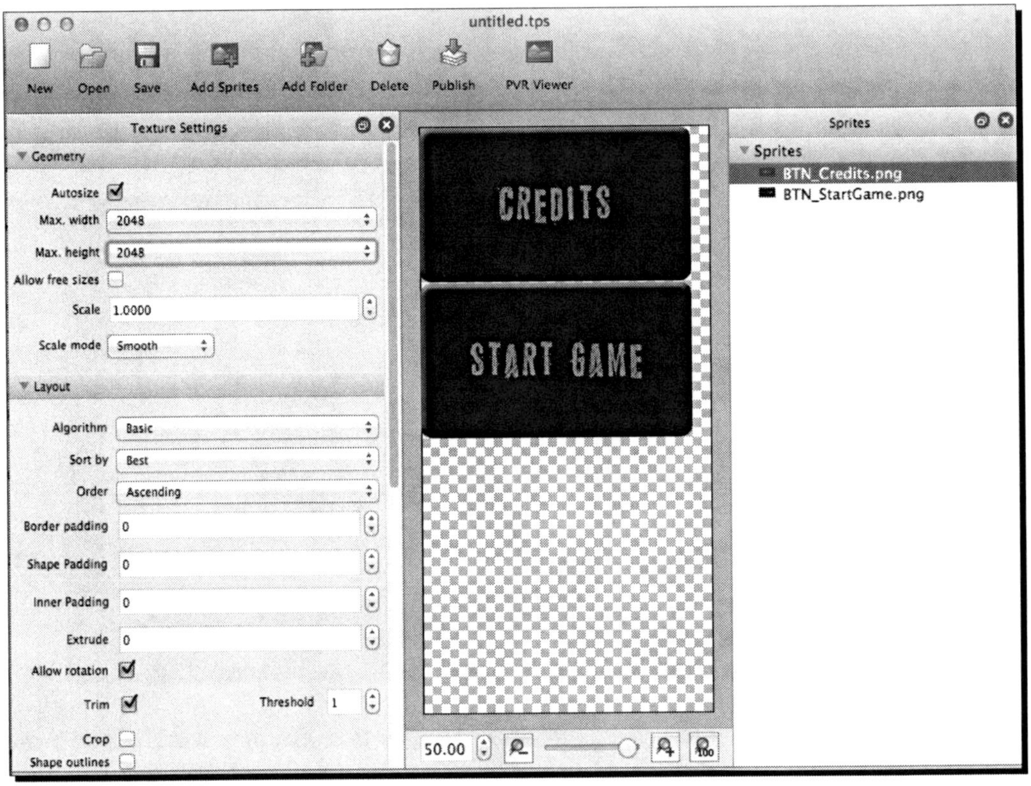

4. We want to use the minimum amount of texture memory possible so set the **Max. width** and **Max. height** to the smallest power of 2 possible. Your texture will still need to be square so you're looking for the smallest number that box width and height can be set to simultaneously. In our case it is 512. If **TexturePacker** cannot find a way to fit your textures into that size it will turn the text red.

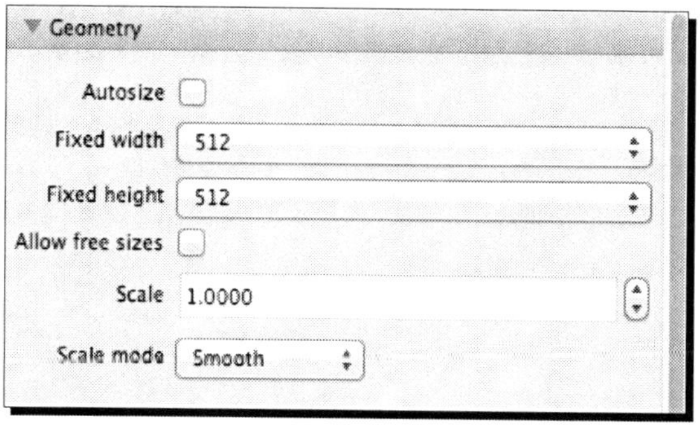

One benefit that you may not have noticed at this point is that before we were creating textures as large power of 2 textures so that Unity would accept them. Here TexturePacker is identifying the empty space in the textures and optimizing the amount of space each texture takes. In this case we actually have additional space where we could pack more textures if we needed to.

5. In the **Output settings** (scroll the left pane to the bottom) set the **Data format** to **JSON** (Javascript Object Notation) and set the directory to your project's `Assets` folder. Set the name of the file as `gui` and change the extension of the `.json` file to `.txt`, as Unity expects text assets to end with a `.txt` extension.

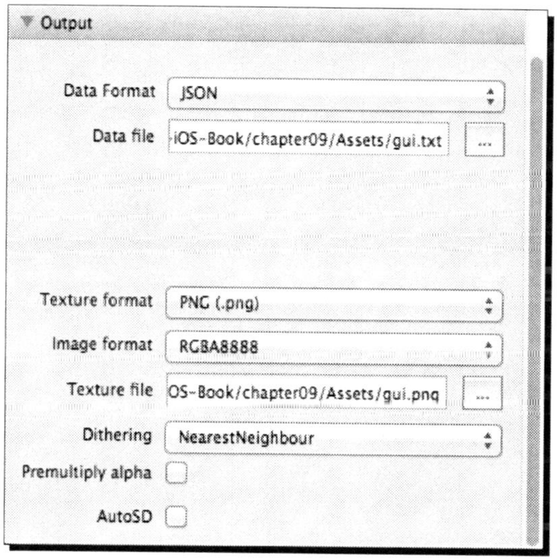

6. Press the **Publish** button in the toolbar and the appropriate files will be created in your `Assets` folder.

We are now done with everything we need from TexturePacker.

7. Download the UIToolkit library from Prime31's github repository by visiting the website at `https://github.com/prime31/UIToolkit`:

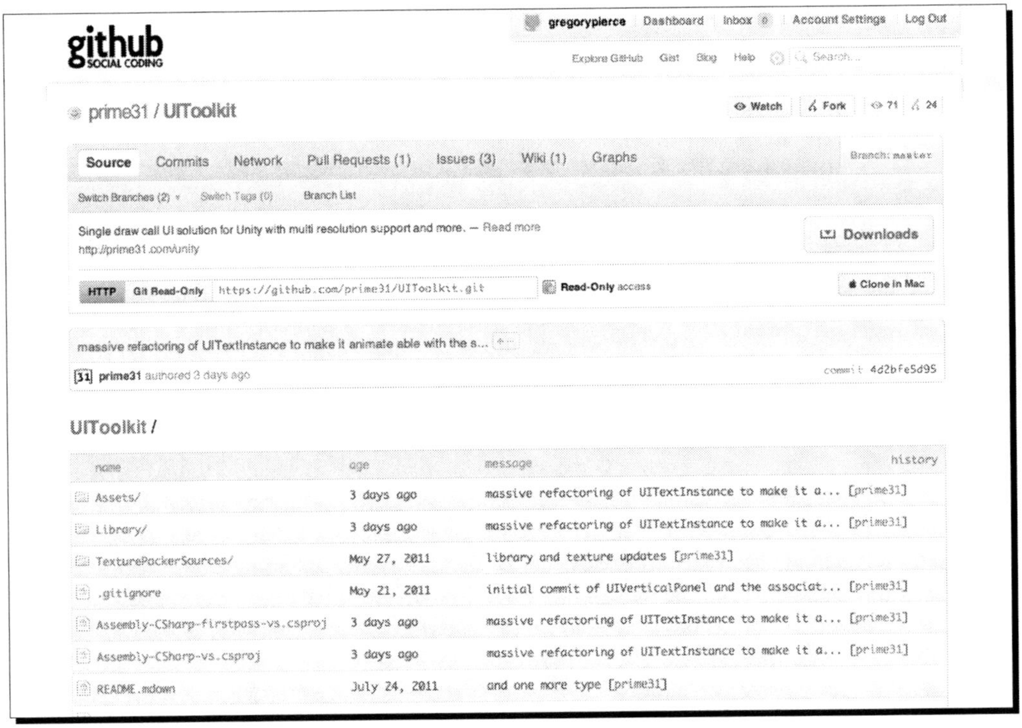

8. Select download and choose the .unitypackage option:

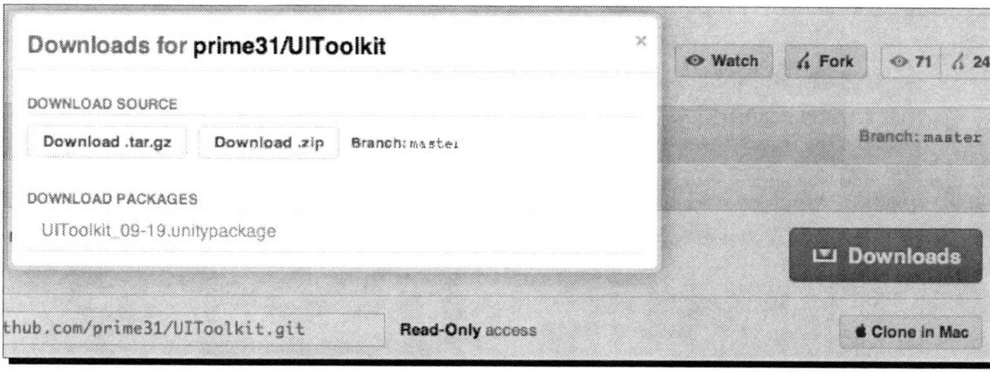

9. After it downloads, install the Unity package, importing all of the items in it:

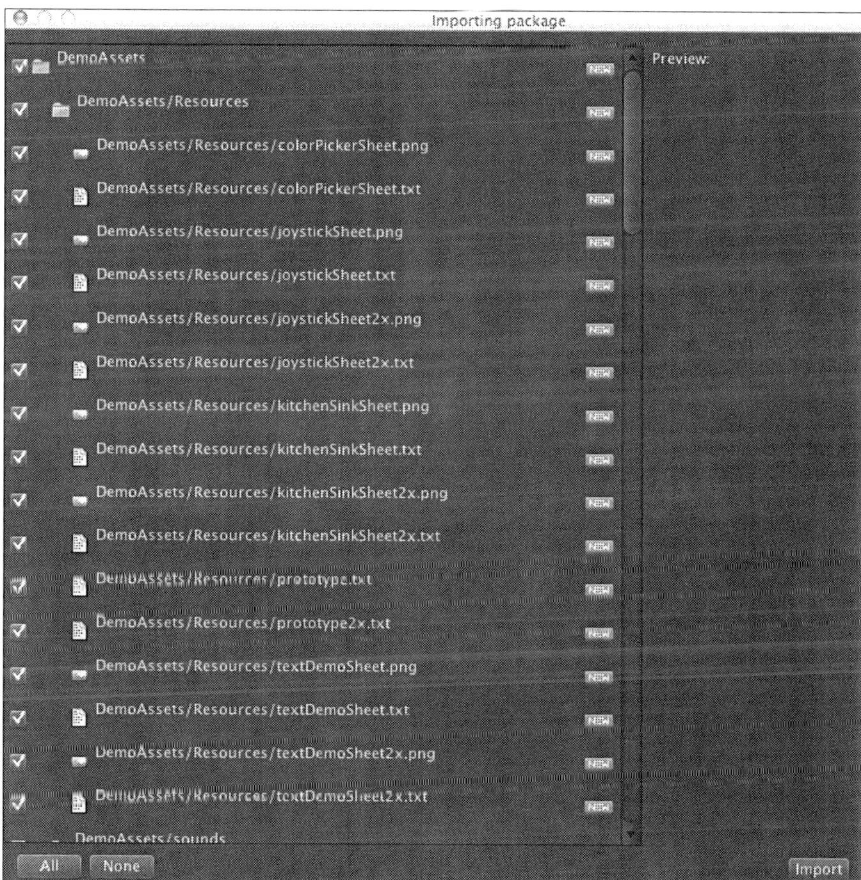

10. So that we can examine the 2 different approaches to render GUIs separately, create a new scene for this approach, and name it UIToolkit.

11. To make sure that our UI components are segregated from the rest of our scene, we want to put them on a particular layer in Unity. Layers are collections of components that can be accessed or manipulated as a collection. If you are familiar with Photoshop, the concept is similar.

12. In Unity, create a new Layer for our GUI to be drawn on by accessing the Layers through **Edit | Project Settings | Tags**:

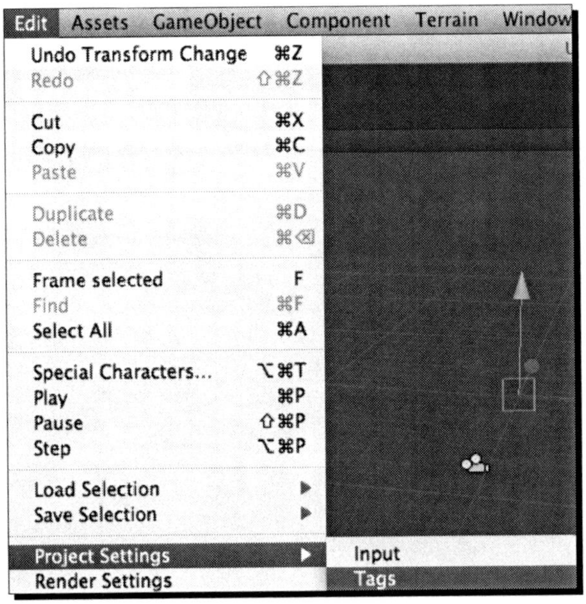

13. Select **User Layer 8** and set the Layer name to **UI Layer**:

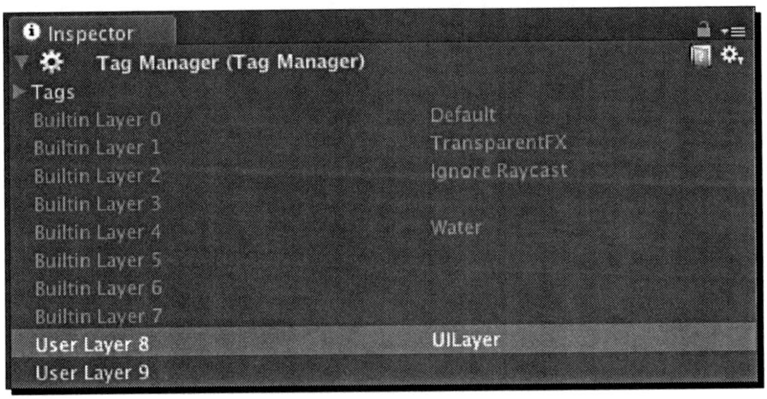

14. Create an empty game object, name it **GUIObject** and set its position to 0,0,0:

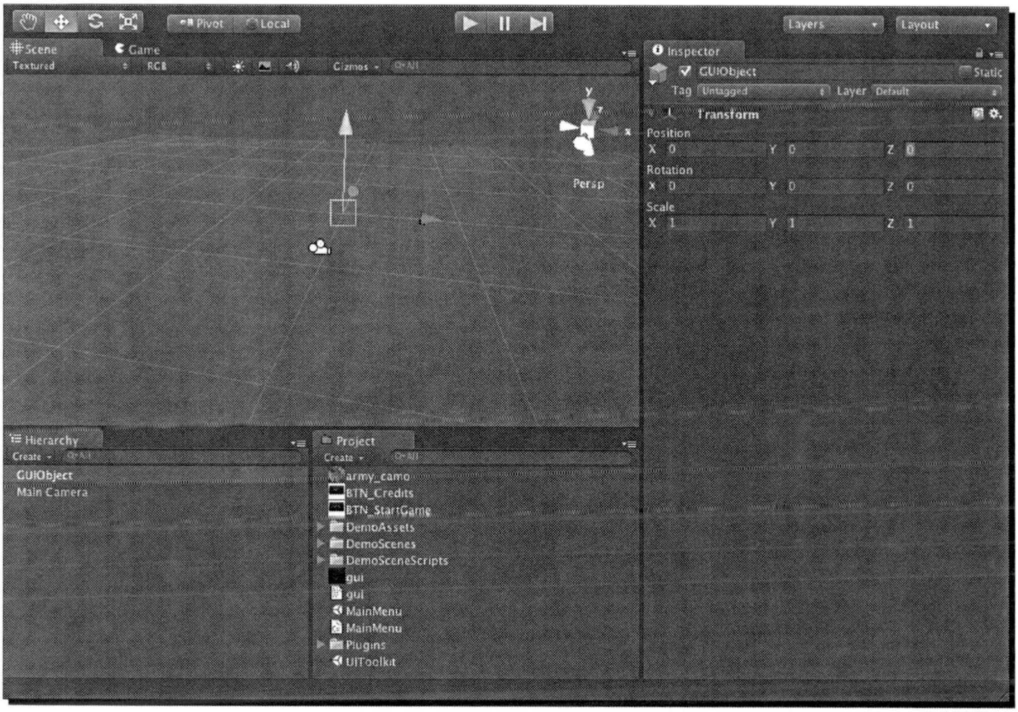

15. Expand the `Plugins` folder in the **Project** view and you will find the **UIToolkit library. Expand UIToolkit** and drag the UI script onto the **GUIObject**:

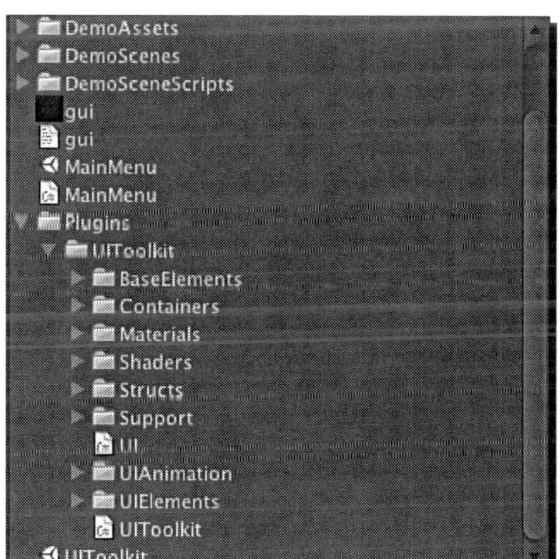

16. Select the **MainCamera** object in the **Hierarchy** view and remove the **UILayer** from the **Culling Mask** to ensure that the UI does not get drawn more than once:

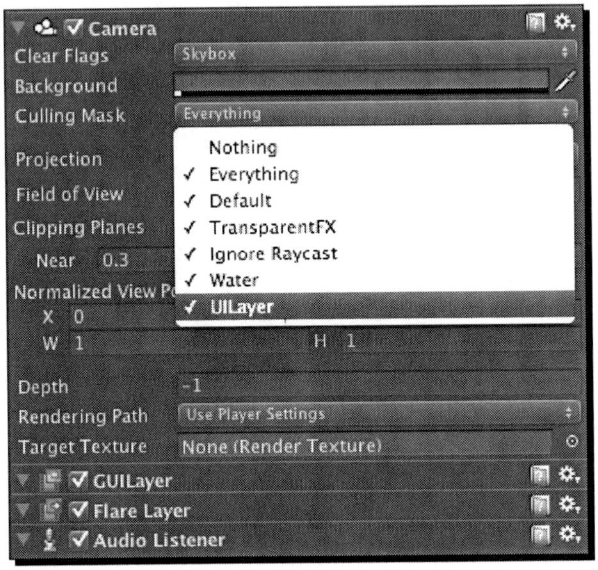

17. Once you select the **UILayer** the **Culling Mask** should be displayed as **Mixed** as shown in the following screenshot:

18. Create a new empty game object called **UIToolkit** and make it a child of the **GUIObject** we created earlier that contains the UI script:

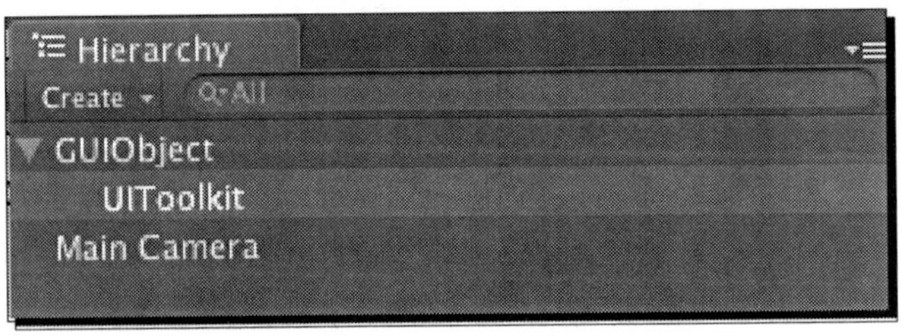

19. Drag the **UIToolkit** script from the `UIToolkit plugins` folder onto the UIToolkit game object in the **Hierarchy** view:

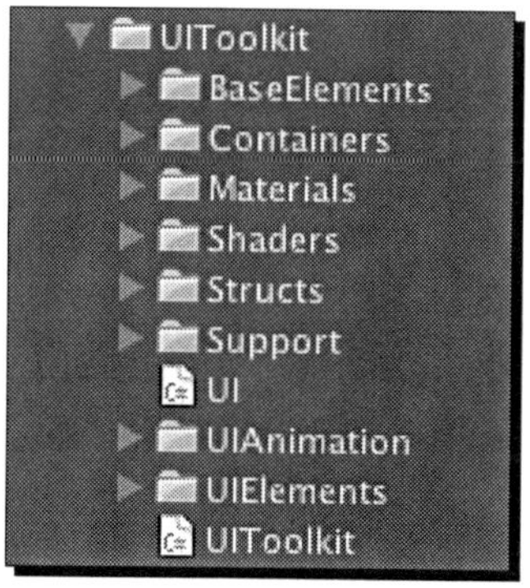

20. Select the **GUIObject** node in the **Hierarchy** view to bring up its inspector. Tell it we want the UI to be drawn on the **UILayer** by selecting the drop-down next to the **UILayer** entry and selecting the layer that the UI is to be drawn on – which we have also called **UILayer**:

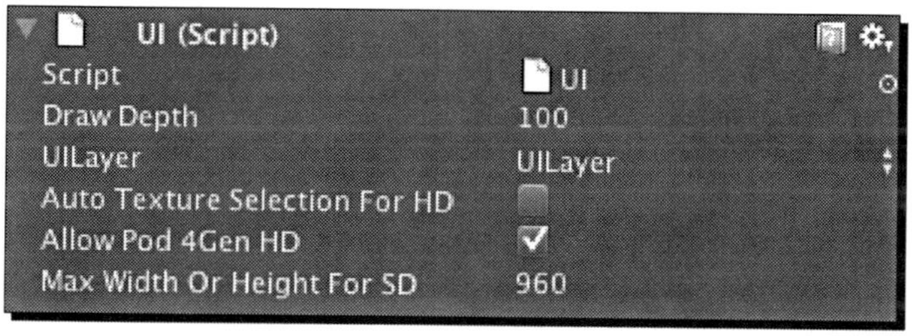

21. To wrap up our configuration we need to tell **UIToolkit** which TexturePacker config we're using. Select the **UIToolkit** node in the **Hierarchy** view to bring up its inspector. In the **Texture Packer Config Name** enter the name of the config that we saved, in this case **gui**:

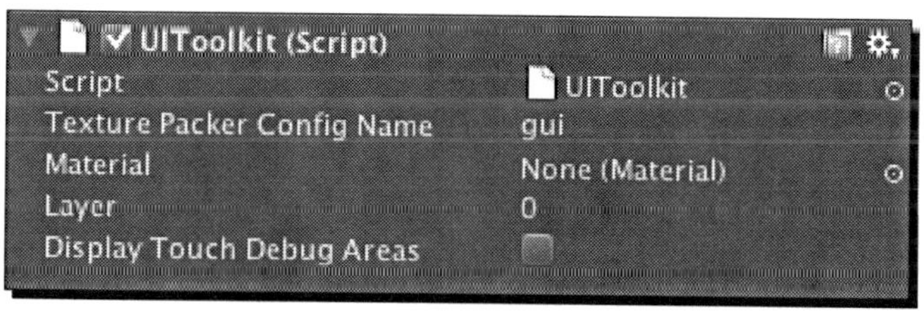

Now we're ready to create our GUI using the textures we used in Texture Packer.

22. Create a Script called `UIToolkitGUI` and let's add a button to the screen using this new approach:

```
using UnityEngine;
using System.Collections;

public class UIToolkitGUI : MonoBehaviour {

  // Use this for initialization
  void Start () {
    var mainMenuButton = UIButton.create("BTN_StartGame.png",
    "BTN_StartGame.png", 0 , 0 );
  }

}
```

Note that the UIToolkit button class takes a normal button state and a pressed button state. As we didn't have both we just used the same texture for both. The last two arguments are the position on the screen where we want this button to show up.

23. Press play and our button will show up on the screen.

What just happened?

We just created our GUI using the open source and free library UIToolkit from Prime31. We have accomplished the same thing as our original menu, but with a single draw call. While we could have accomplished similar with UnityGUI, the performance would have gotten progressively worse the more complex the user interface became, as each control added and each GUIStyle rendered results in another draw call.

In addition, we've come up with a more optimal way to get textures into the UI. Unity, by default, will not allow you to use a non-power of 2 texture for rendering which will result in lots of wasted texture memory at each texture. With this approach we can pack a large number of textures into a single larger texture, which is in itself more efficient, and render textures of wildly different shapes without sacrificing much in texture memory efficiency.

Summary

In this chapter we have learned how to build a UI for our game. We have explored setting up a UI using the Unity GUI APIs, as well as setting up a UI using the leading third party plugin Prime31 UIToolkit.

Specifically, we covered:

- How to build an immediate mode GUI with the standard GUI library
- How to build a GUI using the Prime31 UIToolkit
- Some concerns about GUI performance

Now that we are finished putting together the UI, we need to handle more complex gameplay scripting for our game – which is the focus of our next chapter.

10

Gameplay Scripting

We've come a long way in the past few chapters and have created a great deal of our game, but we still need to do a bit of work to implement some of our gameplay concepts. In this chapter we'll explore some of the gameplay scripts needed to implement the play mechanics of our game.

In this chapter we shall learn:

- How to add a particle system to our imported models to simulate a weapon
- How to use animation to drive events in the game
- How to handle ragdoll physics on our character and enemies
- How to keep score and trigger events based on gameplay

With these basics we'll have the core of an actual game's play mechanics completed and all we'll need to do is add this to the world the characters live in.

Gunplay as gameplay

As our game is a shooter, one of the primary gameplay mechanics we need to provide is a mechanism through which guns can fire projectiles and hit other objects in the world. While there are many ways to accomplish gunfire in the game such as simulating the gunfire or creating game objects that represent projectiles, the more efficient mechanism to represent gunfire is a particle system. By attaching a particle system to our gun object, we can easily draw a representation of projectiles being fired at objects in the game world.

Particle Systems in Unity support physics, collision, and memory management in a way that is particularly efficient for mobile devices. The only issue to watch for is that the fill rate (the rate at which the screen can be filled or drawn) for mobile devices is not as high as that of their desktop cousins. Similarly, if you perform actions such that the engine must redraw certain areas of the screen repetitively, you will see the same fill-rate issues. So if you have a lot of particles that are taking up large sections of the screen, you will likely have a performance issue. We will discuss this in much greater detail during the optimization chapter.

Time for action – Readying the weapon

For this example we will create a new project called gun range so that we can easily test our gameplay without having to build and deploy the entire project. Whenever you are making a large play mechanic change to your game, it is often useful to do this in isolation so that you can be more agile in your development. Large projects can get cluttered pretty quickly so it's best to test in simple projects:

1. Create a new project called **GunRange**. Save the scene in the project as **level_0**.
2. Import a static gun model and put it in a hierarchy group called **Weapons**.
3. Next we need to ensure that the weapon is pointed along the Z-axis. We accomplish this by rotating the model so that the business end (that is, the end our projectiles will come out of) is pointed along the positive Z-axis.

As we will attach this entire weapon and its gunfire particle system to the character as a prefab, we want to make sure that we define everything at this point relative to the coordinate system of the prefab. This is so that when it is attached to our character, or other object, it behaves properly.

What just happened?

We just imported a gun model to our scene and aligned it to the Z-axis. We did this relative to the prefabs, coordinate system and not specifically to the game's coordinate system. We did this because we want projectiles being fired along the prefabs Z-axis regardless of what else is going on in the world's coordinate system.

It doesn't really matter which axis you align the weapon to (so long as you adjust your model and scripts), but it makes logical sense to align the weapon so that it is pointed down the Z-axis so that when we fire projectiles they are going down the positive Z. Why? In the traditional orientation for 3d graphics, movement along the positive Z-axis represents things moving away from the camera – so it makes sense to use that here.

Firing projectiles

We have two approaches that we can use to add a particle system to our weapon. We can either add it directly to our gun's Game Object or we can add a child Game Object to the gun that does the actual emitting. The approach you choose really depends on how much flexibility you need versus your desire to have more objects in the hierarchy.

If you add the particle system directly to the gun's Game Object, the particles will be emitted from the center of the Game Object and that would not be visually correct. The more universal case is to create a Game Object that will serve as the emission point and attach that to a point on the weapon. This is the approach we will use for our project.

Time for action – Adding a particle system

1. Create an empty game object from the **GameObject** menu and select **Create Empty**.

2. Name this game object **MuzzlePoint**.

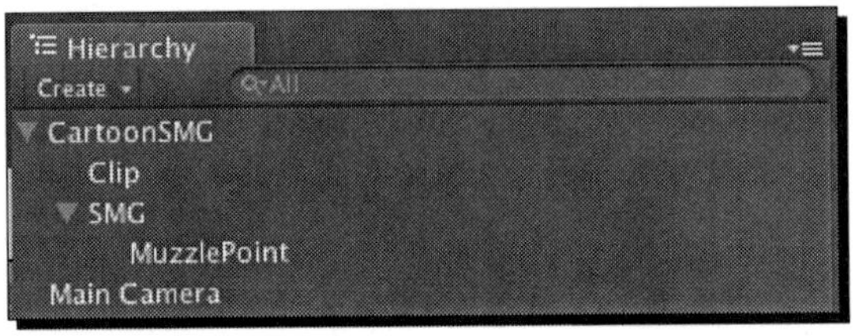

3. Select the **MuzzlePoint** game object in the **Hierarchy** view to bring up the components associated with it.

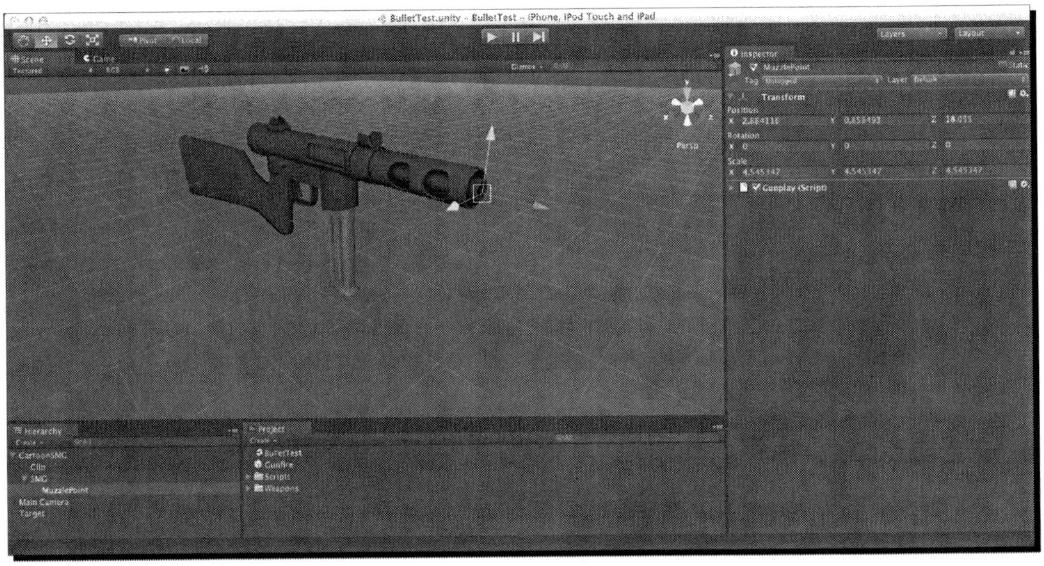

4. In the **Component** menu select **Ellipsoid Particle Emitter** so that it has a particle system associated with it.

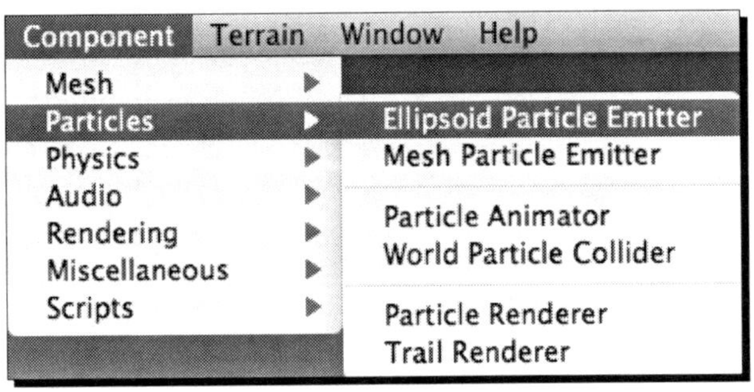

5. Position the **MuzzlePoint** game object on your gun model in Unity to designate where the projectiles should be emitted.

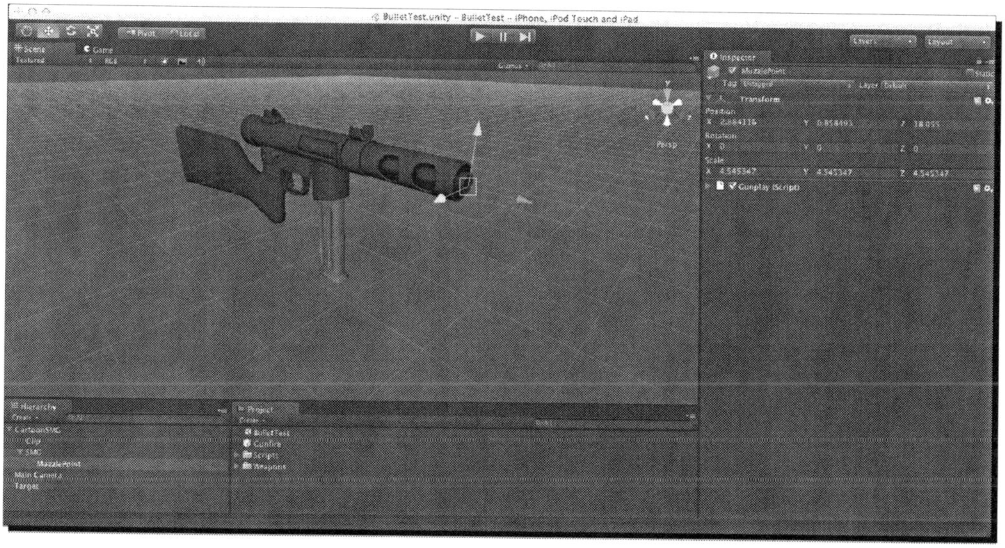

6. The next thing we need to do is have our particle emitter actually emit particles. Since we set up our weapon so that it was pointing down the Z-axis, it is pretty easy to configure our particle system so that it will send the particles down the positive Z-axis as well.

   Remember that since we've made this particle emitter a child of our gun, we want to make sure that the coordinate system we define for it is relative to the origin of the gun model. You will need to adjust it from the gun model's origin to position it properly on the gun, but realize that the coordinate system for the **MuzzlePoint** is relative to that of the gun.

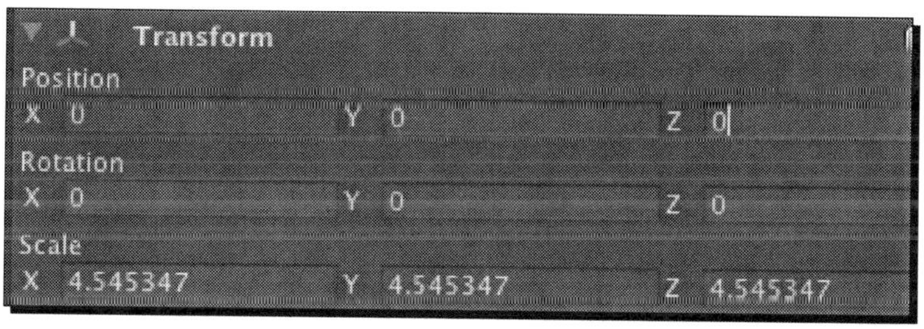

Since we've made this a child of our gun model, we want to configure it to be at the gun models, origin. You may have to adjust this for your particular model, but you should make sure you start at the gun model's origin.

Since we are creating a particle system that represents bullets, we want to have all of our projectiles moving along the same axis. To accomplish this with an **Ellipsoid Particle Emitter**, we change the Ellipsoid for the emitter to only emit particles along one axis, the Z-axis in this case. If we didn't do this, we would have particles that would spray along random axes.

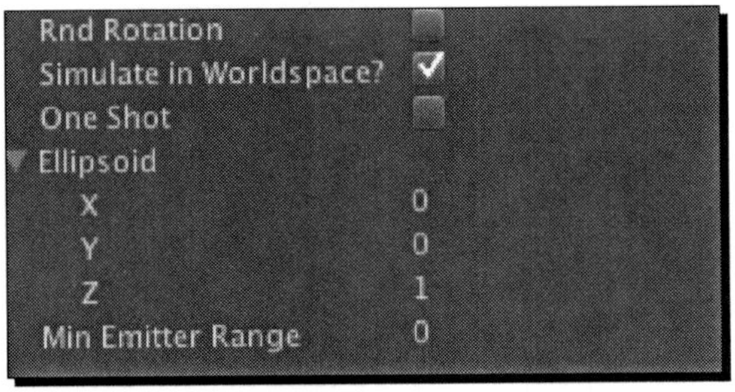

7. Finally, we need to add a simple script, call it Gunfire, to our **MuzzlePoint** game object that is tied to the fire button of our gun and we're done.

```
using UnityEngine;
using System.Collections;

public class Gunfire : MonoBehaviour {

   public GameObject muzzlePoint;


   // Use this for initialization
   void Start () {
      muzzlePoint = GameObject.Find("MuzzlePoint");
   }

   void fireWeapon() {


      muzzlePoint.particleEmitter.Emit(1);

   }

}
```

8. Import the soldier model into our scene as done previously.

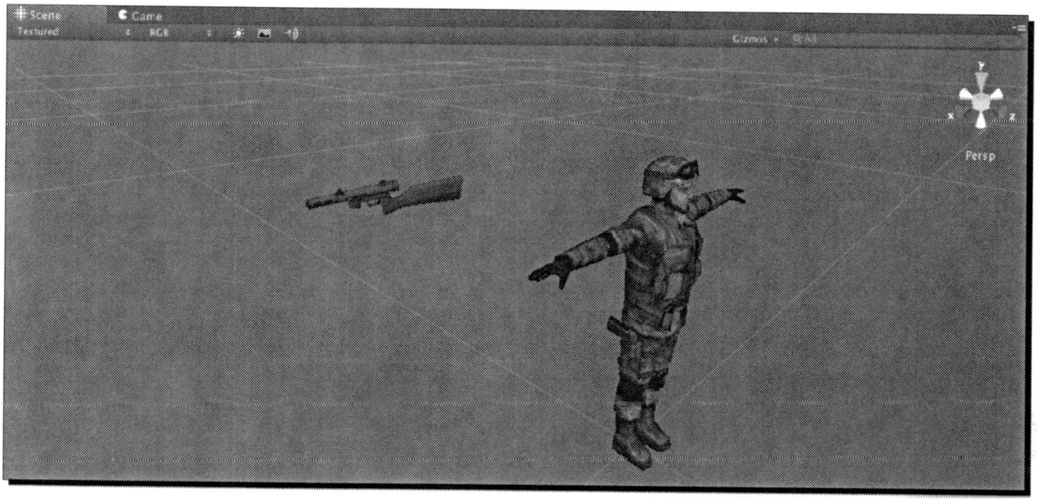

9. Adjust the gun in the soldier's hierarchy such that it is a child of the hand so that the soldier is carrying the item and will move in sync with the player as they move.

10. Update the **Gunfire** script adding a `GUI.Button` to simulate our fire button in the real game.

```
using UnityEngine;
using System.Collections;

public class Gunfire : MonoBehaviour {

   public GameObject muzzlePoint;


   // Use this for initialization
   void Start () {
      muzzlePoint = GameObject.Find("MuzzlePoint");
   }

   void fireWeapon() {

      muzzlePoint.particleEmitter.Emit(1);

   }


   // Update is called once per frame
   void OnGUI () {
      if ( GUI.Button( new Rect(0,0,50,50), "Fire" ) )
      {
         //Debug.Log("Firing the weapon");
         fireWeapon();
      }
   }

}
```

11. Run the game and press the fire button.

What just happened?

We just gave our weapon the ability to fire particles that represent bullets. We have also attached that weapon to our normal player so that it is an integral part of our player and will move as the player animates in the scene. We now have one of the fundamental building blocks for a game that involves shooting as a primary play mechanic.

Currently our particles have a default appearance, but if we want to change that appearance we can simply add a Particle Renderer component to this **MuzzlePoint** game object. We can then change the appearance of the particles by providing our own texture that is representative of what our bullets will look like.

Let the animation drive

There will often be times where there is a lot of contextual information in the animation data that has been given to us by our animators. In our case we have an animation where our character will go through a throwing animation to represent throwing a grenade, but currently we have no way of actually putting a game object into the world that will respond to this. One certainly wouldn't want to hard code the frame of animation that the throw represents, as this is likely to change throughout the course of the game. We can, fortunately, associate any arbitrary part of an animation with a callback in Unity.

Animation Events

In Unity's animation system we have the ability to associate events with arbitrary parts of an animation. Unity refers to this capability as Animation Events. With an Animation Event we can have the animation system execute scripts and consequently drive some of the logic of the game. Animation Events can be added to any Animation Clip that you have imported from your modeling environment or any ad hoc animation you create using the **Animation** view.

Time for action – Adding animation events

1. To add an event to our soldier's animation, select the character and examine the **Animation** view.

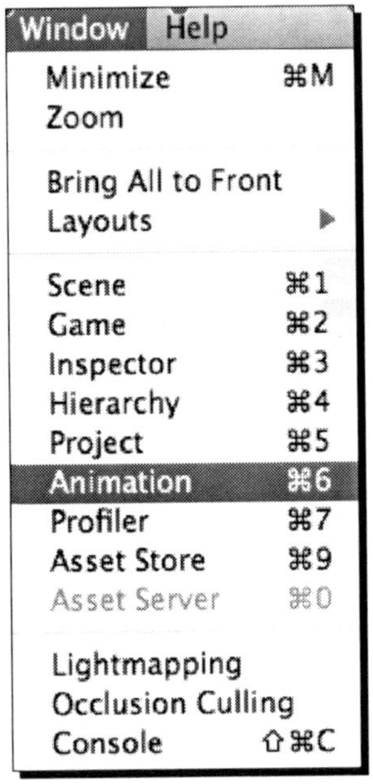

Above the animation data are two tracks – the top-most track shows all of the events added for this animation. The bottom track shows all of the defined key frames for our animation data.

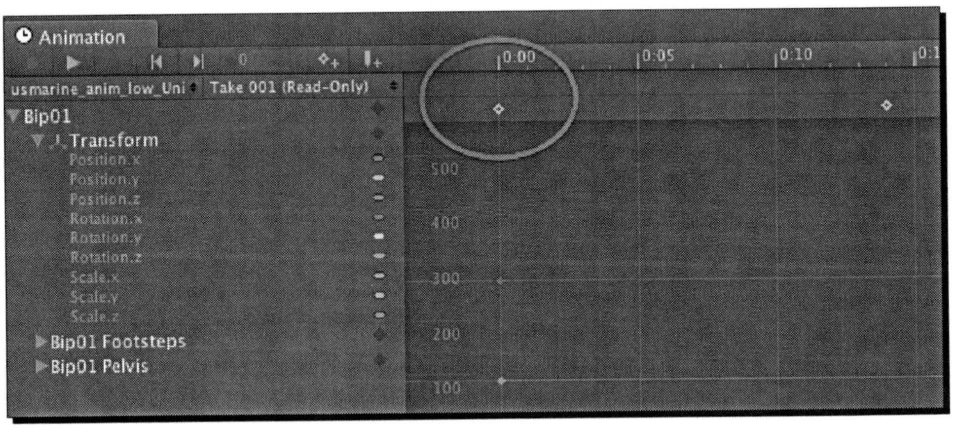

2. Create a C# script called `GrenadeToss` and make it a child of our soldier object.

3. Delete the `Start()` and `Update()` methods in the class and create a method called `TossIt` in the class and add a log statement to it. The `Start()` and `Update()` methods are not necessary for our purposes.

```
using UnityEngine;
using System.Collections;

public class GrenadeToss : MonoBehaviour {

  // Use this for initialization
  void TossIt () {
    Debug.Log("We have arrived at the toss point of the script");
  }

}
```

4. Next, scroll through the animation in the **Animation** view until you get to the point in the animation where you want to have the throw take place.

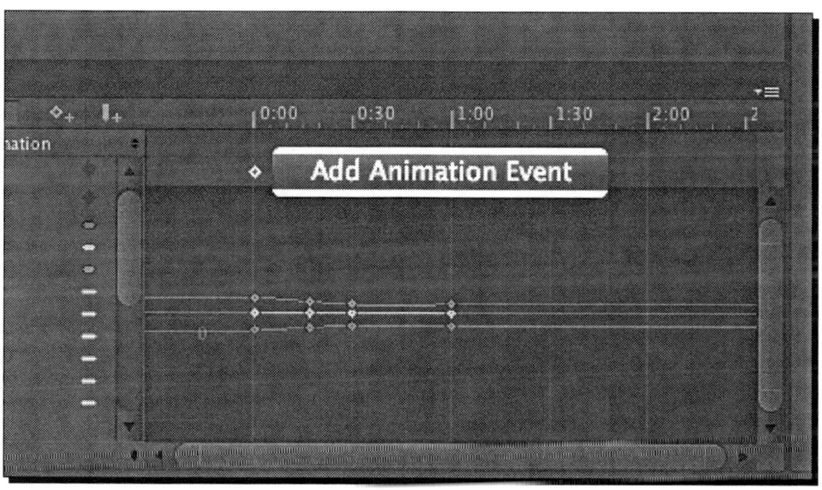

5. Create a new Animation Event by clicking on the **Add Animation Event** button. You can also accomplish this task by clicking on the event track above the animation data. An **Edit Animation Event** dialog will appear that will allow you to configure the script function that will be called when that event is reached.

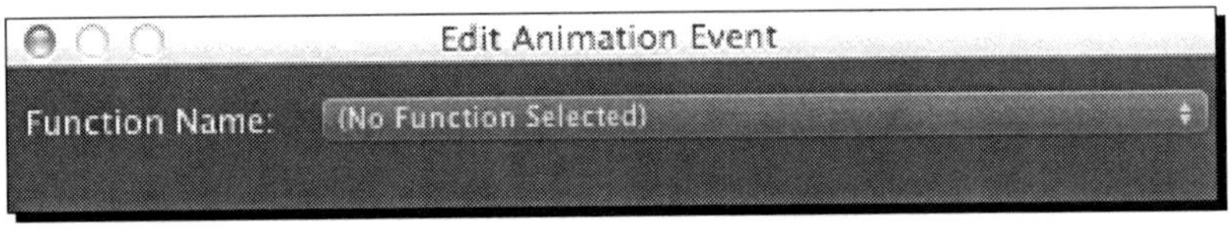

6. Open the list box and you will see a list of all of the functions that can be called.

7. Select the `TossIt()` function.

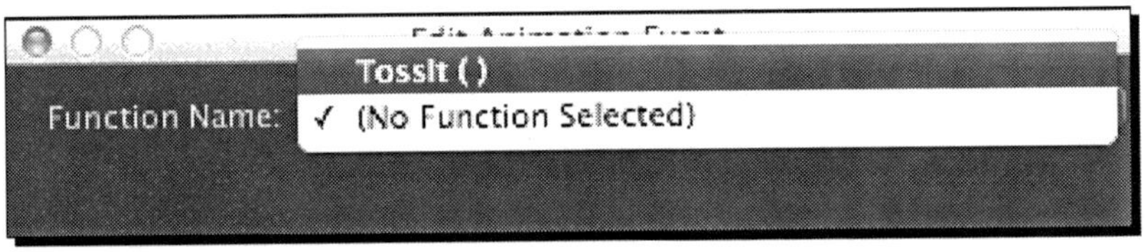

8. Press the play button for the animation. If everything is successful, you will see the log message printed out when that frame of animation is reached.

9. Create a folder called `Grenade` in the `Weapons` folder of the project.

10. Create a new Prefab object called **Grenade** as a simple sphere, stretched in one dimension.

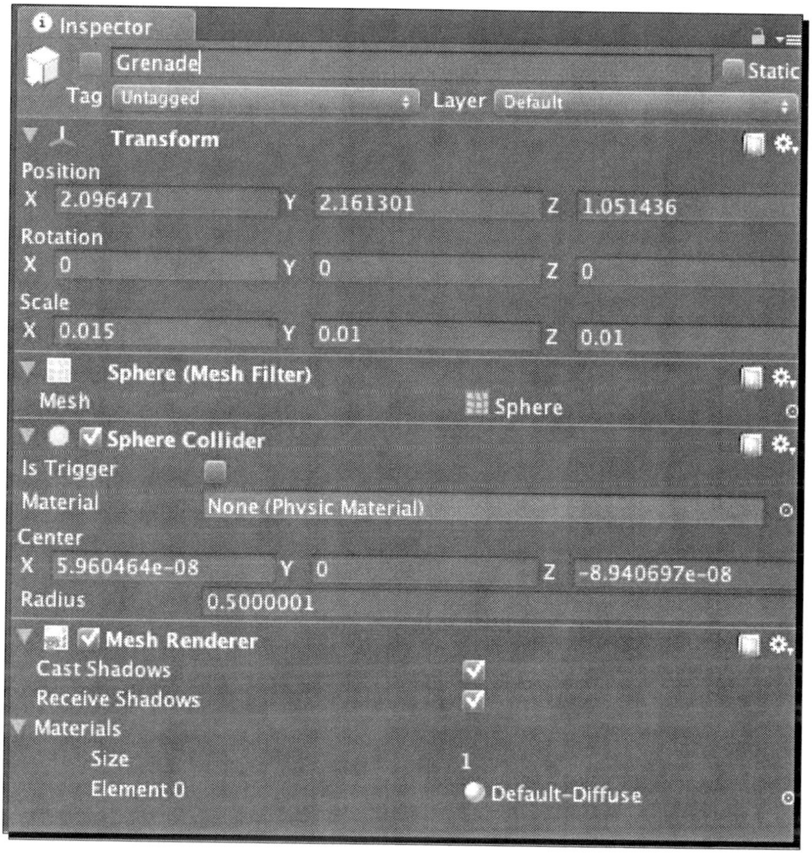

This is the object that we will create when the character reaches the animation position for `TossIt()`.

11. Update our `GrenadeToss` script to instantiate a game object when the player reaches the `TossIt()` function of our script. Since we want this object to be simulated by the physics system, we want to create it as a **Rigidbody**. Accomplish this by selecting the Grenade object from the hierarchy and add a **Rigidbody** to it.

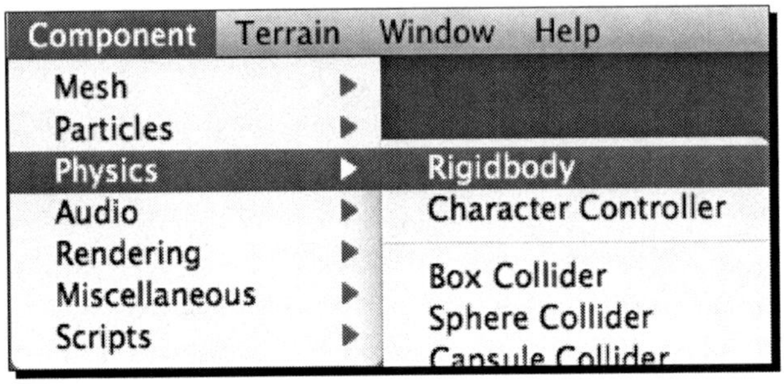

Now every Grenade object we instantiate will be simulated by the physics system.

12. We also want to instantiate this grenade at the location of the hand when we reach this point in the animation. Since all of the parts of our soldier model are named, we can use the Transform of that object after we look it up from the hierarchy.

```
using UnityEngine;
using System.Collections;

public class GrenadeToss : MonoBehaviour {

  public Rigidbody         grenade;

  // Use this for initialization
  void TossIt(){
    Debug.Log("We have arrived at the toss point of the script");

    Transform handLocation =
      GameObject.Find("LeftHandIndex1").transform;

    Instantiate( grenade, handLocation.position,
      handLocation.rotation );

  }
}
```

What just happened?

We have just added some realism to our game and provided some flexibility to our artists. By importing our animation data and then associating an event with it we have created a path to drive gameplay behavior entirely based on the scripts. We can expand this further by allowing the artists to model weapons behavior in animations and as the modeled bullets are ejected from the gun, we can update our ammo counter such that it and the animation are in perfect sync.

Further, we have provided functionality for the player to create a new game object on demand and put it in the game world, driven by the physics engine.

You are already dead

Now that we have a player that can fire a gun, we need to have the projectiles fired from that gun to collide with enemies and for those enemies to take damage when hit and be destroyed.

To accomplish this we will add a Particle Collider to our gun system and add a damage script to our enemies so they can respond to being hit by projectiles.

World Particle Colliders

The World Particle Collider is what is used to detect collisions between particles and other colliders in a scene. The other colliders in the scene can be any one of the normal spheres, boxes, capsules, and wheel or mesh colliders that Unity can assign to a game object.

Time for action – Detecting collisions

1. Import the Target Dummy model from the project assets folder.
2. To ensure that your game objects have collision data, be sure to check the **Generate Colliders** setting in the Import Settings for your mesh.

> In many cases, however, it is less costly and reasonably accurate to use a simple sphere or box collider for your enemies. If you want to do location specific damage, this is one of the cheaper ways to accomplish the effect on mobile devices.

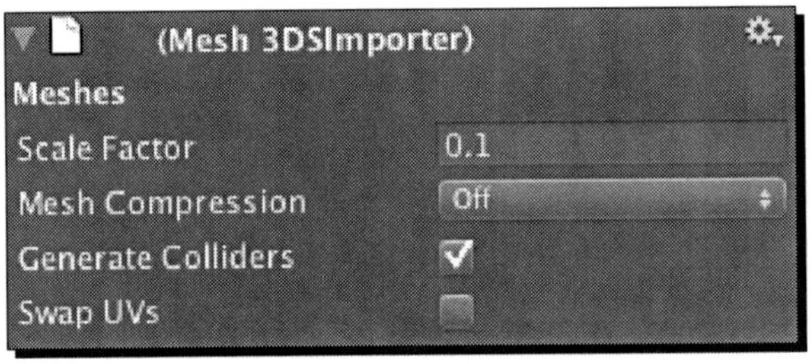

3. Now that we have collision data for our target game objects, we need to add a particle collider to the particle system we created earlier. We do this by selecting the component in the **Component | Particles | World Particle Collider** menu.

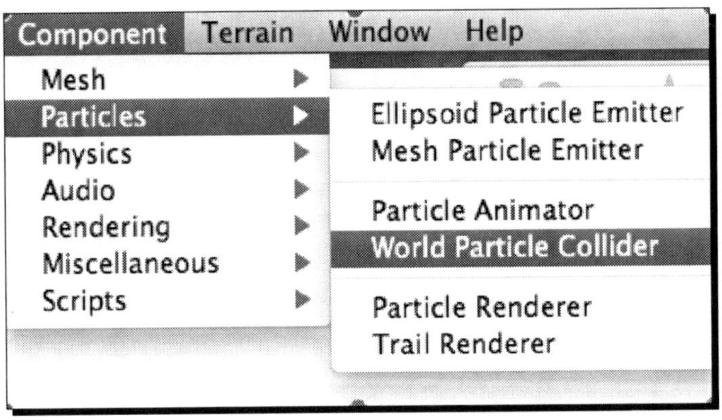

By itself this will result in particles colliding with other objects, but what we really want is for the game objects to be notified when the collision happens so we can have our target react to being hit.

4. To do this we select the **Send Collision Message** in the **World Particle Collider** so that each particle game object and the game object involved in the collision receive a collision message.

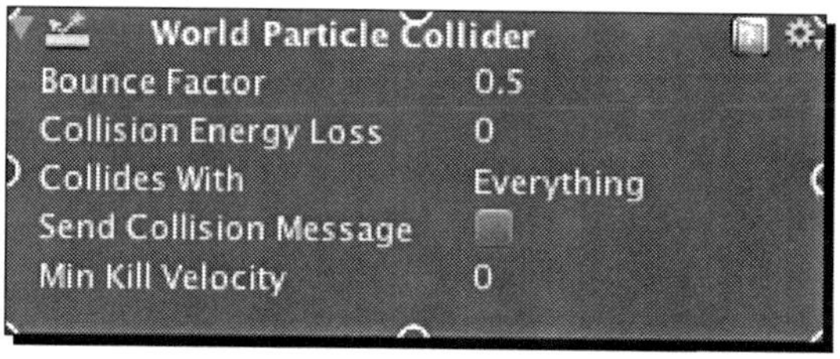

We can look for this event in scripts that we attach to any object we want to receive collision events from the particle system.

5. Create a script called `Damage` and attach the collision script to the Test Dummy objects that will process the damage.

```
using UnityEngine,
using System.Collections;

public class Damage : MonoBehaviour {


   void OnParticleCollision()
   {
      Debug.Log("Hit!");
   }

}
```

6. Update the `OnParticleCollision()` method to update the health of the object that has been hit by the particle. When the health of that item reaches zero, remove the test dummy from the game.

```
void OnParticleCollision()
  {
      HealthScript healthScript = GetComponent<HealthScript>();
      healthScript.takeHit(1);
      Debug.Log("Hit!");
  }
```

Here we are going to have our Damage script communicate with a `HealthScript`, which will define the health of our target dummy objects and remove them when they have run out of health.

7. Attach the `HealthScript` to the target dummies.

```
using UnityEngine;
using System.Collections;

public class HealthScript : MonoBehaviour {

   public int         initialHealth;
   private int         currentHealth;

   // Use this for initialization
   void Start () {
      currentHealth = initialHealth;
   }

   public void TakeHit( int damage ) {
      currentHealth = currentHealth - damage;

      if ( currentHealth <= 0 )
      {
         Destroy( this.gameObject );
      }
   }
}
```

Here we will simply remove the game object after it has taken enough damage by telling the game object that this script is attached to to destroy itself. If we wanted this object to explode or take some other behavior we could Instantiate an explosion prefab at this game object's location when we destroy the original object.

What just happened?

We have now handled the other part of our gameplay. The player can fire a weapon, the projectiles will be emitted using a particle system and when the particles come into contact with another object the damage can be calculated and this object removed from the game.

Playing with (rag) dolls

Up to this point we have simply removed enemies from the game when they have taken damage from our weapons. However, we want the enemies to respond realistically to damage from weapons based on the physics properties of the damage. In particular, when a grenade impacts an enemy, the force of the blast – something that is not currently simulated at all, should toss them around.

To accomplish this we will use Unity's Rag Doll system and assign it to our target dummies, so that when they take damage, physics will drive their motion.

Time for action – Attaching a rag doll

1. Create a new scene in the project.
2. Create a ground plane and texture it.
3. Import the target dummy model into the scene.

4. Create a Ragdoll by selecting **GameObject | Create Other | Ragdoll...**

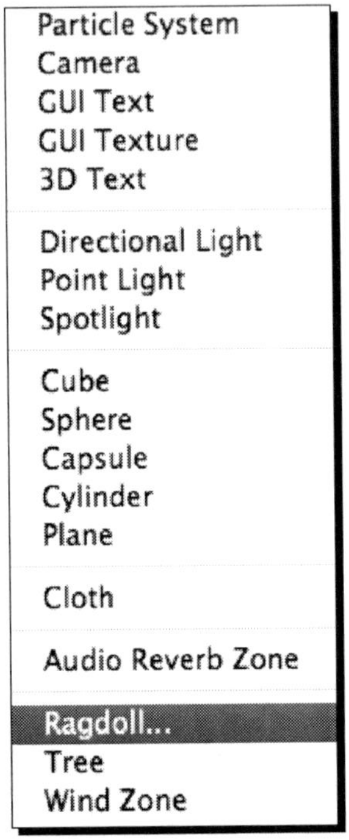

5. Next we need to map the skeleton of our target dummy model to the bone hierarchy of the rag doll. Unity makes this simple by providing a Ragdoll wizard with which we can perform the mapping between the two bone hierarchies.

6. Select the circle to the right of the Ragdoll item to bring up a list of transforms that you can connect it to.

7. Drag and drop the **soldier (Transform)** onto the **Root** of the item in the list for the Ragdoll nodes that are to be mapped.

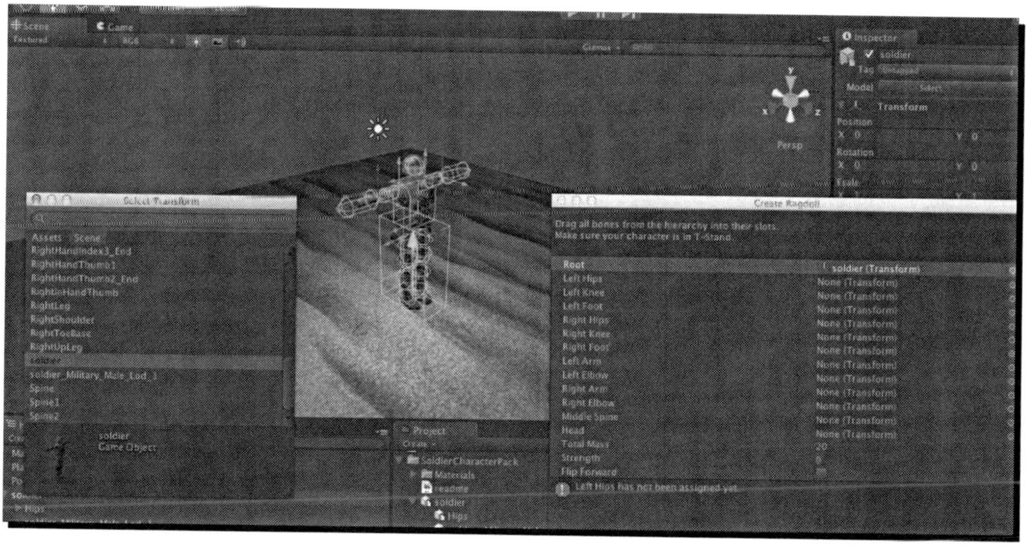

8. Select the root of the Soldier model in the **Hierarchy** view so you can see the Ragdoll mapped onto the geometry of the soldier.

9. Examine the scene by pressing the **Play** button.

What just happened?

You will note that the physics system has simulated the various forces on the rag doll and it has collapsed, as gravity is the only force on the dummy and there is nothing preventing it from falling to the ground plane.

This brings up the first problem that we have to solve – we need our model to be rigid until we want it to be impacted by the world of physics. We can accomplish this by either turning off physics until the character is in a state where it should not be in control of its actions, such as in the case of an explosion, or we need to attach the character to some other system that prevents it from slumping over.

We have attached rag dolls and rigid body physics systems to our enemies so that they can animate properly when hit affected by the physics of explosions and other in-world physics simulations. When we turn on the rag dolls, Unity uses physics, as opposed to our animation data, to determine what happens to the character. This results in a more realistic reflection of the world.

Summary

In this chapter we walked through all of the basic requirements for gameplay in our game.

Specifically, we covered:

- How to equip a character with weapons
- How to have the character move through the animations of firing the weapons
- How to display the projectiles using a particle system
- How to have the weapons impact enemies
- How to create weapons that have Rigid Body physics and how to assign Rag Dolls to objects.

Now that we have a better understanding of gameplay scripting knowledge under our belt, it's time to look at how to optimize our game for optimal performance on the target device. While the scripts provided will work on any platform, as we'll see in the next chapter, there are some particular tricks to making them perform optimally on the iOS platform.

11
Debugging and Optimization

Now that we have a nearly completed project it's time to start working on getting as much performance out of the system as possible. While we would normally address performance throughout the development process, I felt it was important to look at the project further along, so that we could see how to reengineer the product based on some questionable decisions we might have made earlier in the project. By doing it this way it will be possible to see these decisions within the context of how we might normally build an application.

In this chapter we shall:

- Learn about debugging options in Unity
- Learn how to profile a mobile application
- Learn about object pooling and why it's crucial on mobile devices
- Learn how to optimize lighting with Beast Lighting

This chapter is where we will highlight some of the key differences between making a game for Unity and making one for Unity on a mobile device. This chapter will make the biggest difference between our application being a hit and it just bring a pretty showpiece that people uninstall a few hours after launching it.

Debugging

Unity possesses a debugger that is a first-class citizen with the rest of the Unity platform. The debugger will allow you to put breakpoints directly in your Unity scripts, and while the game is running on the target device, allow you to pause the game's execution to enable observation or tweaking of variables. This is a very powerful approach that is often times missing when developing for a device. In the past, the best one could do is emit sounds or change screen colors when certain conditions were met. Today you can watch the values of variables change, make modifications to scripts that are executing on the device, and change the flow of execution of the game dynamically without much impact to the game's frame rate. So let's take a look at how we make this magic happen.

Debugging a running application on real hardware is something that you need to be very comfortable with. While Unity can do an admirable job of helping you simulate your content on your Mac, there is nothing that beats knowing how your application will perform in the wild.

A breakpoint is a place in your game where you want to pause the execution of the application for debugging purposes. As the Unity scripting environment, MonoDevelop, is integrated with the Unity IDE, and consequently the runtime, we can insert breakpoints in our scripts, which will trigger the pause in execution.

Time for action – Using breakpoints

1. Position the carat on the line that you want to pause execution on and use the hotkey combination **Apple-** to create the breakpoint. For many keyboard-centric developers this is the preferred way of doing things.

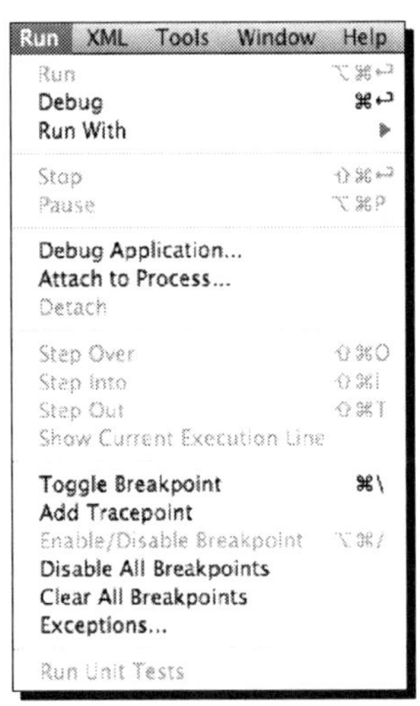

The other method is to click on the spine area to the left of the code and line numbers. If you are more a mouse-centric developer, you will find this to be the more natural way for setting breakpoints.

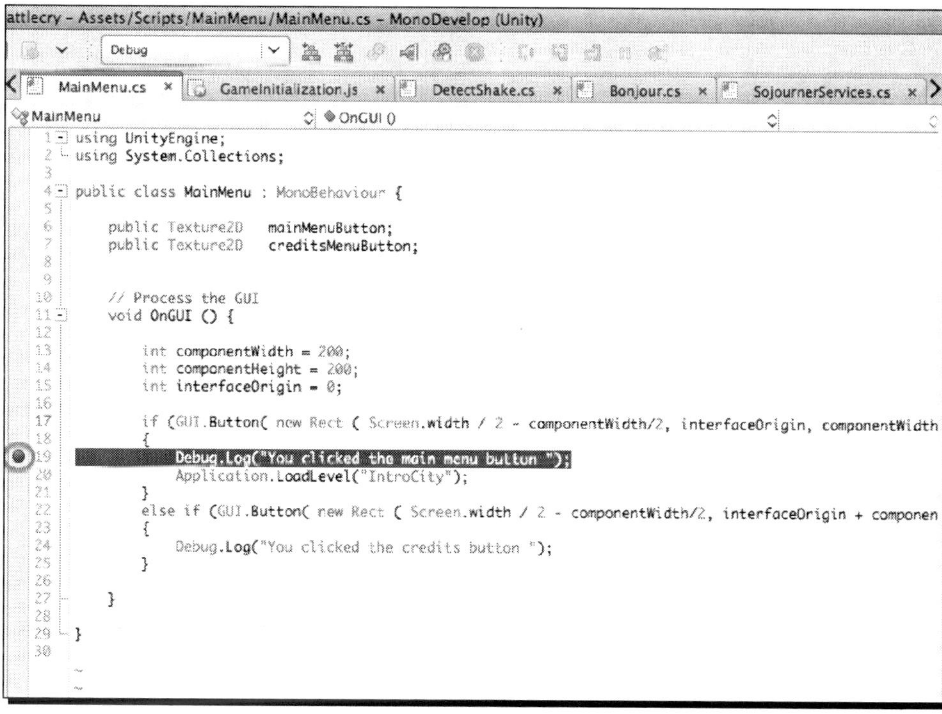

2. Observe that the line that you created the breakpoint on is highlighted with a red circle in the spine next to the code. This represents an active breakpoint.

To deactivate a breakpoint, simply click on the red circle or press **Apple-** again and the breakpoint will be removed.

It should be noted that if you create a breakpoint on a line that contains no actual code, the break point would actually execute on the next line of executable code.

3. Run the application.

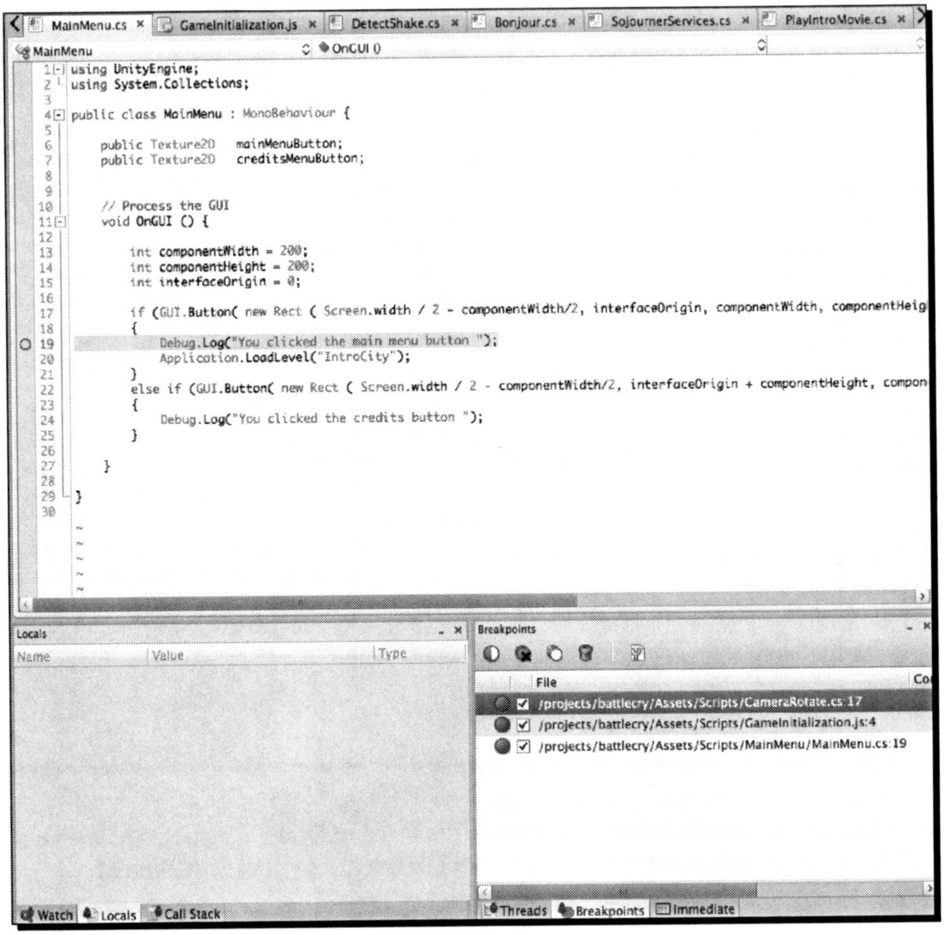

We can now observe that the application stops on the line where the breakpoint was located. This gives us an opportunity to observe the state of the application at the time when the breakpoint is reached. Many times it is useful to put a breakpoint inside of some control structure, such as an `if` statement, to see if the conditions which should trigger it are ever met.

What just happened?

You have just created a breakpoint within your application and had your app stop on the line specified. When the application is in this state it is paused so that you can examine and/or change the state of any variables of the application.

Time for action – Debugging the application

The process of getting the debugger to communicate with the running application and provide data to the user is known as attaching the debugger to the process.

1. Deploy and run your game on your iOS device. Make sure that the device is on the same WiFi network as the machine that will be doing the debugging and then select the iOS device that you want to attach to.
2. Select the **Debug** button in the toolbar:

MonoDevelop will then launch the Unity editor and after some time start the execution of your application. Your application will begin running in the player and stop when the first breakpoint in your code is encountered:

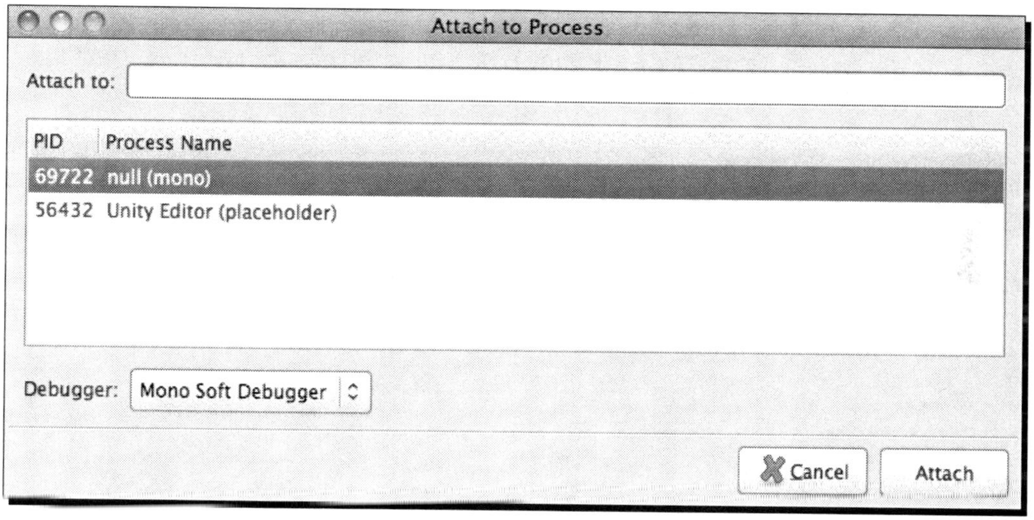

3. Select the game that you want the Unity debugger to attach itself to. In this image we see the Unity Editor as one process we can attach to and another referred to as "null (mono)." This is your game running on your iOS device. Select this instance of your game.

What just happened?

We have just attached our debugger to an instance of our game that is running on our iOS device. This is very useful as we can get real debugging information from our actual device. When testing an application it is important to do this, as there will be times when an application will run fine within Unity on the PC, yet fail on an actual device.

Time for action – Stepping through the game

Once you have reached a breakpoint and examined variable values at that point, the next thing you will want to do is step forward in the application so you can watch the application change over time. There are several options available to you for stepping forward through the application depending on what your intentions are. The following screenshot shows these options: **Step Over**, **Step Into**, **Step Out**, **Pause**, and **Detach Debugger**:

1. Press the Step into icon so that the application will start.
2. As you can see below, the application is paused at the breakpoint. The current line of execution is highlighted in yellow:

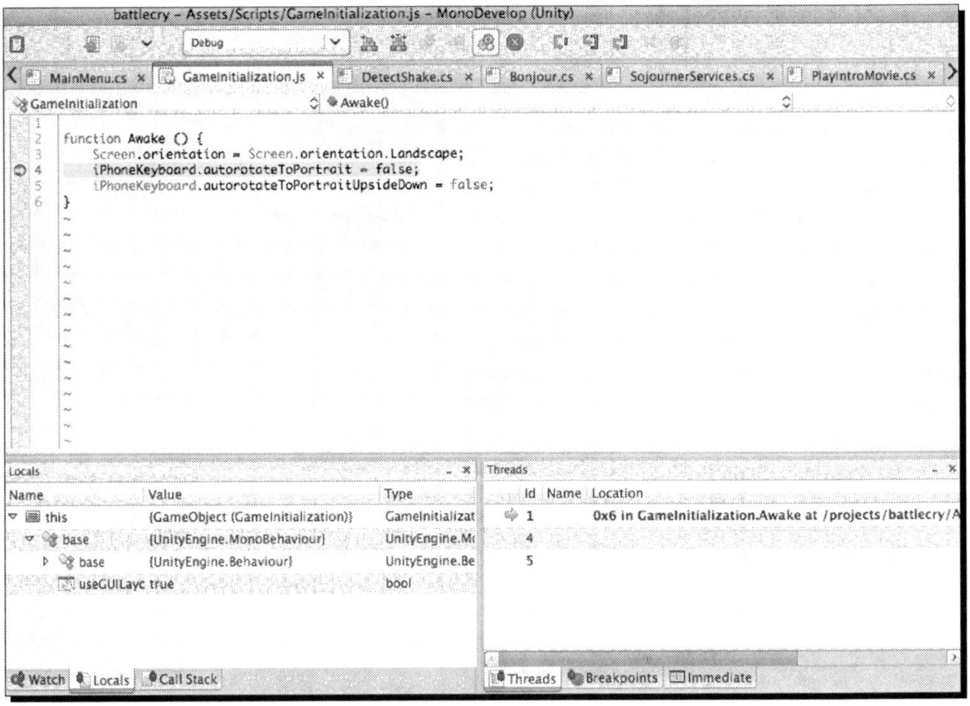

As mentioned earlier, when the debugger is attached, you can get the value of any variable in your game. However, it would be cumbersome to have to constantly look for each individual variable, especially if there is a variable that we want to examine over time. You can accomplish this by setting up a watch for a variable of interest and observe its value as it changes.

3. Create a new watch by selecting the **Watch** tab in MonoDevelop. Enter the word **Screen** into the **Watch** tab to have MonoDevelop open an autocomplete dialog showing all of the attributes of the **Screen** object:

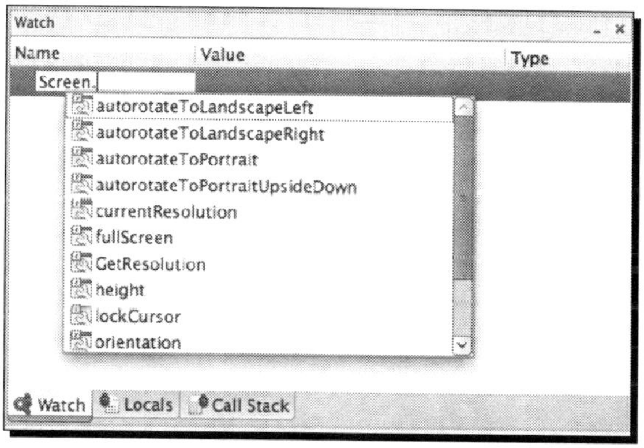

We can see here that **Screen** has a **currentResolution** attribute attached to it.

4. Select **currentResolution** so that a watch is created for this variable. If the variable you've selected is an object, you will see a triangle to the left of it. Clicking on this triangle will display any attributes of the object as shown in the following screenshot:

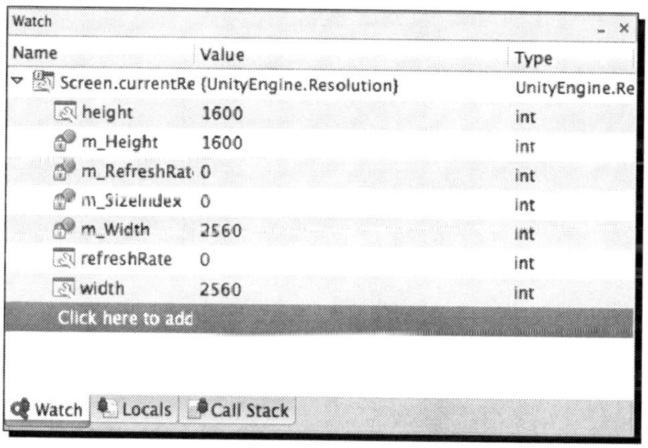

Here we are able to see all of the attributes of the **Screen.currentResolution** object.

What just happened?

We have just stepped through our application using the attached debugger and added a watch so that we can observe a variable as it changes over time. Adding watches is a common way to examine variables as they change during the execution of the game. As you begin writing complex scripts, creating watches will help you determine whether or not the correct behaviors are happening at runtime.

Profiling

We've been going along building our game and running it for sometime and it appears to be performing okay, but to really determine how our game is performing, we are going to have to profile. Profiling is the act of gathering information about how each part of our game is performing so that we can optimize the code or assets that are causing performance bottlenecks.

We could make some assumptions about how the game is running and start blindly optimizing code because it should be faster to do it a certain way, but in reality, the biggest performance wins won't be obvious until you see what the profiler is telling you about the game. To successfully profile an application one has to really look at the data objectively as poor performance could result from texture sizes, shaders, scripts, physics, draw calls, or even something as simple as adding fog.

So let's go through our current application and walk through the process of profiling it.

Time for action – Fine tuning the application (Pro Versions)

Now we're going to take our application and tune it so that it performs well, and has consistent behavior, regardless of where we are in the environment.

1. Start the Profiler by selecting it from the **Window** menu (**Window** | **Profiler**):

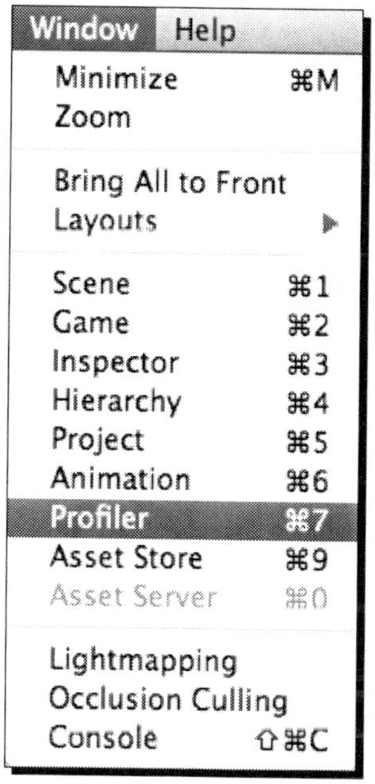

The profiler will start and display the profiling interface for Unity. If you are familiar with the XCode tool Instruments you will find many of the same design and interface concepts in the Unity profiler:

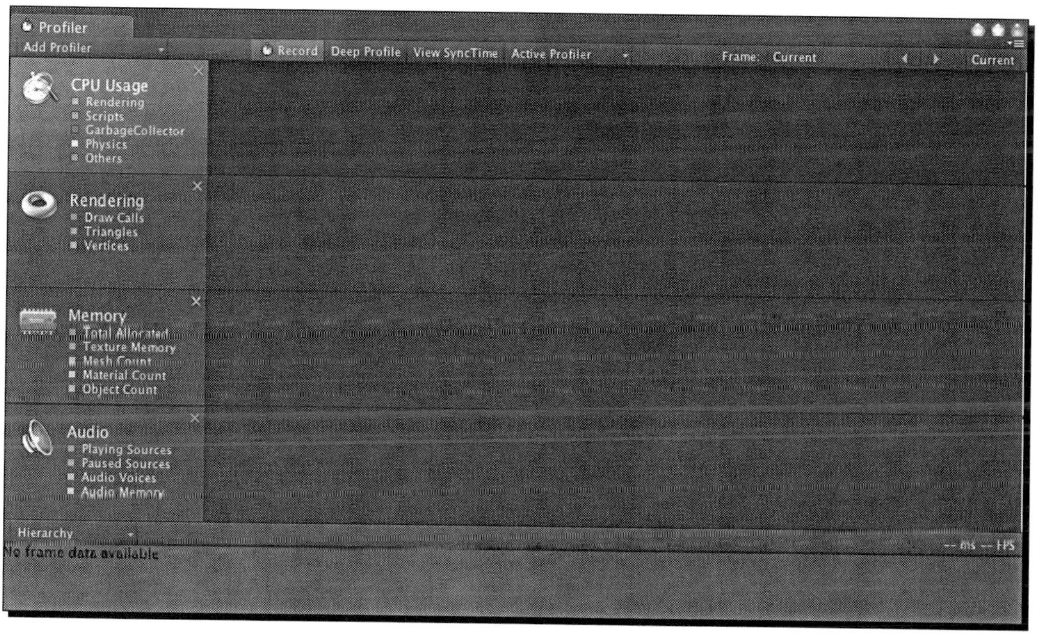

The **Profiler** will display metrics across a range of different settings: **CPU Usage**, **Rendering**, **Memory**, **Audio**, and **Physics**. You can remove profilers by clicking on the X in the upper-left corner of the **Profiler**.

2. Remove the **Audio** profiler by clicking on the X in the upper-left corner of the **Profiler**:

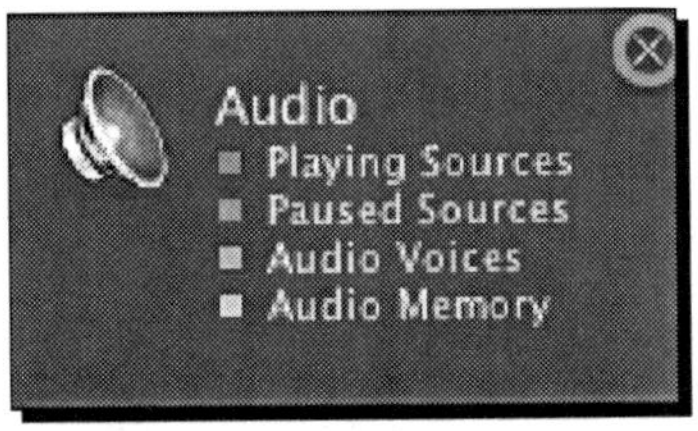

3. Add the **Audio** profiler back by clicking on the **Add Profiler** drop-down and selecting the **Audio** profiler:

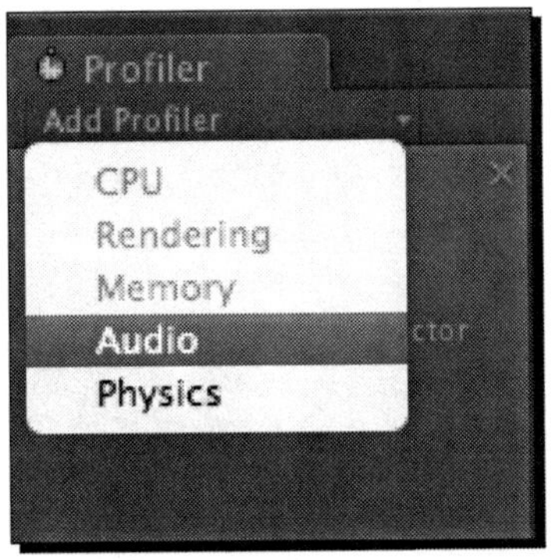

The profilers that are already added will be greyed out. In this example both **Audio** and **Physics** can be added to the **Profiler**.

4. Start the game by pressing the **Play** button. Immediately you will see the profiler fill with data from the profiling session:

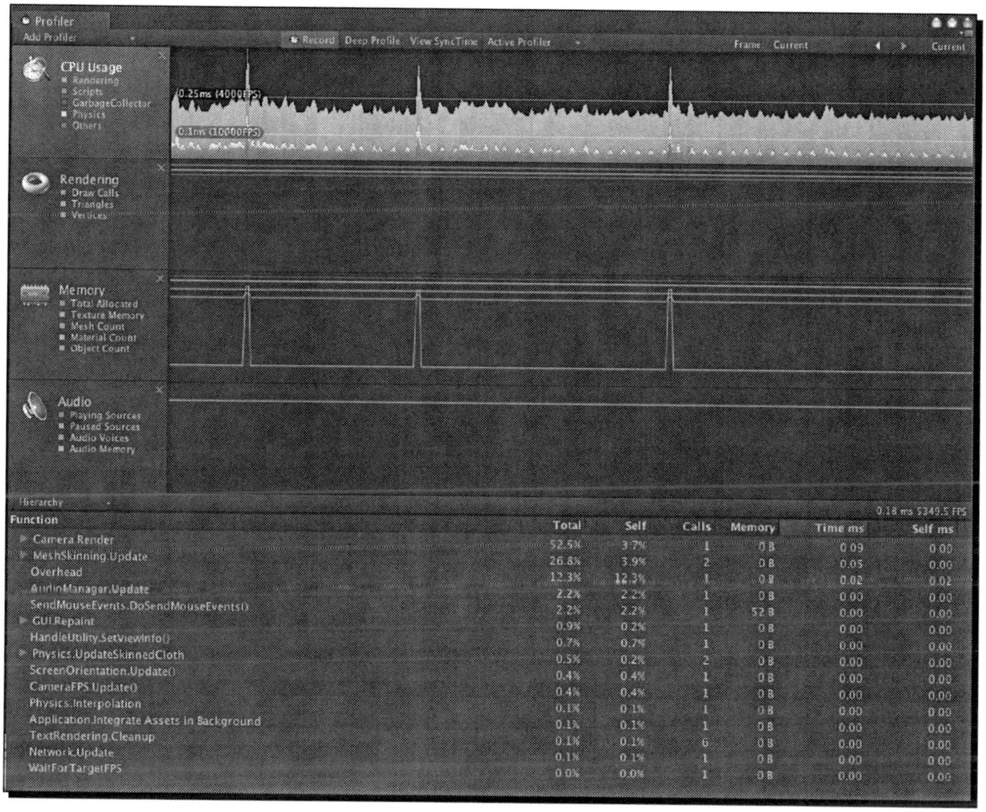

What just happened?

We have used the build in Unity profiler to examine the performance of our application and explore the different metrics that it is returning so that we can gain some insight to the bottlenecks in our application. Now that we've done this we can identify some hot spots and look at a few ways to fix the issues that we uncover.

Object pooling – Into the pool

As we have learned from our profiling session, one of the largest performance detriments on the mobile platforms is the constant creation and destruction of GameObjects. As you probably noticed earlier when we were testing out firing our weapons, there were noticeable pauses in the game every so often. Let's examine why this happens.

When an instance of the class `GameObject` is created in Unity on a mobile device, the device must allocate memory for this new instance of `GameObject` and potentially clear out memory that is used by some other object that may not be visible. This process, known as garbage collection, takes just enough time that it causes the pauses that you experience in the game. The reason this happens is due to the limited amount of memory available on the target devices and the time it takes to collect the old object. Java developers, particularly those that were brave enough to write games for the platform, are very familiar with the issues associated with garbage collection.

Typically, one will resolve some of the issues associated with garbage collection through the use of an object pool. An object pool allows one to allocate a number of objects up front and cycle through them such that new objects are never created. In the case of our weapon example we would allocate a number of objects in our game object pool that represent the max number of projectiles we want to be able to display at one time. As projectiles reach a certain distance from the player, we can remove them and free up a new object in the object pool for objects that are going to be visible next.

This particular implementation of an object pool was created by the Unity3D forum member and has an extension for particle systems as well as audio.

```
using UnityEngine;
using System;
using System.Collections;

using UnityEngine;
using System.Collections;
using System.Collections.Generic;

public class ObjectPool : MonoBehaviour
{

  public static ObjectPool instance;

  /// <summary>
  /// The object prefabs which the pool can handle.
  /// </summary>
  public GameObject[] objectPrefabs;

  /// <summary>
  /// The pooled objects currently available.
  /// </summary>
  public List<GameObject>[] pooledObjects;

  /// <summary>
```

```
/// The amount of objects of each type to buffer.
/// </summary>
public int[] amountToBuffer;

public int defaultBufferAmount = 3;

/// <summary>
/// The container object that we will keep unused pooled objects
/// so we dont clog up the editor with objects.
/// </summary>
protected GameObject containerObject;

void Awake ()
{
  instance = this;
}

// Use this for initialization
void Start ()
{
  containerObject = new GameObject("ObjectPool");

  //Loop through the object prefabs and make a new list for
  //each one.
  //We do this because the pool can only support prefabs set to it
  //in the editor,
  //so we can assume the lists of pooled objects are in the same
  //order as object prefabs in the array
  pooledObjects = new List<GameObject>[objectPrefabs.Length];

  int i = 0;
  foreach ( GameObject objectPrefab in objectPrefabs )
  {
    pooledObjects[i] = new List<GameObject>();

    int bufferAmount;

    if(i < amountToBuffer.Length) bufferAmount = amountToBuffer[i];
    else
    bufferAmount = defaultBufferAmount;

    for ( int n=0; n<bufferAmount; n++)
    {
```

```
            GameObject newObj = Instantiate(objectPrefab) as GameObject;
            newObj.name = objectPrefab.name;
            PoolObject(newObj);
          }

          i++;
        }
      }

      /// <summary>
      /// Gets a new object for the name type provided.  If no object type
      /// exists or if onlypooled is true and there is no objects of that
      /// type in the pool
      /// then null will be returned.
      /// </summary>
      /// <returns>
      /// The object for type.
      /// </returns>
      /// <param name='objectType'>
      /// Object type.
      /// </param>
      /// <param name='onlyPooled'>
      /// If true, it will only return an object if there is one currently
      /// pooled.
      /// </param>
      public GameObject GetObjectForType ( string objectType , bool
        onlyPooled )
      {
        for(int i=0; i<objectPrefabs.Length; i++)
        {
          GameObject prefab = objectPrefabs[i];
          if(prefab.name == objectType)
          {

            if(pooledObjects[i].Count > 0)
            {
              GameObject pooledObject = pooledObjects[i][0];
              pooledObjects[i].RemoveAt(0);
              pooledObject.transform.parent = null;
              pooledObject.SetActiveRecursively(true);

              return pooledObject;

            }
            else if(!onlyPooled) {
```

```
          return Instantiate(objectPrefabs[i]) as GameObject;
        }

        break;

      }
    }

    //If we have gotten here either there was no object of the specified
    //type or none were left in the pool with onlyPooled set to true
    return null;
    }

    /// <summary>
    /// Pools the object specified.  Will not be pooled if there are no
    /// prefab of that type.
    /// </summary>
    /// <param name='obj'>
    /// Object to be pooled.
    /// </param>
    public void PoolObject ( GameObject obj )
    {
      for ( int i=0; i<objectPrefabs.Length; i++)
      {
        if(objectPrefabs[i].name == obj.name)
        {
          obj.SetActiveRecursively(false);
          obj.transform.parent = containerObject.transform;
          pooledObjects[i].Add(obj);
          return;
        }
      }
    }

}
```

The `ObjectPool` code is very straight-forward. It exposes several public variables so that you can configure it from the Unity IDE itself. The `ObjectPool` implemented here is designed to pool a variety of classes of objects at once. You don't need an implementation for each type of `GameObject` you want to pool. The **ObjectPool** stores each of the object types you want to pool in the `ObjectPrefabs` array.

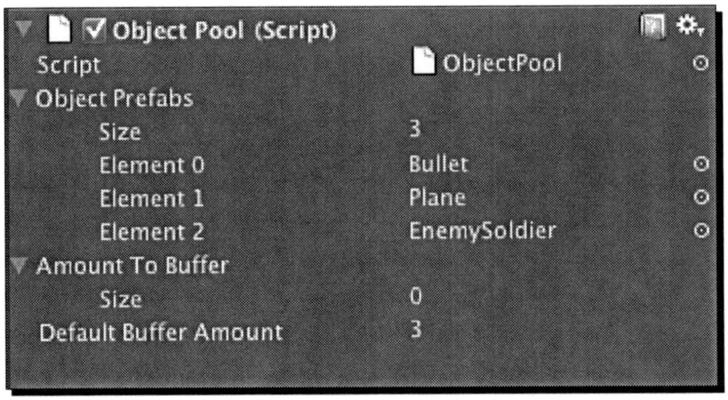

By default the pool will create a maximum of three objects of each type. If you want to configure the amount of objects that an individual object can have, expand the **Amount To Buffer** element and set that size.

Time for action – Optimizing with the object pool

Now that we have a game object pool and the ability to profile our application we can look at how this optimization improves our application's performance. We will do this by replacing the `GameObject` instantiation approach that we took to creating projectiles when the player fires his weapon.

1. Connect the game to the profiler following the previous *Time for action* and run it, firing a large number of projectiles:

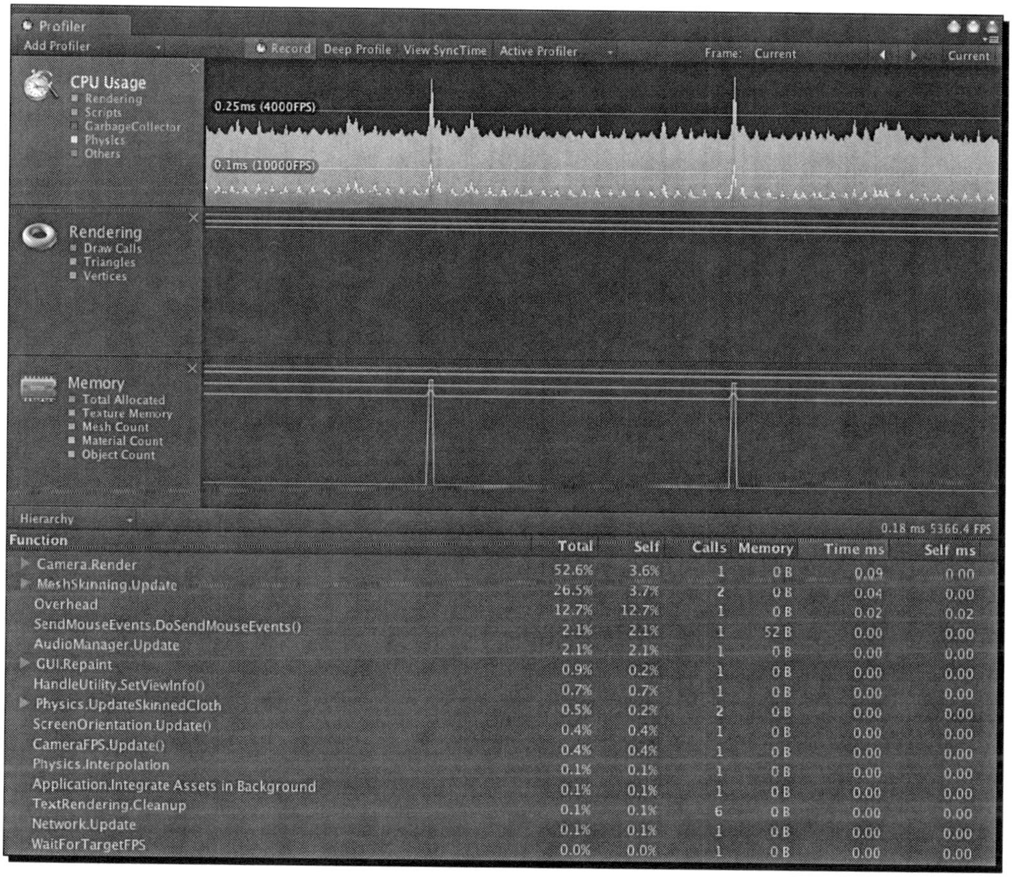

What we can see from this object profile is that performance dips considerably when the weapon is fired. The reason for this is because we are creating GameObjects on the fly. We can see here that when these objects are removed from view and collected, the performance of the application becomes more consistent. Things like this are a smoking gun and we have an optimization that can be made to improve performance of the game.

2. Create a **GameObject** called **PoolManager**:

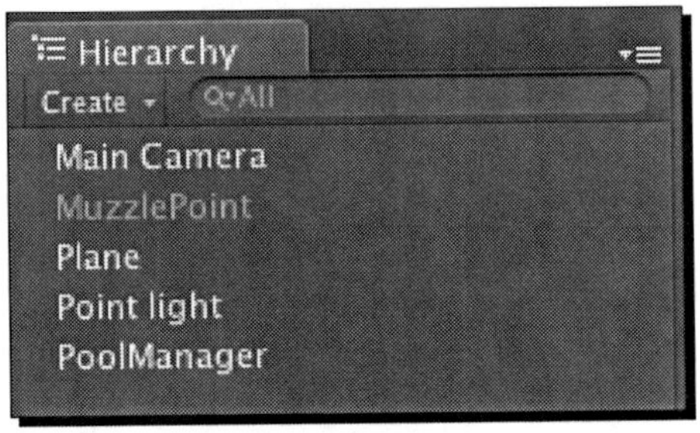

3. Add the **ObjectPool** script to the **PoolManager**:

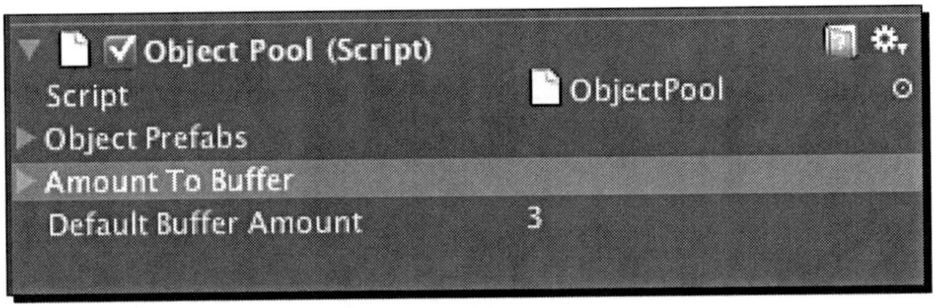

4. Add the prefabs that you want to pool to the **Object Prefabs** array. You can accomplish this by dragging a prefab from the **Hierarchy** view onto the **Object Prefabs** array:

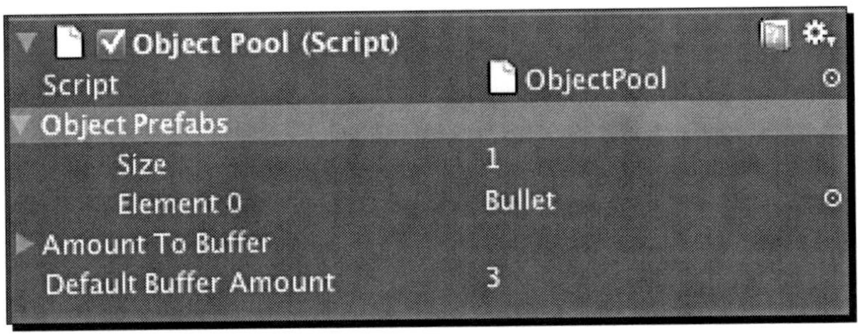

5. Replace the existing `fireWeapon` script with the optimized `fireWeapon` script that uses the **Object Pool**:

```
void fireWeapon()
{
        GameObject bullet = ObjectPool.instance.GetObjectForType(
"Bullet" , true);
```

```
        bullet.transform.position = spawnPoint.transform.position;
        bullet.transform.rotation = spawnPoint.transform.rotation;
}
```

What we have done here is replace the `GameObject.Instantiate()` method that we were originally using for creating new bullets from our weapon.

6. Start the game again and look at the **Profiler** profile. Fire a lot of projectiles and examine the performance.

What just happened?

We have just improved the performance of our application using object pooling. As you can see, the performance of the application is consistent now. This is what we are aiming for – a consistent frame rate.

Instead of paying the penalty for creating and deleting large numbers of `GameObject` instances, we are instead creating a pool of those objects and simply changing their position, rotation, state, and visibility. This is an old trick that was frequently employed in gaming that was lost in the age of modern computers and graphics capabilities, but is just what we need on mobile devices to ensure optimal performance.

Unleash the beast

So often when you're trying to improve the performance of your application you will have to make trade-offs between the visual presentation of your application and its performance. This time we will perform optimizations that will enhance both the performance and visual quality of our application is by using the integrated Beast lightmapping system from Illuminate Labs.

The goal of lighting in our game is to provide a realistic depiction of our world. Normally the objects in the world would have some base material or texture that describes their natural surface. The lighting algorithms used by the engine would then compute the effects of the lights on the pixels or texels of the object's surface when it is rendered.

Lightmapping, as its name implies, is the process of utilizing lighting data (emissive properties, real lights, and so on) and casting rays from these lights as if they were active in the scene. The engine will then take the actual effect of these lights and store it in texture maps that will be mapped onto textures at run time (Unity refers to this process as baking the lights). As a result you can have a very complex lighting environment based upon a computationally intensive number of lights. You can also have all of this information baked into the texture maps of the scene, resulting in increased visual quality without the expense of having lights within your scene.

As lighting is one of the more expensive operations you can perform on mobile devices, using lightmaps represents a major performance win. While lightmapping will eventually be replaced with per pixel lighting in shaders, today's mobile hardware isn't quite up to the task.

So let's look at how we can make this work for our application.

Time for action – Generating Beast lightmaps

To illustrate how lightmapping can improve our application we're going to take our City level scene and add Beast lightmapping to it.

1. The first step in preparing our scene for lightmapping is to ensure that any object that we want to have lightmaps generated for is declared static. Unity uses this declaration to make assumptions that the object won't move, scale, or change in any way during the scene. Remember, we only want to bake lightmaps on static geometry, as we're generating lighting based on the location of lights in the scene at a given time. If we tried to use this approach on objects that moved, for example, you'd find that even though an object changes its orientation with respect to a light, the lighting and shadow calculations would look as if the object were in a different place:

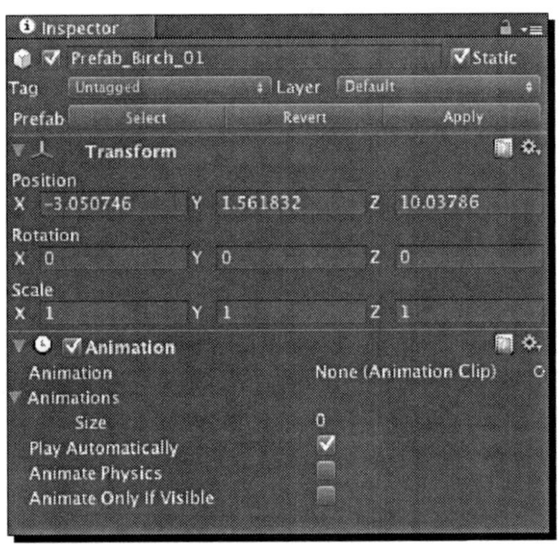

   Here we have specified that one of our birch tree prefabs is **Static**. Similarly we can add the same settings to the terrain.

2. Add a light to the scene using **Game Object | Create Other | Point Light**. Position this light in our scene. This is the light whose lighting effects we want to bake into our scene. Now that our objects are defined as being static, let's add a light to the scene that we want to bake to our objects:

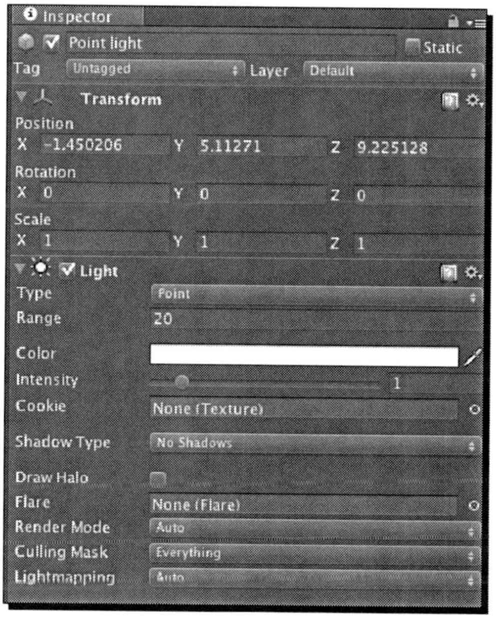

3. Observe the scene to see what everything looks like when the lighting is rendering normally. This will give us an idea of what the lightmapped scene should look like if we perform the operation properly:

Now that we've provided some lighting data for the lightmapper to work with, we can start the baking process.

4. In the **Window** menu select the **Lightmapping** option to bring up the Beast lightmapping interface:

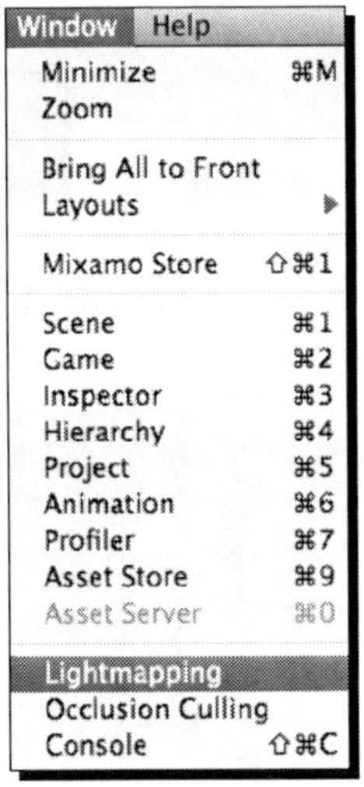

This will open the Unity Lightmapping interface which allows us to configure the Beast lightmapping session:

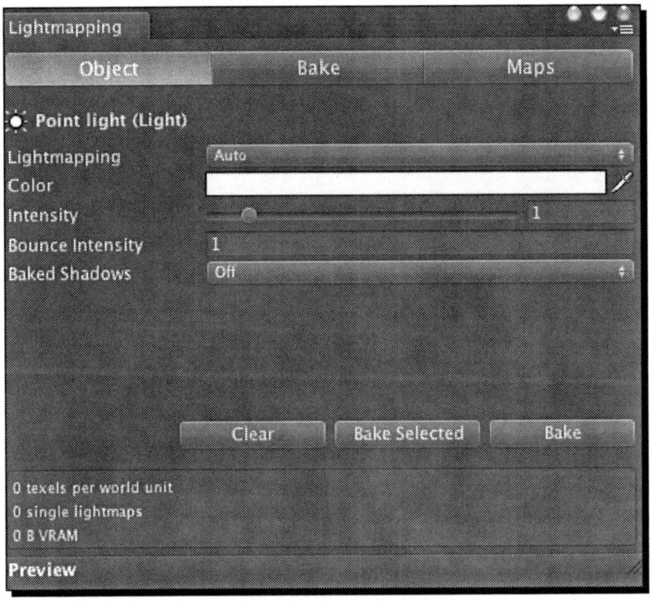

5. With the interface is open, select the **Point light** we added to the scene and click on the **Bake** tab:

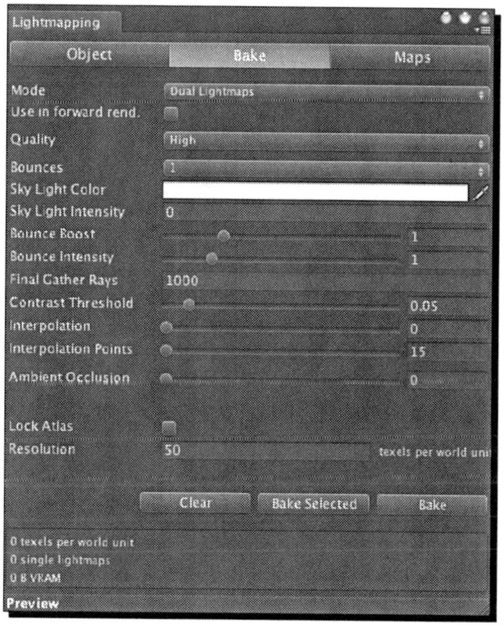

6. We can take our simple light and have it baked into the lightmaps of the scene. Press the **Bake** button and observe the debug output window:

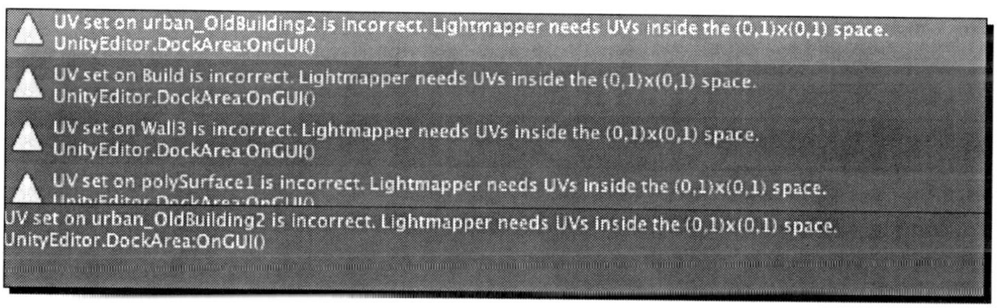

The output window is telling us that it is unable to bake the lights because there is no UV data for the geometry in our scene. Remember that our lightmaps are texture maps that are being added as a texture map and, as such, if the geometry does not have UVs generated properly it cannot generate the lightmaps.

7. Select the geometry that Unity is reporting does not have UV data and select its **FBXImporter**. Click on the **Generate Lightmap UVs** button to ensure that Unity generates the UV information for this piece of geometry:

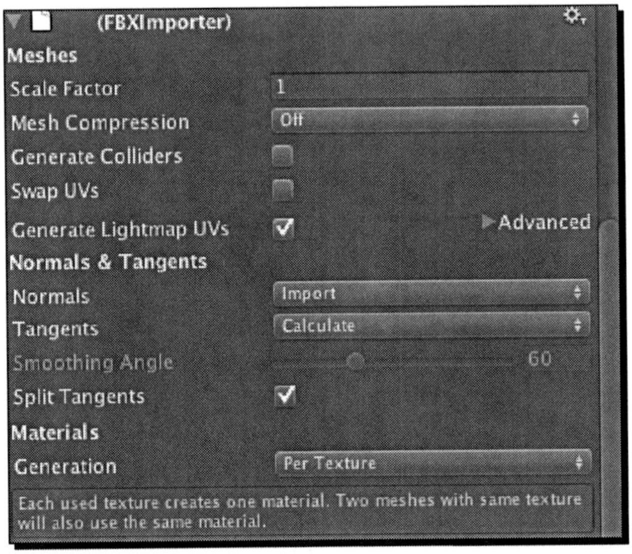

Now when you bake the scene, Unity will be able to generate a properly lightmapped scene.

8. Select the **Point light** in the **Hierarchy** view and delete it from the scene. When you run the game you will note that the game looks exactly the same as it did before but it is now running without the performance overhead of the lights in the scene.

What just happened?

What Unity is doing behind the scenes is taking all of the assets and scripts from the Unity IDE and putting together a player that will be able to playback the content and all of its scenarios based on input from the user. This is a very important concept to understand as the content within the Unity IDE is largely platform agnostic and can be readily redeployed after a simple recompile within the Unity environment. This player is the the actual application that is deployed to the iOS device.

Summary

In this chapter we learned a little bit about the topic of debugging, profiling and optimizing Unity projects. We've really only just scratched the surface on the subject, however, as game optimization can fill a book in its own right and much of it is related to the design of a particular application.

Specifically, we covered:

- How to attach the Unity debugger to a running application
- How to profile a Unity application
- Using object pooling to improve mobile application performance
- Using Beast lightmapping to improve performance and visual quality

Now that we've profiled our application and worked specifically to improve its performance it's time to investigate monetization of our game and publish it on the AppStore.

12

Commercialization: Make 'fat loot' from your Creation

According to the American Marketing Association, marketing is the process of planning and executing the conception, pricing, promotion, and distribution of ideas, goods, and services to create exchanges that satisfy individual and organizational goals. While most people equate marketing with advertising, marketing encompasses market analysis, value proposition, product differentiation, market strategies, and so on. While we don't need all of this in order to build our game, we need to examine portions of marketing to determine what is the best way to bring it to market and make money from all our hard work. Should we charge 99 cents, should we give it away and depend on advertising, or should we try to license the game to a third party? These are all questions that this chapter will help us answer.

In this chapter we shall discuss:

- How to add IAds to a product
- How to add In-App purchases
- How to publish content to the Unity Asset Store
- How to publish the final version of our product
- How to track success with iTunes Connect

This is our final step to putting out a quality application that generates revenue and produces happy customers – our number one priority.

So let's get on with it...

Business model generation

At the time of writing there are over 200 million iOS devices in the hands of consumers, nearly 15 billion downloads of applications from the App Store, with over 2.5 billion dollars being paid to developers in App Store sales. While this alone would have the average developer salivating, one must also consider that there are over 300,000 applications in the App Store with a growth rate of 11,000–15,000 applications per month. As such, one cannot depend on simply shipping a title and expecting it to make money. You will need an approach for how to target customers, get your app on their device and extract money from them – and that approach is commonly referred to as a business model.

While normally one would discuss this as the first topic when planning to build a revenue generating venture, most people's eyes would glaze over in the first chapter and they'd put the book back on the shelf.

As the Apple App Store ecosystem has developed, four successful business models have emerged as viable ways to capitalize on your creation: pure app sales, advertising, In-App purchases, and marketplace component sales.

Pure app sales

This is the traditional approach to publishing applications on the App Store. You produce an application, set a price based on some pricing strategy, and then release it to the App Store and wait for customers to purchase your application.

Advertising

The advertising model is typically used for applications that are distributed for free, though some applications charge money and still include advertisements. Nevertheless, as the game is started or played, the application makes a request to an ad network to include ad content somewhere in the game. As people watch these ads or interact with them, the ad supplier pays the application creator.

In-App purchases

The In-App purchase model is quickly establishing itself as the business model of choice for mobile applications. There are two models generally used with In-App purchases. In the first model one develops a form of currency and players use that currency to purchase items in the game world. In the second model, developers sell additional weapons, tracks, vehicles, and so on, which are then added to an existing game to enhance the player's experience.

Marketplace component

While not truly a model for selling a game, selling components on a marketplace is something you can consider if you are building components and prefabs for your game and either decide that they are no longer useful for you, or that you want make some money without publishing an entire game. In addition, if you develop a novel solution to a common development problem, you should sell it on `www.gameprefabs.com` or within the Unity Asset store itself.

There isn't anything preventing you from choosing just one of these business models or implementing all of them in a single product. The only thing you need to do is balance your desire to make money with the end-user experience. So long as you aren't very intrusive into the user playing your game, the model will not annoy the users, but if they begin to feel as if you're fleecing them, you will kill the goose that lays the golden egg.

Time for action – Readying your app for sale

We've finally reached the point that we've been waiting for. We're going to prepare our game for distribution to customers, set a price, and then publish the application for sale. Unlike the developer portal that we've been using up to this point, to publish our content for consumption we need to use the **iTunes Connect** portal located at: `http://itunesconnect.apple.com`.

1. Log into the **iTunes Connect** portal using the credentials you normally use to connect to the developer portal:

2. Select the **Manage Your Applications** link to start the process of adding an application:

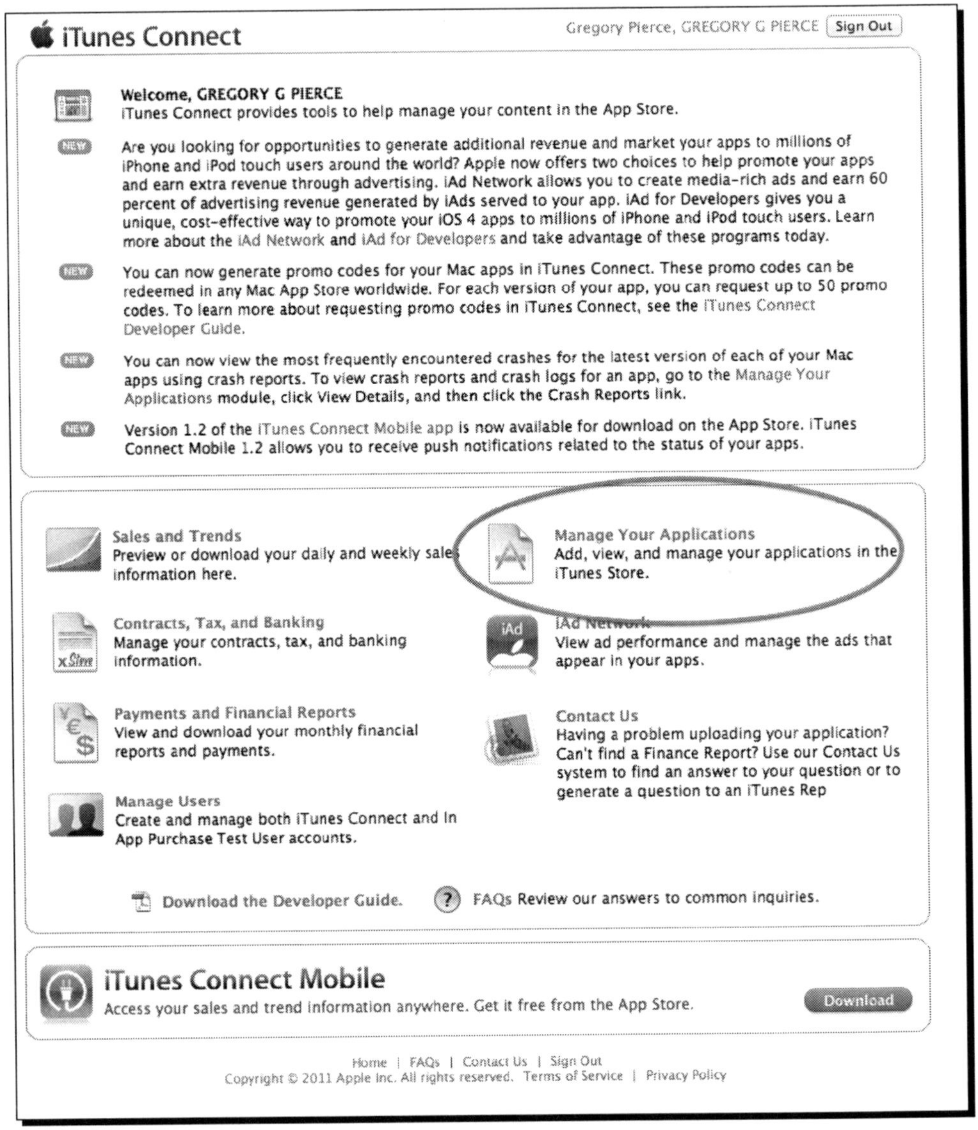

3. Select the **Primary Language** for your country and enter the name of your company or the name under which you will be doing business legally:

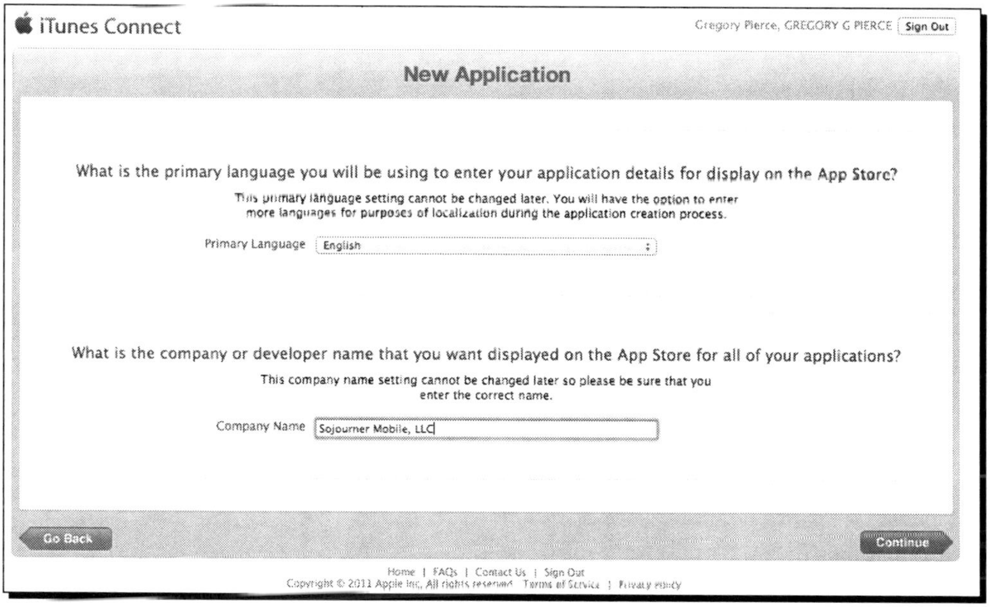

4. Next you need to tell **iTunes Connect** which type of application you're going to create. If you have the ability to create both iOS apps and OSX apps simply select the iOS icon:

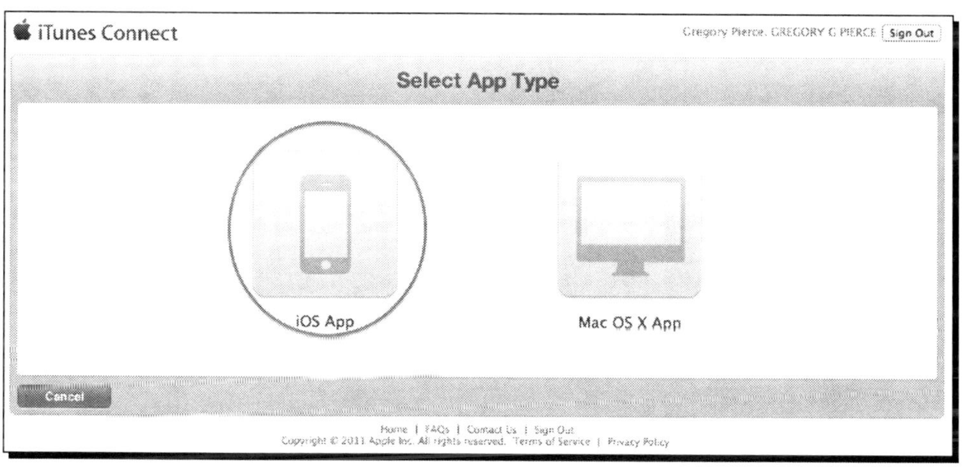

5. Now that **iTunes Connect** knows what type of application we're trying to create enter the **App Name, SKU Number**, and **Bundle ID** that represent your application:

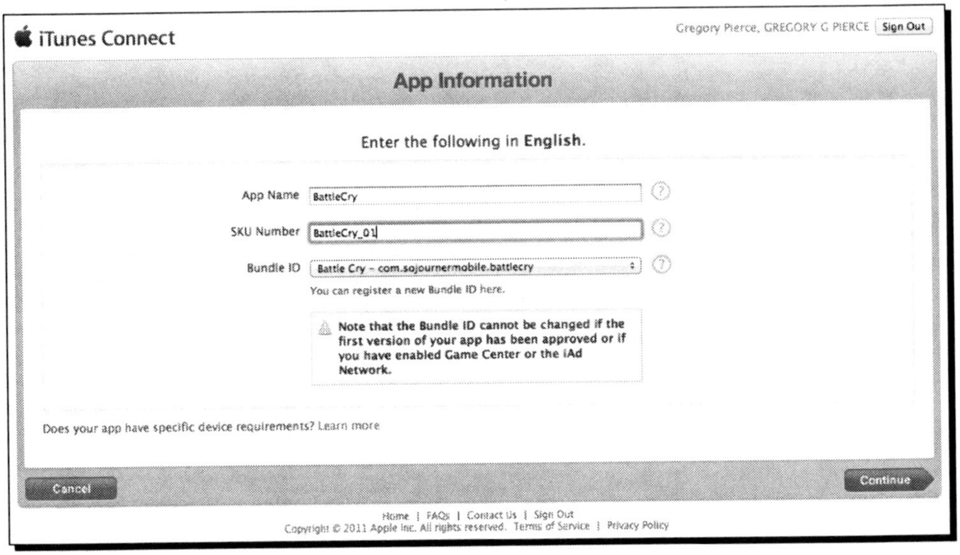

6. After entering this information its time to set your price. Enter a date for when this product will be available. Set the price to be **Free**. Press the **View Pricing Matrix** option to see what other options you have for pricing.

> If you want to provide a discount for educational institutions through mass purchases, check the checkbox for this option.

The second option **Custom B2B App** is for applications that are being offered to business customers for volume purchases (`http://www.apple.com/business/vpp/`). If you check this box your game will not be available on the regular app store.

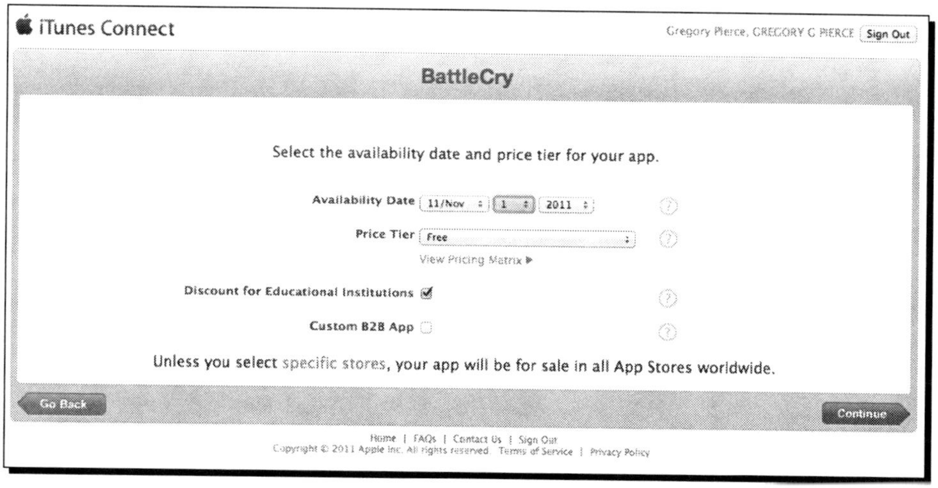

7. Next enter the metadata for the game. This is the information that will be used to populate the iTunes app store page:

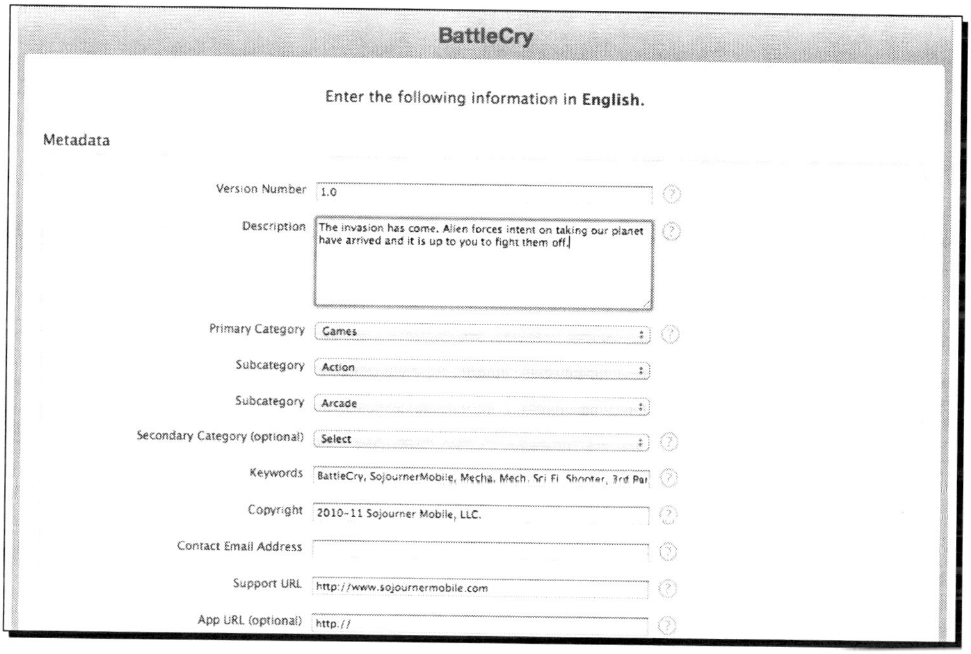

8. To ensure that the application is rated and targeting the appropriate audience select the appropriate options for the application. Most importantly make sure any ratings of maturity and violence are properly represented or your application will be rejected. If your application has prolonged graphic, sadistic, sexual, or nude content it is not permissible to sell this content on the app store:

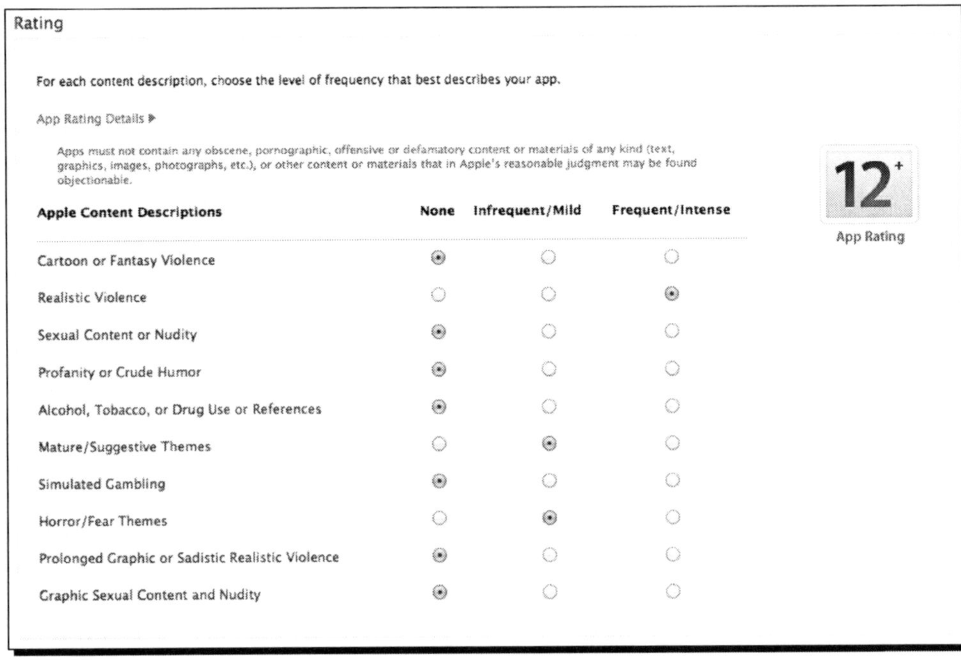

9. The final step is to provide **iTunes Connect** with artwork, which will be used on the iTunes store. Depending on your target platform you will have to provide up to three pieces of artwork.

   The **Large** version of your app icon is the one that will be used in the App Store. It must be at least 72 DPI and a minimum of 512x512 pixels (it cannot be scaled up). It must be flat artwork without rounded corners.

   iPhone and iPod touch Screenshots must be either a `.jpeg`, `.jpg`, `.tif`, `.tiff`, or `.png` file that is 960x640, 960x600, 640x960, 640x920, 480x320, 480x300, 320x480, or 320x460 pixels, at least 72 DPI, and in the RGB color space.

   iPad Screenshots must be either a `.jpeg`, `.jpg`, `.tif`, `.tiff`, or `.png` file that is 1024x768, 1024x748, 768x1024, or 768x1004 pixels, at least 72 DPI, and in the RGB color space:

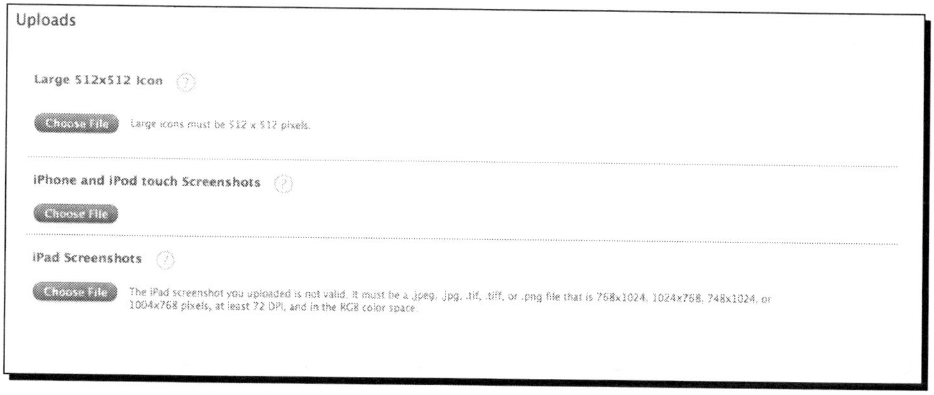

10. Now that all of the app settings have been configured, the app is ready for distribution. Under the version of the app you will note that the status is **Prepare for Upload,** which means that Apple is waiting for us to upload our game for review.

Select the application icon so that we can upload the final binary version of our game for review:

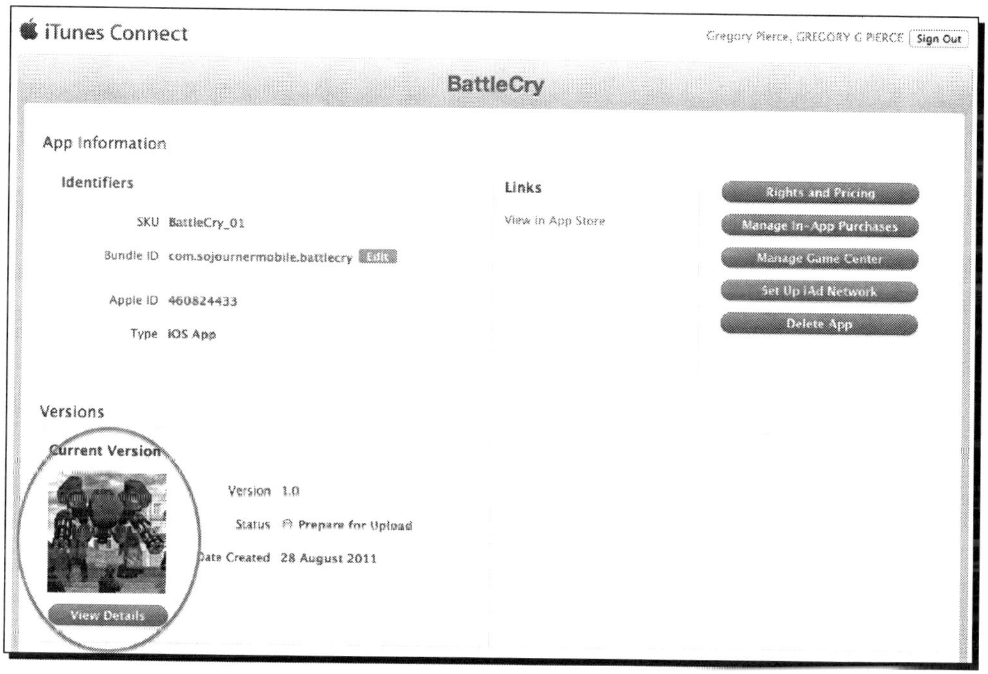

We are now ready to publish our application with the price we've set and, if it passes review by Apple, it will be available on the date that we specified as the availability date above.

What just happened?

We have just created all of the metadata for iTunes to sell our application. The remaining step before final publication is to submit the final binary to Apple. We will cover that after we have added the other components of our business model to the application.

Time for action – Adding iAds

One of the low hanging fruit for generating revenue from your application is introducing an advertising model to your existing game. You can easily display an ad in the main menu or in the loading screen of your application and not adversely impact the user experience of your customers, yet generate a reasonable amount of revenue.

As Unity itself doesn't provide functionality for adding iAds to an application, we will illustrate how to acquire this functionality using the Prime31 plugin. While it is certainly possible to also implement custom plugins, this is outside the scope of the book. More importantly, it is a better use of our time to build the application:

1. Visit the website `http://www.prime31.com` and download the iAds plugin:

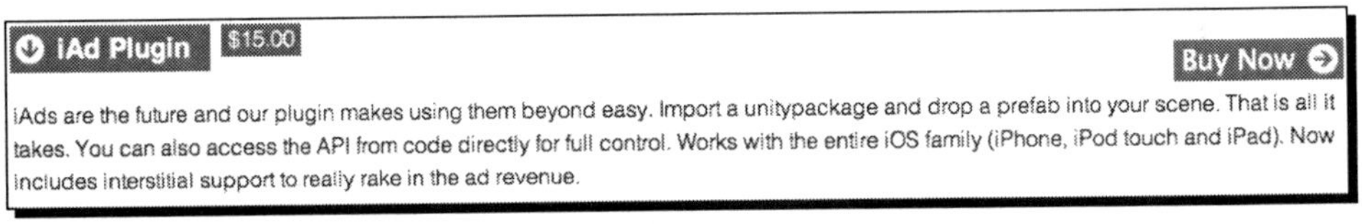

   While the plugin itself isn't free, you should make more than the cost of the plugin in ads to justify its purchase.

2. Import the purchased unitypackage by importing a custom package through the **Assets | Import Package | Custom Package** menu command:

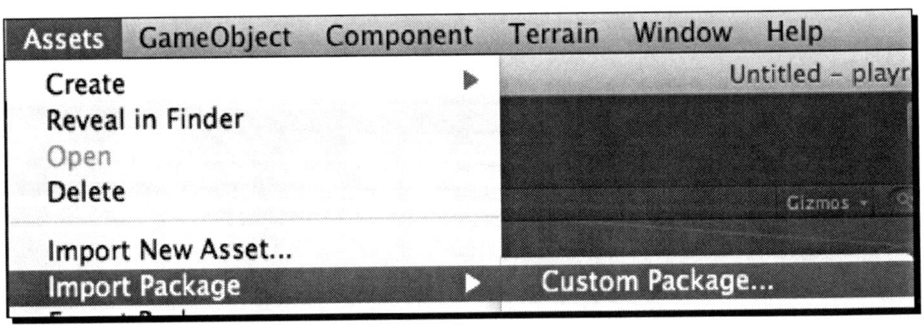

3. Select the unitypackage on your machine so that Unity can begin importing its assets:

4. Unity will now begin importing the plugin and display a dialog confirming that you wish to import all of the assets from the package into the project:

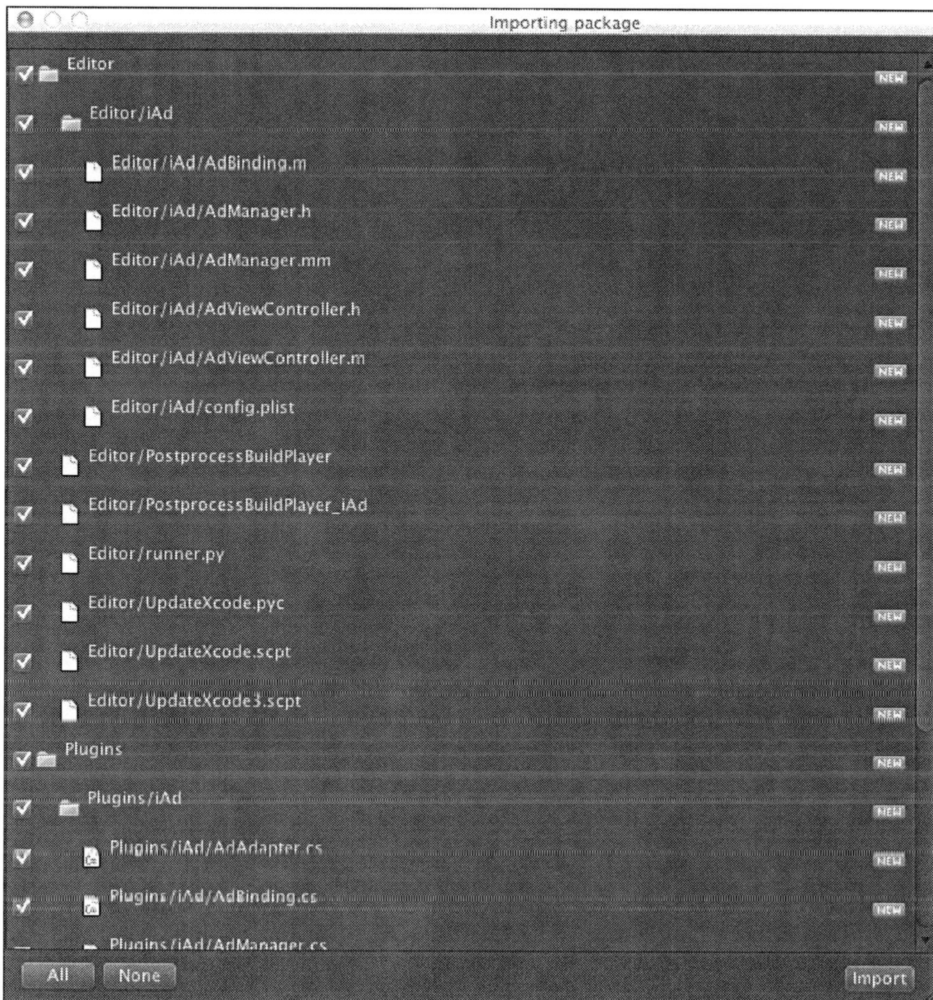

Make sure you have all of the items selected and press the **Import** button. When the import process is completed you should have two new nodes in the **Hierarchy** view:

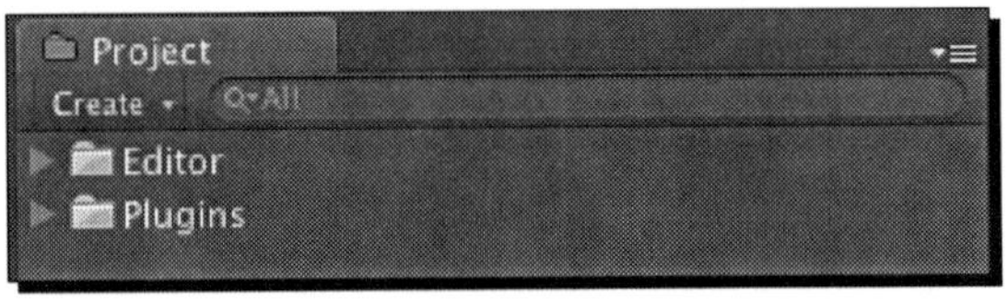

5. The iAds system comes with a ready-to-use Prefab for displaying ads, so let's drag that into our scene.

Now that this is added, our application is ready to display ads.

6. Open the application in iTunes Connect and select the **Set Up iAd Network**:

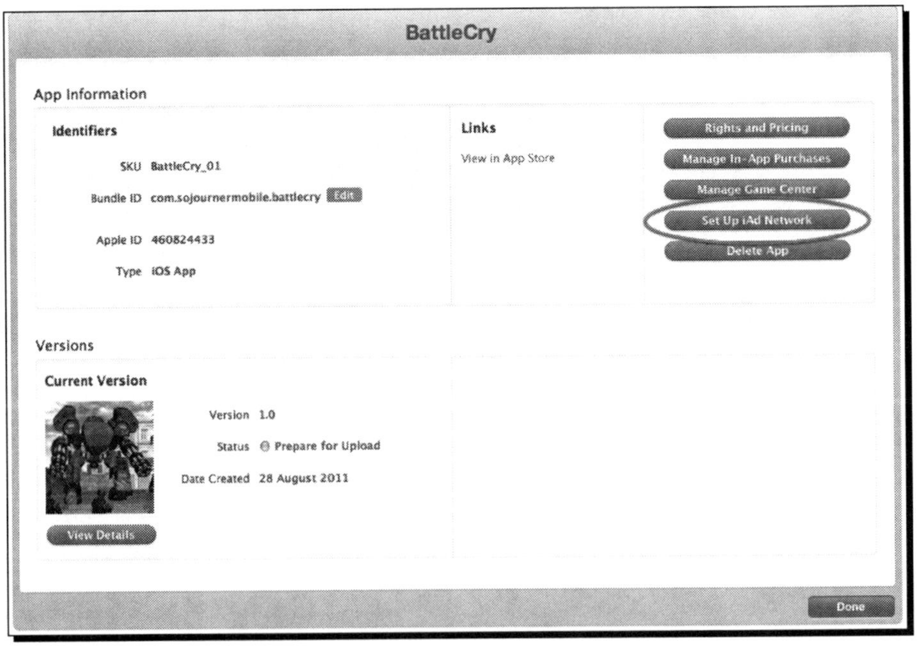

7. Enable the iAd advertising network for your application by selecting the **Enable iAds** button:

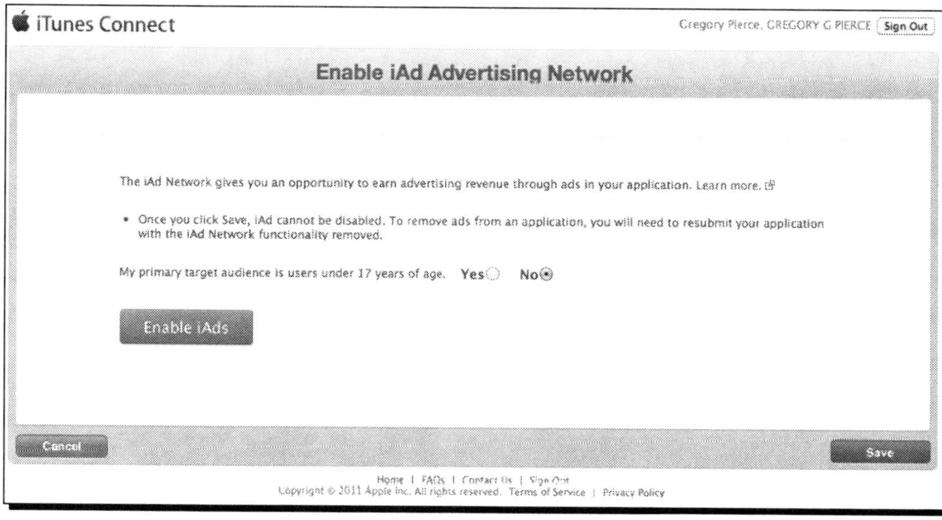

Be sure to set your primary audience appropriately. This will ensure that you are delivering advertisements appropriately for your target audience.

What just happened?

We have just added the iAd network to our application. When running our game, we will now see an iAd advertisement appear in the main scene of our application – purely driven by Apple's demographics and advertising engine. As people interact with the ads in our game you will get a check from Apple.

In-App purchases

An In-App purchase within a game provides users with the ability to purchase upgrades, access levels, weapons, or other content by transacting with the App Store. The App Store will then communicate with the game to notify it that a purchase has been authorized and that the content should be unlocked within the game. All of this takes place within the iOS SDK and the App Store commerce systems, so you will not have to deal with credit card transactions or the security of commercial transactions across the wire. Apple will handle the entire process and you will receive money in your account the same way you would with regular application purchases.

Internally, In-App purchases are accomplished using the iOS SDK Store Kit API. This API is responsible for communicating with the App Store and collecting payments from the user:

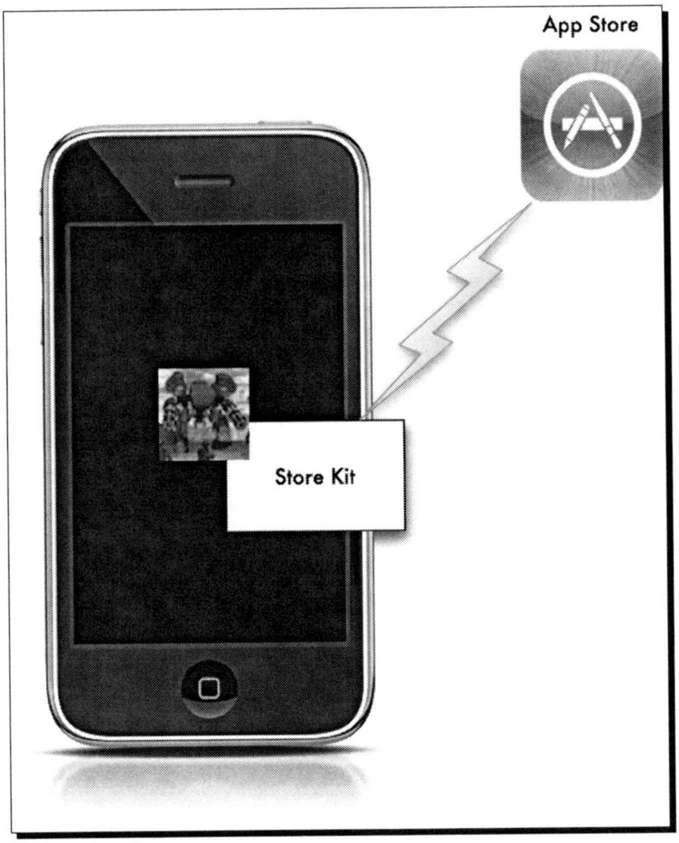

To date, Unity does not provide a channel within the iOS version of the Unity product for an application to add In-App purchases to games so, as with iAds, we will have to rely on a third-party plugin to implement this functionality. As before we will use a plugin from Prime31 – the StoreKit plugin.

Subscription types

There are four different types of In-App purchases: non-consumable, consumable, subscriptions, and auto-renewing subscriptions:

- **Non-consumable** In-App purchases represent a class of items that you purchase once and have access to continuously. These purchases can be transferred between devices on the same iTunes account. Examples of non-consumable items include game levels, weapons, vehicles, and other permanently available items.
- **Consumable** In-App purchases represent a class of items that, as the name suggests, are purchased and then consumed by the player – requiring an additional purchase each time the player wishes to use the item. Examples of consumable items include experience points, health kits, turbo boosts, ammo packs, and so on.
- **Subscriptions** are similar to magazine and newspaper subscriptions that last for a limited duration and then require the user to renew after that duration has expired. While not typical in gaming circles, an example of a subscription might be a defensive coach in a football game, which allows the player to not have to call defensive plays. The coach would be available for the duration of the subscription and after it expires the game would require the player to call defensive plays again.
- **Auto-renewable subscriptions** are those that allow the user to purchase In-App content for a set duration of time. At the end of the duration, the subscription will automatically renew, with iTunes charging the user, unless the user opts out. Examples of the auto-renewable subscriptions are the same as normal subscriptions except that the player continues to have the defensive coach until they cancel the subscription.

Delivery models

In-App purchases can use one of two delivery models with iTunes, the built-in model and the server model.

In the built-in product model, everything required for your application to deliver In-App purchases to your customer is built in to your game. This means that all of the consumable and non-consumable In-App purchases are already built into the game. Accordingly, this means that all purchase access would be defined through application identifiers. As an individual application would be responsible for maintaining these preferences they can become lost when a user moves between devices, so you must ensure that any preferences, that would preserve that state are stored in application preferences, as they are backed up by iTunes. Another solution is to use iCloud, or similar, to host these application preferences off of the device:

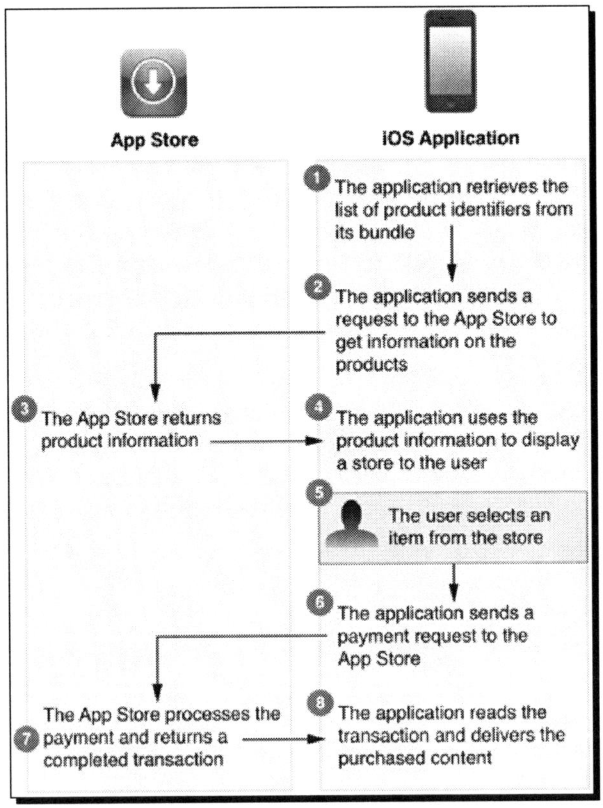

In the server product model a separate server maintains the In-App purchase content as well as the transactions with the App Store. The App Store, application and the server then orchestrate confirming purchases and delivering content to the iOS device. In this model a game would deliver new levels or other content directly to the application. While this model is compelling, at the moment it does not work well with Unity iOS applications, as Apple requires that all of your content be distributed in the application on the App Store. It is included here for completeness:

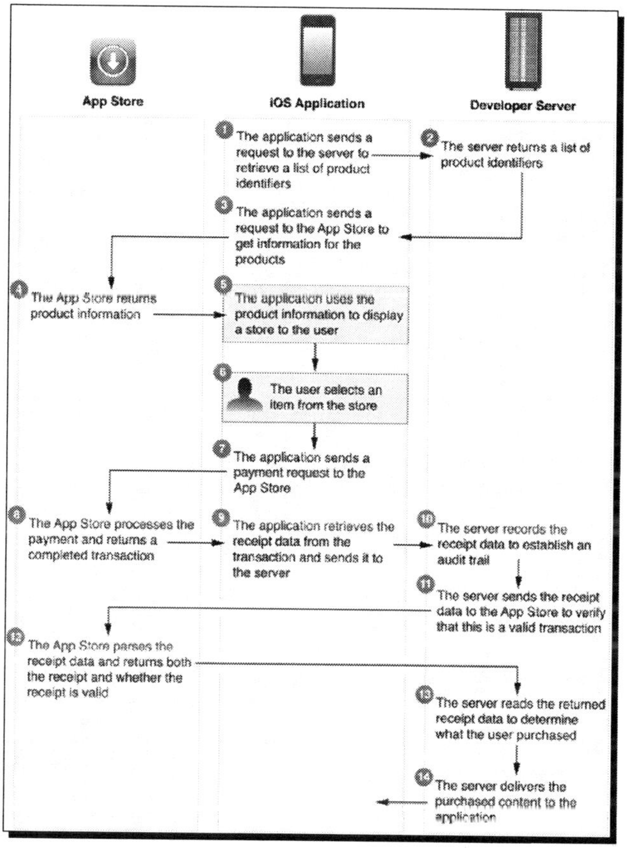

As the In-App purchase process does not provide the capability to patch an application, and since Unity will not directly load content that is not in the application bundle, it is expected that all of the content that you plan to deliver through In-App purchases will be delivered in a version of your application in the App Store.

Time for action – Adding In-App purchases

1. The first step in defining In-App purchases is to add the purchase types to the application in **iTunes Connect**. On the application profile page, select the **Manage In-App Purchases** link in the portal:

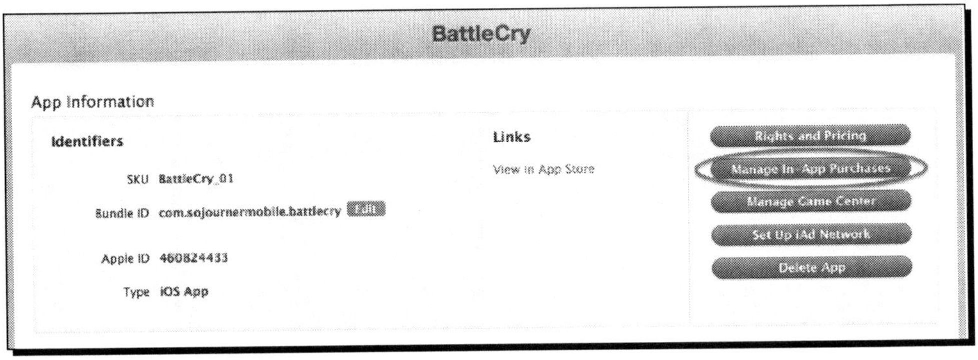

2. On the **In-App Purchases** screen select **Create New** to start the process:

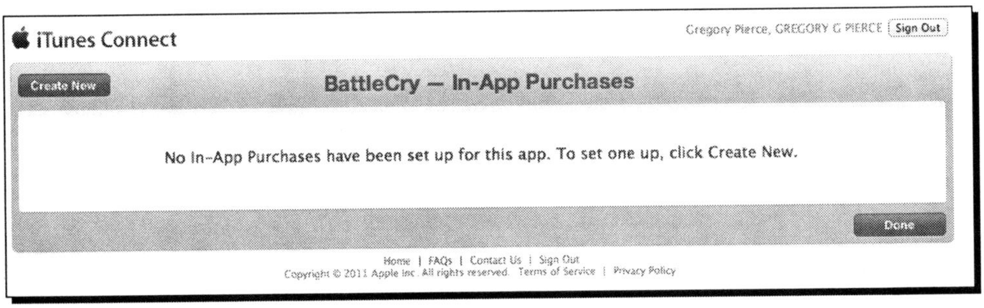

3. Next we want to set up an In-App purchase that represents a new gun type for the user, so select **Non-Consumable**:

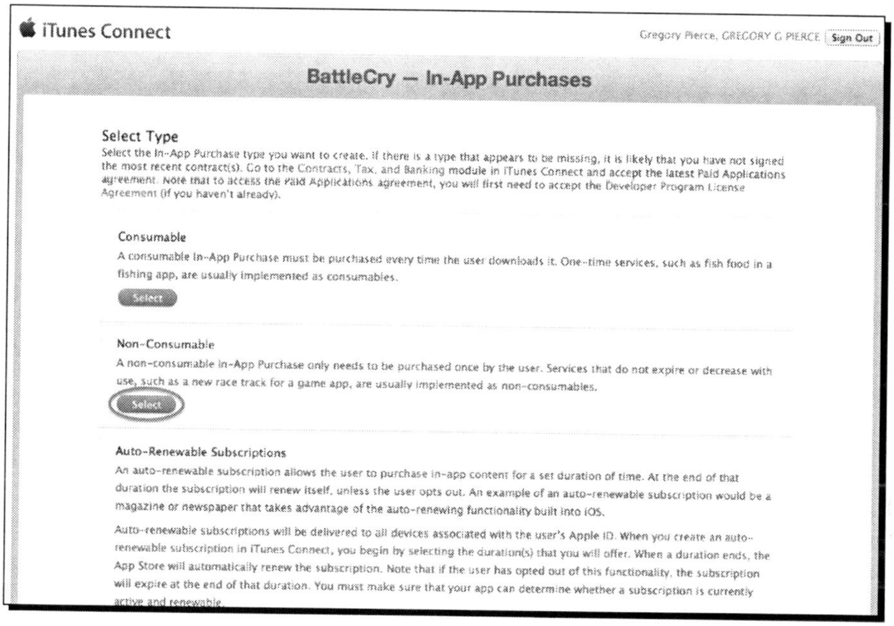

4. In the details area provide a **Reference Name** and a **Product ID** for the product. The **Product ID** is what you will use to refer to the product in the Store Kit APIs later. You can call your product ID whatever you want, it is for your own internal purposes. You should follow the naming convention you used for your product to ensure that you will not have any name collisions between products, versions, and so on:

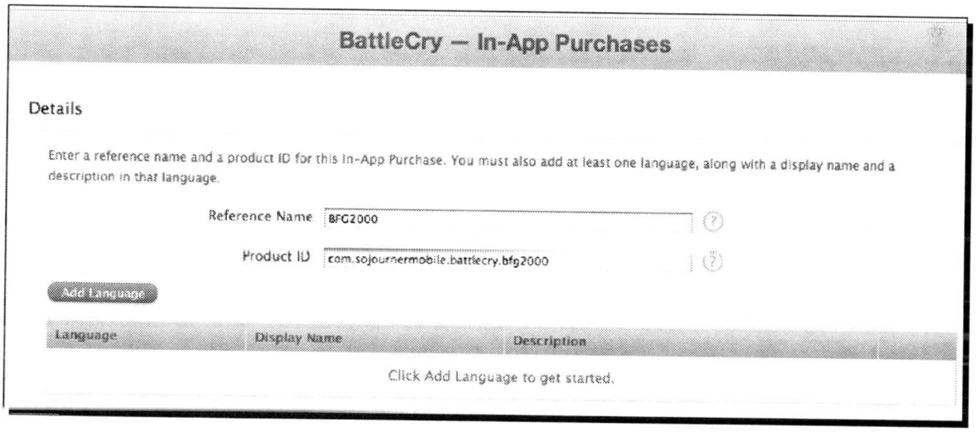

5. As iOS applications and iTunes support localization you need to set the language for how your product will be displayed in the store. Select **Add Language** and enter the store details for the product.

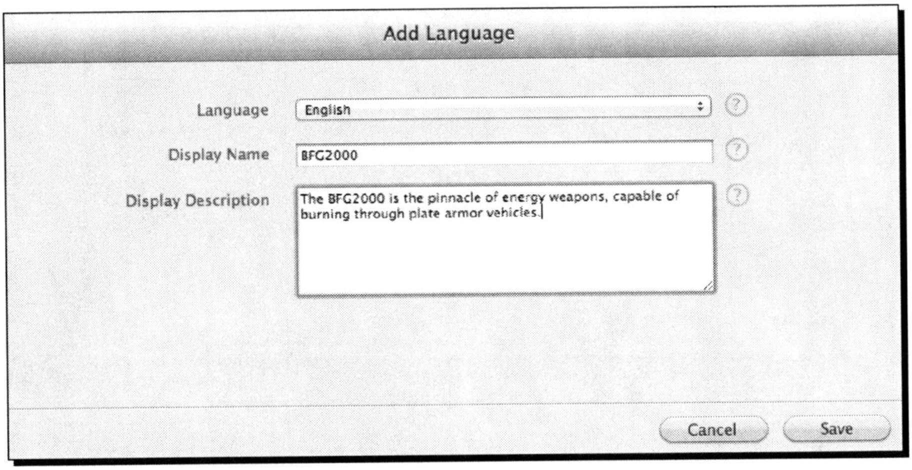

6. Next set the pricing for the product. The tiers for **In-App Purchases** are similar to those of regular iTunes App Store purchases:

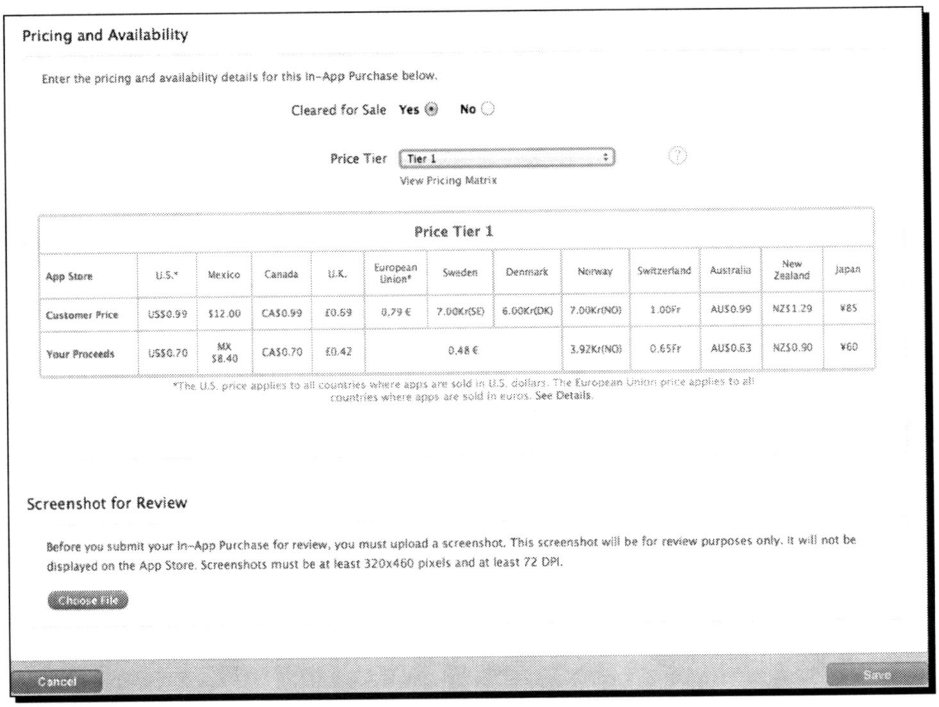

7. Next we need to add a screenshot for the App Store review team. It's not entirely clear how this screenshot is used, but you will not be able to submit your In-App purchase without this 320x240 image:

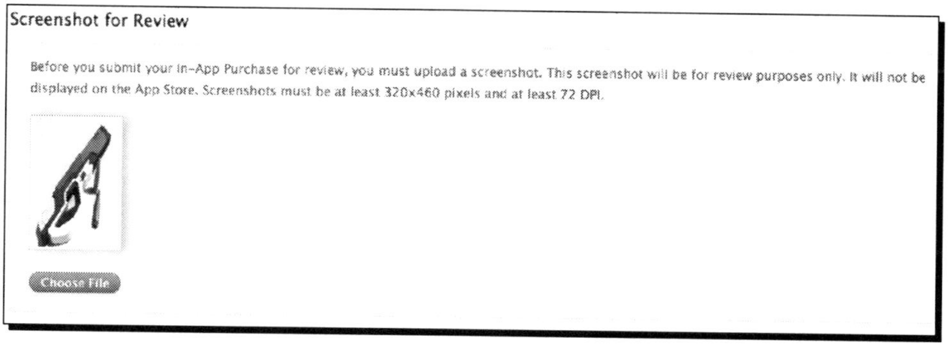

8. With this update completed, review the In-App purchase list to ensure that the details entered match what is submitted for your game:

> The purchase is currently pending review.

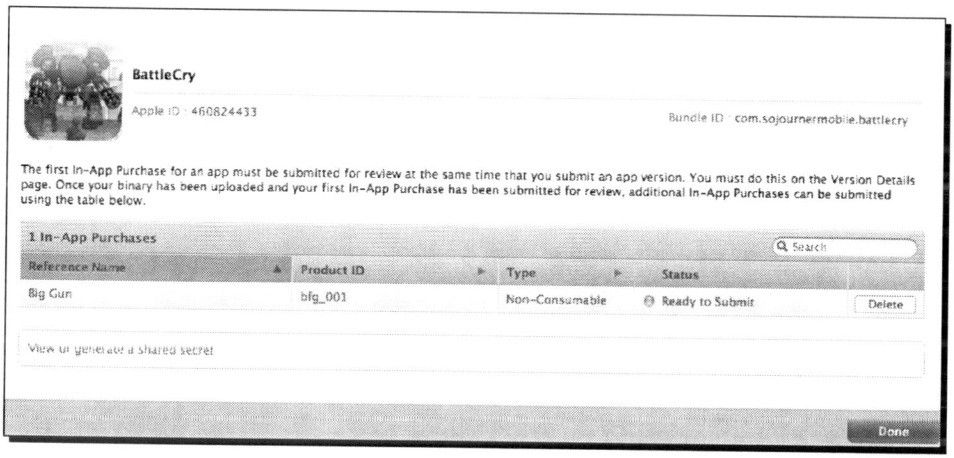

With this completed we can write the plugin code necessary to access this In-App purchase within our Unity game.

9. Drag the StoreKitManager prefab from the Prime31 Plugin into the scene. The StoreKitManager is responsible for communicating with the native Objective-C libraries on the iOS device to handle integration with the Apple StoreKit API.

10. Drag the StoreKitEventListener prefab into the scene. As StoreKit events happen on the iOS device, the StoreKitEventListener will receive notifications about them from the operating system.

11. To keep things simple we will create a simple GUI Button that when clicked will cause the user to purchase the BFG weapon.

12. Create a new script called InAppPurchases:

```
using UnityEngine;
using System.Collections.Generic;

public class InAppPurchases : MonoBehaviour
{
#if UNITY_IPHONE
  void OnGUI()
  {
    if( GUI.Button( new Rect( 0, 0, 50, 40 ), "Purchase BFG" ) )
    {
      bool canMakePayments = StoreKitBinding.canMakePayments();

      if ( canMakePayments )
      {
        StoreKitBinding.purchaseProduct( "bfg_001", 1 );

      }
    }
#endif
}
```

What just happened?

We have just created our second channel of revenue, In-App purchases. We have just created a mechanism through which the user can purchase the BFG weapon for use in the game by pressing a button on the game interface.

Time for action – Adding content to the Unity Asset Store

During the development of your game you may have developed assets such as music, artwork, or plugins that you want to share with other users of the Unity community. The Unity Asset Store offers a channel for distributing these works through the Unity IDE itself and provides a 70 pecrent revenue share with you – making it a way to make money on your game even if you choose to not deliver it to the Apple App Store. In fact, there are entire game projects available on the Unity Asset Store that can help developers get started. We're going to submit part of our game project to the Asset Store so that people can download it and learn from it in their development projects:

1. The first step in publishing content to the Unity Asset Store is to create an account. If you've been following along you have already created a customer account and can skip this step. Otherwise open the Unity Editor and choose **Window | Asset Store**.
2. Select **Create Account** and complete the account creation process:

3. Download and review the Asset Store Provider Agreement from (`http://download.unity3d.com/assetstore/asset-store-provider-distribution-agreement.pdf`). Read through this document to understand the relationship between Unity Technologies and the Asset Store providers.

4. Download and review the Asset Store Submission Guidelines from (`http://download.unity3d.com/assetstore/asset-store-submission-guidelines.pdf`). These guidelines outline the various conventions required when submitting content to the Asset Store.

5. In the **Asset Store** window search for the **Asset Store Tools** and download them. It is represented in this image with the Unity icon:

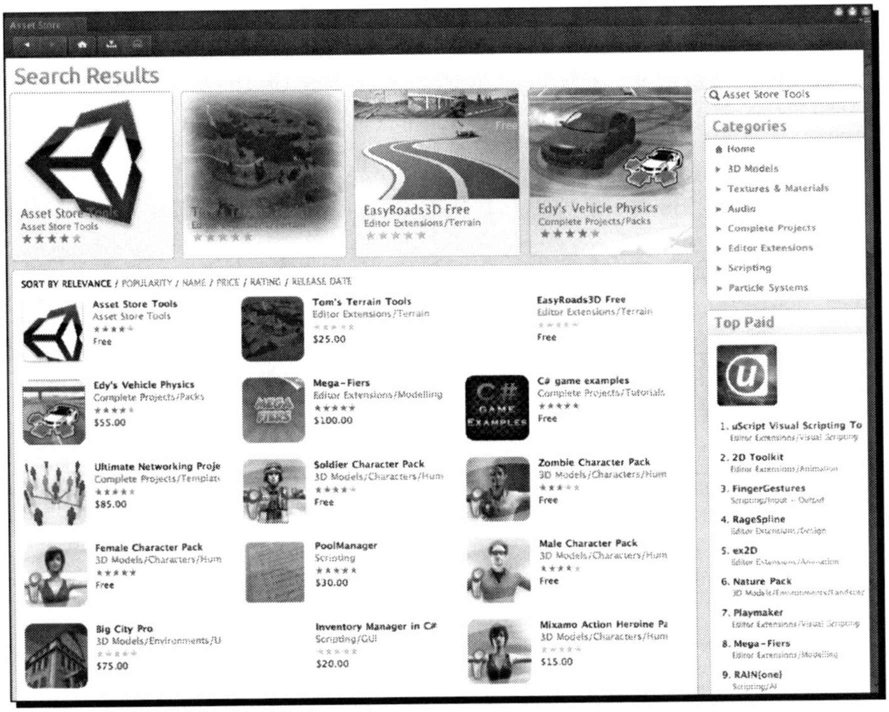

6. Once downloaded, import the **Asset Store Tools** package just as you would any other Unity package. These tools have the framework and scripts necessary to prepare content for submission to the Asset Store:

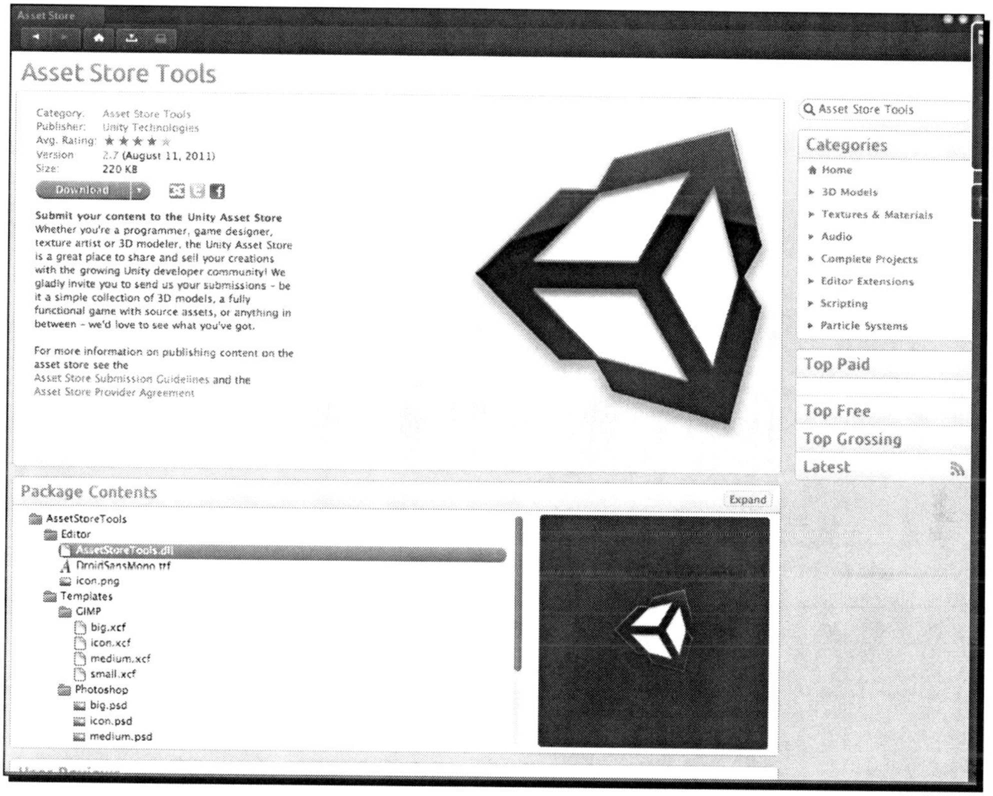

7. Under the **AssetStoreTools** hierarchy of the downloaded plugin you will find a `Templates` directory. This directory contains all of the image templates that you will want to modify for submission to the Asset Store. These key images are what the Asset Store will use for creating its own store pages:

Image Type	Size	Description
Big	1010x389	Used to promote a package when the package is the primary item on screen. The live area where you should put your image is 550x330
Medium	460x250	Used to replace big images when a smaller view size is required. The live area where you should put your image is 285x200.
Small	200x258	Used to promote images in smaller box views. The live area where you should put your image is 175x100.
Icon	128x128	Used for downloads and list views

8. Update your images to adhere to the layout suggestions from Unity Technologies to ensure that text displays properly and that your images are not cropped when displayed in the store:

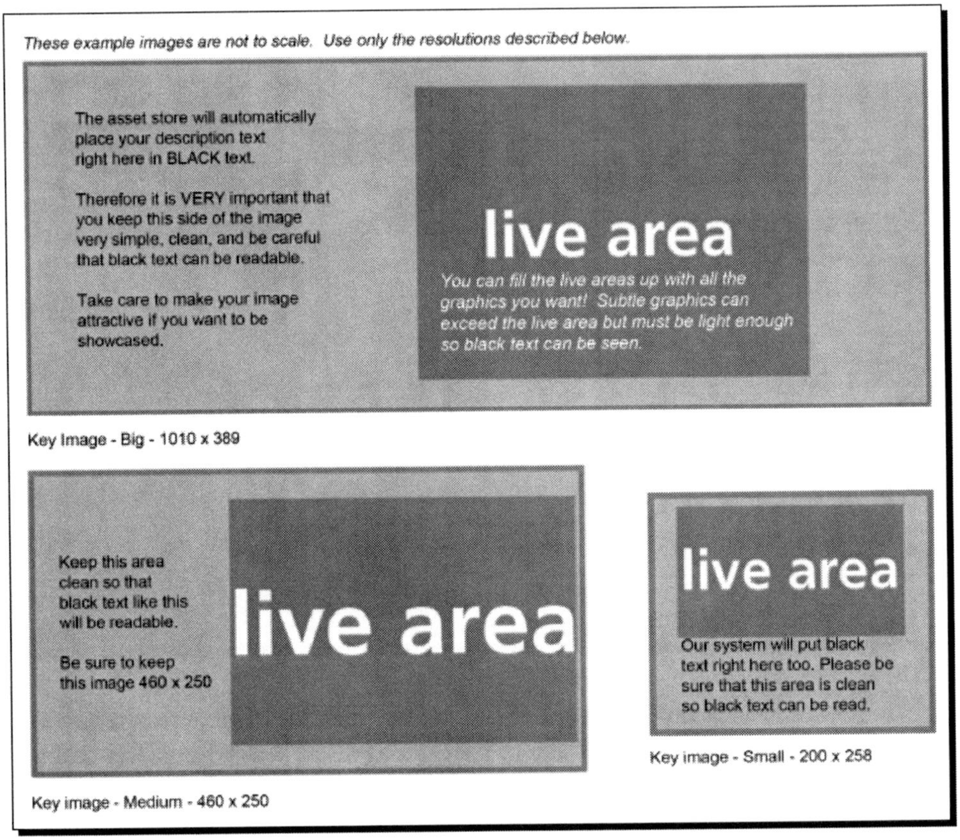

9. In the game project create an `AssetStore` directory. All of the assets you want to distribute go under the root folder of the project. In our case we're distributing the entire game project so we don't have to do anything special as the Asset Store packager will copy our folder structure and assets as-is when distributing content to end users.

10. In the `AssetStore` directory, create a folder called `Screenshots` for your key images. These screenshots should be a minimum of 640x480. These are images that can be viewed by customers when they are evaluating your assets in the Asset Store:

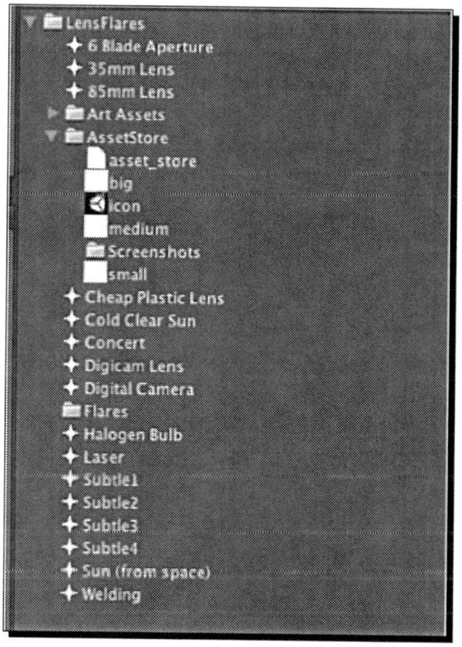

11. Launch the Unity Asset Store **Package Manager** that will generate the package necessary for submission for the Asset Store:

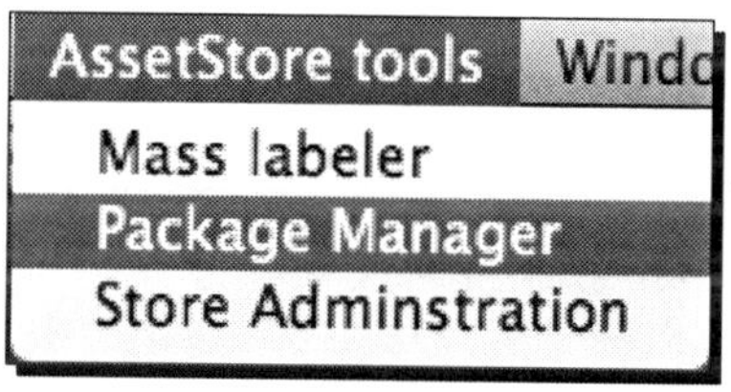

What just happened?

We have just published our game project to the Unity Asset Store for purchase by other developers. This is one of the final revenue streams that we have available to us as content developers and allows us to sell something as simple as music, artwork, scripts, or entire games for other developers to purchase.

Measuring success with iTunes Connect

Once your game product has been released on the market, you're going to want to measure success so that you can determine the best ways to grow your market opportunities and maximize revenue. Your channel for gathering this information is iTunes Connect.

Time for action – How is our game doing?

To illustrate the type of content that is possible using Unity3, we're going to get started by getting a real application running on a device. There are a number of steps that you have to perform to get this right, especially if you're a new developer to the iOS platform, so I'm going to take some time to make sure you understand what's going on. iOS development can be very unforgiving if you don't do things the right way, but once you walk through it a few times it becomes second nature.

We are going to walk through each of the steps necessary to produce commercial content for Unity3 that can be deployed to an iOS device:

1. Open the **iTunes Connect** portal at `https://itunesconnect.apple.com` or launch it from the normal iTunes developer portal:

2. Once in the portal, select the **Sales and Trends** link in the portal links. This area houses all of the demographic reports for the content we've published to the App Store:

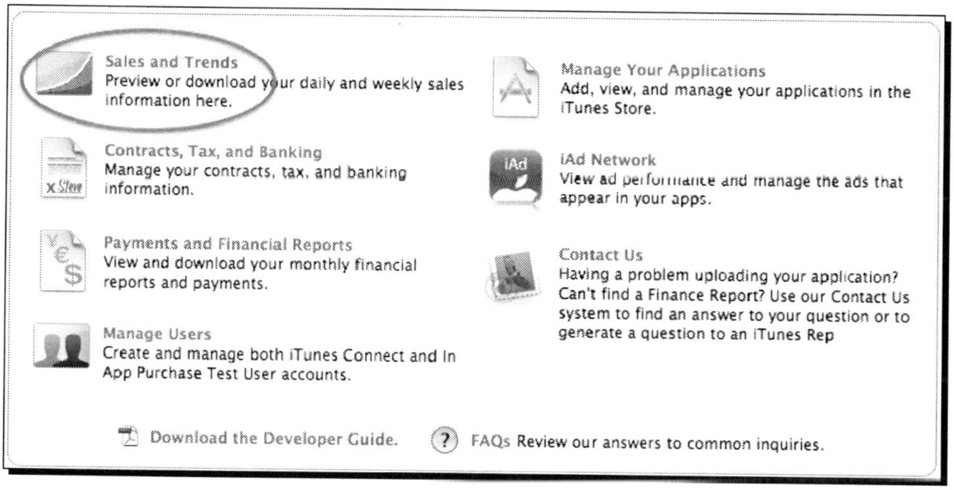

What just happened?

We have just examined how to look at the iTunes Connect portal and determine how to measure the success of your published game. In iTunes Connect you can look at the demographics of the purchasers of the game across a number of different dimensions such as time, geography, device, and so on. This will help you to measure the impact of things such as promotions, advertising campaigns, or the launch of new devices.

Summary

There is one last challenge for you to accomplish that is more important than anything we've done thus far and that is to actually create and publish your own game. There are lots of reasons why people stop short, but realize that you are now armed with all of the information you need to create a game, publish it, and make money doing it. You may not be able to quit your day job, but if you stick with it you may very well one day create the next great gaming brand or game company.

Don't worry about creating the next best game in any one particular genre, don't worry about having the latest and best graphics, don't wonder if that gaming idea will sell a million units (I can't imagine the guys who created *Angry Birds* knew it would take off the way it has) – focus on creating SOMETHING, then create something else and, before you know it, you WILL create something great. But you can't do it if you try to create the next *Skyrim, World of Warcraft, Call of Duty*, or *Crysis* as your first project.

So, rather than say goodbye, I'll say, "See you on the App Store." Good luck and above all else... HAVE FUN!

Pop Quiz Answers

Chapter 1

1	e
2	d
3	false
4	b
5	false

Chapter 2

1	b,c
2	d
3	false
4	false
5	false

Index

Symbols

J

K

L

M

T

U

Thank you for buying
Unity iOS Game Development: Beginner's Guide

About Packt Publishing

Packt, pronounced 'packed', published its first book "Mastering phpMyAdmin for Effective MySQL Management" in April 2004 and subsequently continued to specialize in publishing highly focused books on specific technologies and solutions.

Our books and publications share the experiences of your fellow IT professionals in adapting and customizing today's systems, applications, and frameworks. Our solution-based books give you the knowledge and power to customize the software and technologies you're using to get the job done. Packt books are more specific and less general than the IT books you have seen in the past. Our unique business model allows us to bring you more focused information, giving you more of what you need to know, and less of what you don't.

Packt is a modern, yet unique publishing company, which focuses on producing quality, cutting-edge books for communities of developers, administrators, and newbies alike. For more information, please visit our website: `www.PacktPub.com`.

Writing for Packt

We welcome all inquiries from people who are interested in authoring. Book proposals should be sent to `author@packtpub.com`. If your book idea is still at an early stage and you would like to discuss it first before writing a formal book proposal, contact us; one of our commissioning editors will get in touch with you.

We're not just looking for published authors; if you have strong technical skills but no writing experience, our experienced editors can help you develop a writing career, or simply get some additional reward for your expertise.

[PACKT] PUBLISHING

HTML5 Games Development by Example: Beginner's Guide

ISBN: 978-1-84969-126-0 Paperback: 352 pages

Create six fun games using the latest HTML5, Canvas, CSS, and JavaScript techniques

1. Learn HTML5 game development by building six fun example projects
2. Full, clear explanations of all the essential techniques
3. Covers puzzle games, action games, multiplayer, and Box 2D physics
4. Use the Canvas with multiple layers and sprite sheets for rich graphical games
5. Harness CSS3 special effects to create polished, engaging puzzle games

---

Google SketchUp for Game Design: Beginner's Guide

ISBN: 978-1-84969-134-5 Paperback: 270 pages

Create 3D game worlds complete with textures, levels, and props

1. Learn how to create realistic game worlds with Google's easy 3D modeling tool
2. Populate your games with realistic terrain, buildings, vehicles and objects
3. Import to game engines such as Unity 3D and create a first person 3D game simulation
4. Learn the skills you need to sell low polygon 3D objects in game asset stores

Please check **www.PacktPub.com** for information on our titles

CPSIA information can be obtained at www.ICGtesting.com
Printed in the USA
BVOW042244260212

283787BV00003B/20/P

9 781849 69040